SPA SPECIALTIES
from the kitchen of Lake Austin Resort

To Margo & Joe,
I hope you enjoy the book in the best of health!
Deborah Hart Evans

SPA SPECIALTIES
from the kitchen of Lake Austin Resort

To O'Neil & Nan ~ by Deborah Hart
Hope you enjoy these great recipes!
Much Love ~
Margo & Joe
1996

Cover design and illustration by Kathy Whitley

Book design by Deborah Hart
Lake Austin Resort
Austin, Texas

ACKNOWLEDGMENTS

The completion of this book required over a year of work and the time and talents devoted by many. I would like to thank all of those who made this book possible: Trisha Shirey for indexing; Trisha Shirey, Candy Cates, Jill Schoenborn, Julie Abbott, Robyn Barziza, and Kenny Asklund for typing, editing and assembling; and my husband, Andrew Hart, for his support and for tasting all the recipes.

CONTENTS

INTRODUCTION

I am committed to provide all the necessary tools to begin a healthy lifestyle and am delighted to offer a sound, balanced safe approach to weight loss. Sample menus have been included featuring some of your favorite Lake Austin Resort recipes. All of the recipes used by Lake Austin Resort have been included as well as many of my favorites.

We have included many recipes to give you a base for low calorie, low fat cooking. Experiment with combining the different recipes, create new dishes with the sauces, dressing, etc.; and substitute ingredients for new creations.

It is critical for a successful and permanent weight loss to follow a safe weight loss plan aiming for a 1-2 pound "fat" loss per week. Women should consume 1200-1500 calories per day and men 1500-2000.

The recipes were designed to adhere to the U.S. Senate Select Committee Guidelines outlined on page 4 and the American Heart Association recommendations. It is important to follow these guidelines while following a weight loss program and to continue when you reach your goal weight and begin weight maintenance.

Nutritional breakdowns for each recipe were obtained through computer analysis using *Nutritionist III* by N-Squared Computing. The primary sources for the Data Base for the *Nutritionist III* are USDA Handbooks #8-1 through #8-14. Other USDA sources, Bowes and Church, and manufacturer's data was used when information not included in #8-1 through #8-14 was needed.

The exchange system used in the analysis is the New Exchange System introduced by the American Dietetic Association in October, 1986.

The staff at Lake Austin Resort will continue to provide ongoing information and encouragement to help you continue to achieve your goals. I certainly hope that you will count on us to be here whenever you feel the need for relaxation and renewal.

Best of health,

Deborah Hart
Director

DIETARY GUIDELINES

For many years the medical community failed to acknowledge a relationship between the American diet and the incidence of disease. Finally, in the mid-1970's, the government became so concerned over the decline in health in America that they demanded statistics be compiled and recommendations made for a healthier diet. In 1977, the United States Senate Select Committee on Nutrition and Human Needs reported that "six of the ten leading causes of death in the United States have been linked to our "diet" and "killer diseases" including heart disease, stroke, cancer and various other chronic diseases have reached epidemic proportions in our population. Consequently, Americans are no longer dying from fatal infections but from an affluent diet and lifestyle. The typical American diet contains excess amounts of fat (expecially saturated fat), cholesterol, salt, simple sugars and alcohol.

In an effort to improve the health status of all Americans, the committee published a report entitled "Dietary Goals for the United States." The following guidelines come from this report:

1. To avoid being overweight, consume only as much energy as is expended; if overweight, decrease energy intake and increase energy expenditure.

2. Increase consumption of complex carbohydrates by eating more fresh fruits, vegetables and whole grains.

3. Decrease consumption of sugar and foods high in sugar content.

4. Reduce overall fat consumption from approximately 40% to 30% of total caloric intake. Recommended guidelines for fat consumption are: less than 10% of the fat calories from saturated fat, up to 10% from polyunsaturated fat and the remaining fat from monounsaturated fats.

5. Decrease consumption of foods high in fat and partially substitute polyunsaturated fat for saturated fat.

6. Decrease consumption of butterfat, eggs and other high-cholesterol food sources. (Daily intake should not exceed 300 mg.)

7. Decrease consumption of salt and food high in salt content. (Daily sodium intake should not exceed 3300mg.) The Food and Nutrition Board of the National Academy of Sciences—National Research Council recommends 1100 to 3300 milligrams of sodium daily as a safe and adequate amount for adults. (Equivalent to ½ and 1½ teaspoons of salt, respectively.)

To help implement these guidelines it is important to remember three key ingredients. First, we need the proper *balance* of foods in our diet so that our body can obtain all the necessary vitamins and minerals for healthy functioning. An easy way to obtain a balanced diet is to eat the recommended servings from the Basic Four Food Groups (Meat, Dairy, Fruits-Vegetables, and Grains). See chart on page 5 for Basic four food groups.

BASIC FOUR FOOD GROUPS

FOOD GROUP	RECOMMENDED NUMBER OF SERVINGS PER DAY		
	Child	Teenager	Adult
DAIRY 1 cup milk, yogurt or 1 cup ice milk, sherbert, or frozen lowfat yogurt	3	4	2
MEAT 2 ounces cooked lean meat, fish, or poultry, 2 eggs, 2 ounces lowfat cheese, ½ cup cottage cheese, 1 cup beans, 4 tablespoons peanut butter	2	2	2
FRUIT-VEGETABLE ½ cup cooked or juice, 1 cup raw, 1 medium-sized piece of fruit	4	4	4
GRAIN 1 slice bread, 1 cup cereal, ½ cup cooked cereal, ½ cup pasta	4	4	4

The recommended serving from the four food groups for adults supply approximately 1200 calories.

Second, we need to eat in *moderation* so that we don't consume more calories than we need. By consuming the appropriate number of servings of each food group for our age (and limiting the amount from the other group—fats and sugars), we can reach and maintain our ideal body weight. Third, we must choose a *variety* of foods from the four food groups to obtain all the vitamins, minerals and fiber necessary for a healthy body. Therefore, the optimum nutrition plan is not meant to be an impossible regimen to attain. On the contrary, the best eating plan is one that includes a good balance and variety of foods eaten in moderation.

Combining the U.S. Dietary Goals with the "basic four" (and the three key ingredients *balance, moderation,* and *variety*) results in a low-fat, low-cholesterol, high-complex carbohydrate, high-fiber diet. This type of diet is currently recommended for the treatment and possible prevention of heart disease, diabetes and certain forms of cancer. The American Heart Association recommends a diet that provides 50-60% of the calories from carbohydrates (primarily of the complex type), 15-20% from protein and 30% or less from fat. The major emphasis in this healthier diet is a reduction in fat and an increase in complex carbohydrates. It makes sense that the best diet to follow is not a fad weight reduction scheme to help you drop a few pounds quickly but a sensible eating plan to help provide a lifetime of good health and enjoyment.

IMPORTANCE OF AEROBIC ACTIVITY

by Ellen McCullough

An era modernization and technological advances has forever changed the lives of industrialized America. Advances in medical technology are now controlling diseases once regarded as fatal, but at the same time physical activity patterns have shifted from "work" requiring physical exertion to "work" which is now sedentary in nature.

The majority of reported illnesses and deaths are now more a result of lifestyle than ever before. Cancer, diabetes mellitus, hypertension, mental stress and illness, coronary heart disease, obesity and osteoporosis can all be attributed to modernization: so the hard "work" once seen in the fields is now "hitting the pavement," clad in jogging togs.

Why? What is to be gained from this fitness mania?? Is it really *that* important? If you consider quality of life important, yes!!

So how does one get started? First, realize that not every exercise or exercise program is or should be designed for everybody. Specificity in your goal is the first and most essential point in developing an effective program. Think about your reasons for wanting to exercise. Do you wish to gain muscular strength and body definition; improve cardiovascular fitness; increase your energy level; relieve mental stress; decrease your body fat reserves; or simply increase your flexibility and joint mobility? You may wish to achieve some or all of these goals, but realize there is not one magic form of exercise which will do it all. Learning and understanding the benefits of the various forms of exercise will enable you to be specific about your training program and will lead to success.

If it is muscular strength and endurance or body toning you desire. your program will differ from that which is designed to help you lose body fat. You will want to concentrate on "training" (fatiguing specific muscle groups repeatedly through resistance training) to help strengthen and increase muscle tissue. This form of exercise is also vital in maintaining proper body posture and alignment and assists in strengthening the support tissues of the body, such as your tendons, ligaments, cartilage and connective tissues. It is important to understand that lifting a weight does not necessarily build a muscle. It stimulates the muscle to grow to meet heavier work loads. It is important to note, however, that repeated training sessions will enable your body to adjust to the increased demands, resulting in increased strength and muscular definition. Muscle cells are constantly being broken down into essential amino acids and must be given a chance to rebuild; thus, a proper warm-up (including flexibility exercise), rest, and adequate diet are essential to any good strength building program. Lack of rest can result in muscle loss or susceptibility to injury.

Resistance training, when executed properly and under careful direction, can be credited with increasing bone mineral content and can also aid in the prevention of athletic injury. This is accomplished through the increased strength the body gains to accommodate the stresses of exercise. If you are interested in deriving the many benefits achievable through aerobic training, it is important to note that the intensity, frequency, and duration of your workouts and the type of activity you choose are vitally important to the success of your program.

When an aerobic program is properly designed and followed, one can achieve the following; cardiovascular conditioning (including lowering of the resting heart rate by increasing cardiac output, lowering of your blood pressure, and lowered serum cholesterol percentage—L.D.L.—in addition to lowered percentage of body fat), elevated metabolism resulting in greater metabolic energy expenditure (calories) and an increased energy level, appetite control, the release of endorphins and other biological antidepressants, positive self-image and increased lean body mass. This last result is of particular interest, as after the age of 25, the average American loses up to ½ pound of lean body mass per year and usually replaces it with fat. This tendency often leads to osteoporosis through bone mineral loss. In order to slow this process, exercise which is weight-bearing in nature, combined with a proper calcium rich diet, is essential.

The word "aerobic," however, has become somewhat distorted in the past few years. It does not necessarily mean participating in a high-intensity aerobic dance class where one hoots and hollers while "sweating bullets." In fact, aerobic training exercise encompasses a vast range of activities including swimming, bicycling, walking, jogging, rowing, cross-country skiing, and dancing. Any activity which increases your consumption of oxygen by utilizing the larger muscle groups of the body, is rhythmic in nature and lasts around 20–60 minutes is considered aerobic.

It is essential that you understand your target heart rate zone and stay in your range during exercise to monitor the intensity of your program for effective training. A strict cardiovascular workout would involve a program utilizing a training heart rate at the higher end of your target zone, which differs from the training heart rate when your primary goal is fat utilization. In order to "burn" or oxidize fat (free fatty acids from the blood stream), the presence of oxygen is essential. When one works out in the higher ranges of the maximum heart rate (80–90%), this would be a strict cardiovascular zone. The body is not able to get enough oxygen to catalyze with fat to meet the muscular energy demand and cannot rely fully on fat stores for fuel. The body will then begin using carbohydrate energy or muscle glycogen which is stored in the muscles and is available for immediate release. When one trains at too high an intensity, 90% of the maximum heart rate or above, for too long a time, it is possible to deplete the stores of muscle glycogen which will result in low blood sugar and an overtraining state. If you find yourself excessively tired, sore, unable to sleep, hungry immediately following your workout, and constantly thirsty long after your workout, chances are you are overtraining. Take your resting heart rate in the morning before rising. If your resting rate increases substantially, lower the intensity of your workout and increase the duration.

If your goal is fat loss through an exercise program, you will want to work out at a low intensity training heart rate (60-75% of your maximum) for a longer duration. The body will be assured of getting enough oxygen to the muscles at this intensity, and you will also benefit cardiovascularly.

The benefits can be great from a well-structured aerobic conditioning program, but keep in mind that your success will be better assured if you routinely follow a program which includes a proper warm up and cool down. Too frequently, this is the part of the program which is ignored or given little importance. Preparing the muscles for activity through an active warm up (walking in place, knee lifts, etc.) brings increased blood flow to the muscles, increasing core body temperature. This will stimulate metabolic energy production. Thorough static stretching will also help prepare the body for exercise by increasing the elasticity of the connective tissues, increasing the speed of nerve impulses, assisting your range of motion and helping to lubricate the joints involved in your activity.

Following exercise, a proper cool down will help your body move concentrated blood stores from lower extremities which helps prevent blood pooling. It will also reduce your training heart rate gradually, not radically, and will help heavily contracted muscles to relax.

The key to your success is measurable progress. Frequently we become discouraged because we don't have well-defined goals and we follow the "hit or miss" approach in our programs. Be consistent in your program, be sure not to overdo it.

As with any exercise program, it is advised that you have a thorough physical examination and inform your physician about your proposed fitness program.

TRAINING TIPS

1. Remember to always warm up before any activity with low-level exercise specific to what you will be doing during your workout, and cool down immediately following aerobic activity. To insure success DO NOT OVERDO! Stay within your target zone and listen to your body.

2. Be sure your body stays hydrated. You will lose a lot of body fluids through exercise. This can lead to dehydration, and dehydrated muscles lose efficiency, which may lead to injury.

3. Be conscientious about your form. Throughout exercise remember to keep your posture erect with shoulders over your hips and abdominal muscles tight. Concentrate on deep consistent breathing. Remember: your muscles need oxygen to perform—make sure you're getting enough.

4. Maintain your fitness program during vacation and travel. Bring your fitness bag with you and plan ahead to alter your program accordingly. You can walk anywhere, and if you research the area you are visiting you can find a hotel or local facility which will undoubtedly offer fitness equipment, a pool, etc., to help you stay directed on your fitness goals. (and you'll enjoy your vacation a whole lot more!)

5. Work on the buddy system if possible. Involve a friend or family member in your program with you for encouragement and support. This is also a good safety measure and you'll be more inclined *not* to miss a workout.

6. Arrange exercise schedules early in the week. Plan your workouts in advance and treat them like any other appointment. If you miss it you need to reschedule. This will help you develop a routine which will become second nature. It takes six weeks for a positive addiction to develop.

7. Most importantly, pick activities you enjoy and vary your program from time to time to keep your interest at a peak. Remember: you're doing this for life, so make sure you enjoy it!

TARGET HEART RATE

The purpose of this chart is to help you monitor your heart rate during aerobic exercise. Remember: aerobic exercise can be in the form of walking (vigorously), jogging, bicycling, dancing, swimming, rowing, etc. The important thing to remember is to keep the activity steady and non-stop for a period of about 20-30 minutes minimum. Equally as important as "under working" is "overworking," or rather overtraining. You will achieve the optimum benefits of cardiovascular conditioning and efficient fat oxidation if you stay within the heart rate boundaries set by the following chart.

The pulse can be found over the radial artery which runs along the thumb side of the arm or over the carotid artery which can be found on either side of the trachea (windpipe) on the neck. To take your radial pulse, place your index and middle finger on the wrist about 2 inches above the base of the thumb. Count for 10 seconds. To find the carotid pulse, place two fingers on your Adam's apple in the middle of your neck. Slide the fingers about 1 inch to either side and press *lightly* until you feel a pulse. Count for 10 seconds. (Use one hand only when taking the carotid pulse and be sure to press *lightly*.)

Average Target Zones
(These values represent a 10-second pulse count)

AGE	60%	70%	85%
20	20 (120)	23 (140)	28 (170)
25	20 (117)	23 (137)	28 (166)
30	19 (114)	22 (133)	27 (162)
35	19 (111)	22 (130)	26 (157)
40	18 (108)	21 (126)	26 (153)
45	18 (105)	21 (123)	25 (149)
50	17 (102)	20 (119)	24 (145)
55	17 (99)	19 (115)	23 (140)
60	16 (96)	19 (112)	23 (136)
65	16 (93)	18 (108)	22 (132)

**Note: This chart should not be followed by anyone on medication which slows the heart rate.

LOW-FAT/LOW-CALORIE HINTS

Fat contains two and one-quarter times more calories than carbohydrates or protein. There are 9 calories in a gram of fat compared to 4 in one gram of protein and 4 in one gram of carbohydrate. Fat is even higher than alcohol, which provides 7 calories per gram.

Americans could more than satisfy their nutritional requirements for fat even after cutting one-half to two-thirds of their current fat consumption. Most of the fat we consume is merely empty calories. The average American consumes more than 40% of their daily calories from fat. A typical adult eats the fat equivalent to one stick of butter daily. Too much fat is the major contributor to many of our weight problems. It is also a leading culprit in heart disease and cancer.

The goal is to raise your fat consciousness so that you can cut unnecessary fat calories where they count the least, so you can enjoy them where they really matter to you. When you realize where all the fat is hidden in your diet and how much you add to your food, you'll see that it is really easy to reduce consumption of fat calories drastically.

1. Use no-stick pans or a vegetable coating spray. (Pam or Mazola No-Stick)

2. Sauté with water, stock, bouillon, juice, or other liquid instead of oil or butter. Degrease soups, stocks and stews before eating. Simply refrigerate them, then skim off all the congealed fat that forms on the top. If time is a problem, drop ice cubes in or set dish in sink or bowl of icy cold water, then skim off fat.

3. Steam cook or microwave fat-absorbing vegetables such as eggplant. You can also lightly baste eggplant slices with a little oil and broil or bake.

4. Steam bake corn tortillas in the oven instead of frying. Use a stoneware tortilla warmer or wrap tortillas in wet cloth and then in foil and bake until done, approximately 10-15 minutes at 350°. For tortilla chips (cut tortilla in quarters), tostado or chalupa shells, place tortilla on cookie sheet or non-stick baking sheet and bake at 350° for 15-20 minutes or until crisp. Cool and store in a plastic bag or sealed container. Will keep for about one week.

5. Crackers often contain large amounts of hydrogenated fats (saturated). When buying crackers or baked goods always check the ingredients list on the package. If fat is in one of the first three ingredients the cracker will have a large percentage of fat. Try to substitute a lower fat product. Some nonfat or lowfat crackers that I recommend are:

   Wasa crispbread, Cracottes crackerbread, Kavli Norwegian crispbread, FiberRich bran crackers, Finn Crisp wafers, FiberCrisp crackers, Edward & Sons brown rice snaps, Quaker rice cakes.

6. Substitute nonfat or lowfat "yogurt cheese" for cream cheese, mayonnaise, or ricotta cheese (ex. stroganoff, Mexican dishes, desserts). To keep yogurt from separating when heated, add 1 tablespoon cornstarch before heating. For directions on making yogurt cheese, see page 14.

7. Substitute skim evaporated milk (200 calories per cup, fat free) for cream (717 calories per cup, 94% fat) or half and half (324 calories per cup, 79% fat).

8. Substitute lowfat (2% or less) cottage cheese or dry curd cottage cheese for ricotta. If a smoother texture is desired, process cottage cheese in a blender or food processor. Compare:

cottage cheese (4%)	239 calories per cup	36% fat
cottage cheese (2%)	200 calories per cup	18% fat
dry curd cottage cheese	125 calories per cup	.03% fat
whole milk ricotta	432 calories per cup	34% fat
part skim ricotta	342 calories per cup	17% fat

9. Salad dressings usually use fat (oil or mayonnaise) as a main ingredient. The oil to vinegar ratio is usually 3 to 1. Use one teaspoon oil per serving and use water to make up the difference in liquid measurement. Try experimenting with herbs and herbal vinegars. Or substitute nonfat yogurt or lowfat buttermilk in place of the oil for a creamy dressing.

10. Substitute 2 egg whites for each whole egg called for in recipes. Or use egg substitutes. (Look for egg substitutes that are fat free—some are not.) When making scrambled eggs, quiches, etc., use one whole egg and 2 egg whites for every 2 eggs. One large egg is 82 calories and 64% fat. The egg white is 17 calories and fat free. Also, the yolk contains 274 mg. of cholesterol.

11. If you still want the taste of the high fat food, but want to reduce fat and calories, mix one part mayonnaise, sour cream, or cream cheese, with 2 parts nonfat yogurt.

12. Evaporated skim milk can be whipped and used in place of whipping cream or processed toppings such as Cool Whip which are made with hydrogenated oils. Chill the milk and beaters before whipping. You can add an egg white, dash of sugar, and vanilla or other extract.

13. Bread can be a source of fat. Commercially baked breads are often made with egg yolks and/or hydrogenated oils. Read the label. Choose water bagels rather than egg bagels. Other lower fat choices are raisin toast, sourdough bread and English muffins.

14. For delicious, lowfat garlic bread, coat the bread with a butter-flavored spray and sprinkle with garlic powder. Bake for 5-10 minutes at 350°. Or bake a head of garlic, wrapped in foil, in a 350° oven for one hour. Separate garlic cloves and squeeze soft garlic onto toast and spread.

15. Substitute sherbert, fruit sorbet, frozen lowfat yogurt, frozen juice bar or ice milk for ice cream. In general, the more expensive the ice cream, the higher the percentage of fat.

16. There are few lowfat cakes and cookies, except for angel food cake which is made with egg whites. If you love sweets, it may be worth the time to bake you own from scratch, substituting with lowfat or nonfat ingredients.

17. Substitute vegetable oil for shortening, butter, margarine, or lard. Cut by 1/3, using 2 teaspoons of oil in place of 1 tablespoon shortening.

18. Choose the leanest cuts of beef if you include it in your diet. Select from veal, eye of round, round steak, flank steak, lean stew meat, extra lean ground beef, ground round, skirt steak. For the leanest pork, choose pork loin, center cut ham, pork tenderloin and Canadian bacon. The lowest fat poultry choices are chicken (broilers or fryers), turkey, cornish hen. Avoid roasting hens, duck and goose. Dark meat contains more fat than white meat.

19. Cook roasts, chops, steaks, meatballs, hamburgers, and other meat patties on a raised broiler pan in the oven so the excess fat will drip away.

20. Cut away the visible fat from all meat before cooking. Remove the skin and visible fat from chicken and other poultry.

21. Save the meat renderings in the bottom of the broiler pan to make a natural gravy without added fat. To quickly degrease the meat juice, place it in a heat-proof container. Then submerge the container in ice water 3/4 of the way up. The fat will rise to the top and begin to thicken so you can skim it off easily. Reheat the meat juice and season it with bouillon or herbs and spices to taste. Can thicken with cornstarch (1 tablespoon cornstarch per 1 cup liquid). If flour is used to thicken use 2 tablespoons per 1 cup liquid.

22. Always choose tuna (and other canned fish) packed in water rather than oil.

23. When ordering broiled fish or meats in restaurants, request that no butter or oil be added during their cooking. You can always season the fish or meat to your own taste.

24. Even with visible fat removed, meat and poultry will contribute fat to your diet. If you are a regular meat eater, consider replacing meat several times a week with a healthful vegetarian meal.

25. Avoid processed meats like bologna, salami, sausage and frankfurters. Leaner choices in cold cuts would be sliced turkey breast, turkey "ham," smoked turkey or chicken breast, boiled ham, baked Virginia ham and roast beef.

26. Although most fish are low in fat, the least fatty are the white fish like sole, cod, halibut, flounder, scrod and haddock, along with squid and shellfish (shrimp, mussels, crab, oysters, clams, lobster). Much fatter are salmon, mackerel, and swordfish. Tuna, bluefish, and catfish are moderately fatty. Fatty fish can help protect against heart disease, so try to include fish in your diet two to three times a week.

27. Remember that most recipes call for too much sweetener; reduce the amount by one-half to two-thirds whenever possible.

28. Recipes should not have more than one-fourth cup sweetener for every cup of whole grains or flour.

29. Read the label when selecting margarine. Look for liquid vegetable oil as the first ingredient, followed by one or more partially hydrogenated vegetable oils. Tub margarines usually are more polyunsaturated than stick margarines.

30. Diet margarines or reduced calorie margarines contain water and provide half the amount of fat found in other tub or stick margarines. (Remember although you have cut half the calories, you are still using a product that is pure fat.) Diet margarines can present a problem when using them in baking because of their high water content.

31. Read labels on packaged foods, don't be mislead by "vegetable oil" or "vegetable shortening" labels. Be sure and read the list of ingredients looking for hydrogenated oils which are saturated. Also watch for coconut or palm oil, both highly saturated fats.

32. Reading Labels. The label will give the serving size and will tell you how many servings are in the container. Calories are often listed with number of grams of protein, carbohydrate, and fat. The list of ingredients are in the order of their weight present in the product. For example, a label reads 100% stone ground whole wheat flour, water, honey, sesame oil, and sesame seeds. The product would consist mostly of flour and water.

33. Mix nonfat dry milk powder with stock, stir to dissolve and add to mashed potatoes instead of butter or margarine.

YOGURT CHEESE

Yogurt cheese is a nutritious, nonfat cheese substitute that has the consistency of cream cheese. You can make it overnight as easy as one, two, three. It is a wonderful substitute to use in place of sour cream, cream cheese, mayonnaise, or ricotta cheese. Compare the calories:

ricotta cheese (part-skim)	22 calories per tablespoon
sour cream	30 calories per tablespoon
cream cheese	52 calories per tablespoon
mayonnaise	101 calories per tablespoon
yogurt cheese	**12 calories per tablespoon**

YOGURT CHEESE (METHOD 1)

2   cups nonfat yogurt

Form yogurt cheese funnel (see pg. 425 to order) into a cone with the holes positioned in back of the buttons. Press both buttons securely into holes. The mesh will be inside the cone and will form a point at the bottom.

Place over a container such as a coffee mug or drinking glass. *The container should be tall enough so that the funnel does not touch the whey that drains out.*

Spoon up to 16 ounces of yogurt into the funnel, and place in the refrigerator. Allow to drain until you have the desired consistency: 8–12 hours.

Wash the funnel, rinse, and reuse.

Cheese will usually keep for 1½–2 weeks, refrigerated. Yogurt will condense to half. If you start with two cups of yogurt, you will produce 1 cup of yogurt cheese.

YOGURT CHEESE (METHOD 2)

2 cups nonfat yogurt
15″ × 15″ piece of
  cheesecloth

Spoon yogurt into the cheesecloth. Tie cheesecloth at the top and hang the "bag" over a bowl to catch the whey. Refrigerate and allow to drain 8–10 hours. Keep refrigerated until ready to use. Yogurt cheese can also be made in a paper coffee filter with the holder placed over a coffee mug or drinking glass.

TIPS ON YOGURT CHEESE

1. Check the yogurt you use to make sure it doesn't contain a stabilizer or gelatin base. This yogurt won't separate well. Look for yogurt without gelatin or carrageenan in the list of ingredients.
2. If you cook with the yogurt cheese you need to add cornstarch to the mixture to keep it from separating when heat is applied. Add one tablespoon cornstarch per one cup of yogurt cheese before cooking.

GRAINS AND LEGUMES COOKING CHART

Grain/Legume (1 c. dry measure)	Water	Cooking Time	Yield	Calories per ½ c.
Barley (pearled)	6 c.	1 hour	4 c.	100
Brown rice, long grain	2¼ c.	45–50 minutes	3 c.	116
Kasha (buckwheat groats)	1½ c.	15 minutes	2 c.	208
Bulgur	2 c.	15–20 minutes	2½ c.	200
Cracked wheat	2 c.	25 minutes	2 c.	180
Millet	3 c.	45 minutes	3½ c.	104
Oatmeal, rolled	2 c.	20–25 minutes	4 c.	66
Wild Rice	3 c.	1 hour	4 c.	115
Black beans	4 c.	1½ hours	2 c.	132
Blackeyed peas	3 c.	1 hour	2 c.	109
Garbanzos (chick peas)	4 c.	3 hours	3 c.	171
Kidney beans	3 c.	1½ hours	2 c.	148
Lentils	3 c.	1 hour	2 c.	106
Lima beans	2 c.	1½ hours	1¼ c.	110
Pinto beans	3 c.	2 hours	2 c.	131
White beans	3 c.	1½ hours	2 c.	143

OVERNIGHT SOAKING

Rinse the beans and remove any that are shriveled. Also check for tiny stones. For each pound of dried beans (2 cups), add 6 cups of water. Soak overnight, then drain and rinse. Rinse well.

QUICK SOAKING

Rinse the beans and remove any that float. Also check for tiny stones. For each pound of dried beans (2 cups), bring 8 cups of water to a boil. Add the beans and boil for 2 minutes. Remove the beans from the stove, cover the pan, and allow to soak for 1 hour. Drain and rinse the beans.

Beans should be partially covered and cooked over low heat. Stir gently to keep beans from breaking. Beans may be cooked when you have the time and then stored in the refrigerator for up to a week or frozen for six months.

If it is necessary to add water to beans as they cook, always add hot water. Adding cold water causes the skins to break and beans will become mushy.

STOCKING YOUR PANTRY

Breads/Grains/Legumes

Whole wheat bread
Bulgur wheat
Cornmeal
Cracker choices:
    Wasa crispbread, melba toast, Cracottes crackerbread, Kavli Norwegian crispbread, FiberCrisp cracker, Edward & Sons brown rice snaps, rice cakes
Whole wheat flour
Long grain brown rice
Rolled oats
Wheat bran
Wheat germ
Pinto beans (dry/canned)
Black beans (dry/canned)
Garbanzo beans (dry/canned)
Kidney beans (dry/canned)
Blackeyed peas (dry/canned)
Brown or red lentils
Cannelini or white beans (dry/canned)
Buckwheat groats
Lima beans (dry)
Whole wheat lasagna noodles
Semolina fettucini/linguine
Manicotti shells
Semolina pasta shells
Whole wheat flour tortillas (freezes well)
Corn tortillas (freezes well)

Dairy/Eggs

Parmesan cheese
2% (or less) lowfat cottage cheese
Part-skim mozarella or farmer's cheese
Nonfat or skim milk
Lowfat buttermilk
Nonfat yogurt (Dannon)
Evaporated skim milk (Pet)
Nonfat dry milk powder
Daisy light sour cream
Eggs
Egg substitute (Egg-Beaters)

Fats/Oils

Reduced-calorie margarine (Mazola)
Non-stick vegetable spray (Pam or Mazola No-Stick)

Reduced-calorie mayonnaise (Kraft)
Safflower oil
Olive oil
Sesame oil

Fish/Seafood

Canned clams
Canned pink salmon
Canned tuna (water-packed)

(Other fish used in recipes is best bought fresh)

Fruits

Apples
Bananas
Blueberries (fresh or unsweetened frozen)
Kiwi
Lemons
Limes
Oranges
Peaches (fresh or unsweetened frozen)
Pears
Pineapple (fresh or diced, canned, water-packed)
Seedless raisins
Strawberries (fresh or unsweetened frozen)
Applesauce, unsweetened
Dried apricots

Miscellaneous

Baking powder
Baking soda
Cornstarch
Dry unflavored gelatin (Knox)
Green olives
Dill pickles
Capers
Herbal vinegars
White wine vinegar or champagne vinegar
Balsamic vinegar
Chopped/slivered almonds
Shredded coconut
Chopped pecans
Chopped walnuts
Unsweetened cocoa
Vanilla extract
Almond extract
Clam juice
Horseradish

Dijon mustard
Picante sauce
Tabasco sauce
Ketchup
Worcestershire sauce
Red wine
White wine
Cooking sherry
Rum or rum extract
Diced green chiles (canned)
Chicken stock or low-sodium bouillon
Beef stock or low-sodium bouillon
Vegetable stock or low-sodium bouillon
Soy sauce

Poultry

Chicken breast halves, skinned
Turkey breast slices (cook ahead and freeze)
Frozen ground turkey

Spices/Herbs

Allspice, ground
Basil, leaves
Bay, leaves
Chili powder
Cinnamon, ground
Cloves, ground
Cream of tartar
Cumin, ground
Curry powder
Dill weed
Ginger, ground
Marjoram
Oregano, leaves
Paprika
Black pepper
Red or cayenne pepper
White pepper
Poppy seed
Rosemary
Sesame seed
Tarragon, leaves
Thyme, leaves

Sugar/Sweeteners

Maple syrup
Honey
Light molasses

Brown sugar
Granulated sugar
Apple juice concentrate, frozen
Orange juice concentrate, frozen
Pineapple juice concentrate, frozen

Vegetables

Artichoke hearts, (canned, water-packed)
Asparagus (fresh or frozen)
Bean sprouts (fresh or canned)
Broccoli
Green cabbage
Red cabbage
Carrots
Cauliflower
Celery
Chives
Corn (fresh or frozen)
Fresh garlic cloves
Ginger root
Lettuce (green or red leaf, Romaine)
Mushrooms
Onions (yellow or white)
Green onions
Parsley
Red/green bell peppers
Jalapeño or Serrano pepper (fresh or canned)
Pimentos
Pumpkin (canned)
Sauerkraut (canned)
Shallots
Spinach
Squash (yellow or zucchini)
Tomatoes
Water chestnuts (canned)
Tomato juice (low-sodium)
Tomato paste (low-sodium)
Tomatoes (canned whole, low-sodium)
Tomato sauce (low-sodium)

EQUIVALENTS

Size or Weight of Item	Item	Yield/Measure
1 pound	apples	3 medium (3 cups sliced)
1 pound	bananas	3 medium (2½ cups sliced or 2 cups mashed)
1 quart	berries	3½ cups
1 quart	lemon	2–3 tablespoons juice
1 quart	lemon	1 tablespoon grated rind
1 quart	orange	⅓ to ½ cup juice
1 quart	orange	1½–2 tablespoons grated rind
6-ounce can	frozen juice concentrate	¾ cup or 12 tablespoons
1 pound	raisins	3 cups, loosely packed
8 ounces	mushrooms	2½ cups sliced
1 pound	tomatoes	3 medium tomatoes
8 ounces	tomato sauce	1 cup tomato sauce
6 ounces	tomato paste	¾ cup tomato paste
1 pound	Idaho potatoes	3 medium (2⅓ cups sliced)
1 pound	sweet potatoes	3 medium (3 cups sliced)
1 large	onion	¾ to 1 cup chopped
12 ounces	evaporated skim milk	1½ cups
1 pound	dry beans	2 cups dry beans or 5–6 cups cooked beans
1 pound	brown rice	2¼ cups raw rice or 7 cups cooked rice
1 pound	fettucini, linguine, or spaghetti (2-oz. serving)	8–9 cups cooked spaghetti (1 cup cooked per serving)
1 slice	bread	¼ cup dry bread crumbs or ½ cup soft bread crumbs
1 pound	whole wheat flour	appx. 3½ cups unsifted
1 pound	brown sugar	2⅓ to 3 cups (firmly packed)
1 pound	granulated sugar	2⅓ cups
1 pound	whole almonds, pecans, walnuts (shelled)	4 cups
1 ounce	cheese	¼ cup grated cheese
1 envelope	unflavored gelatin	1 tablespoon gelatin
1 package	dry yeast	1 tablespoon
46-ounce can	juice	5¾ cups
10-ounce box	frozen vegetables	2 cups
16-ounce bag	frozen vegetables	3 cups
20-ounce bag	frozen vegetables	4 cups

SUBSTITUTIONS

1 whole egg	In baking, use 2 egg whites
1 teaspoon allspice	½ teaspoon cinnamon and ⅛ teaspoon ground cloves
1 teaspoon baking powder	⅓ teaspoon baking soda and ¾ teaspoon cream of tartar
1 cup buttermilk	1 cup nonfat yogurt or add 1–2 tablespoons white vinegar in 1 cup skim milk, stir and let clabber (thicken) for 5 minutes
1 ounce unsweetened chocolate	3 tablespoons unsweetened cocoa powder and 2 tablespoons water
1 cup white rice	1 cup long grain brown rice
1 ounce semi-sweet chocolate	3 tablespoons unsweetened cocoa powder, 2 tablespoons water, and 1 teaspoon honey
8 ounces cream cheese	8 ounces nonfat yogurt cheese or 8 ounces Neufchatel
1 cup all-purpose flour	1 cup whole wheat flour minus 2 tablespoons
1 garlic clove	½ teaspoon garlic powder
1 tablespoon fresh grated ginger	1 teaspoon dry ginger
1 teaspoon fresh herbs	½ teaspoon dried
1 cup skim milk	⅓ cup nonfat dry milk powder and ¾ cup water mixed or ½ cup evaporated skim milk and ½ cup water
8 ounces fresh mushrooms	6 ounces canned mushrooms
seeds	oven toasted rolled oats
nuts	diced water chestnuts or toasted Grape Nuts
1 pound ground beef	1 pound ground turkey
1 tablespoon prepared mustard	1 teaspoon dry mustard
1 cup shortening	In baking, ½ cup applesauce or unsweetened fruit juice and ⅔ cup liquid vegetable oil
1 cup butter	1 cup vegetable oil margarine, or 1 cup reduced-calorie margarine
1 cup sour cream	1 cup "Daisy" light sour cream or nonfat yogurt cheese or "Mock Sour Cream" (page 74)

1 cup sugar	¾ cup honey or 1 cup unsweetened applesauce or ½ cup unsweetened frozen fruit juice concentrate
1 cup canned tomatoes	1⅓ cups chopped fresh tomatoes, simmer 10 minutes
1 cup tomato sauce	½ cup tomato paste and ¾ cup water
1 teaspoon Worcestershire sauce	1 tablespoon soy sauce and a dash of cayenne pepper
1 cup light cream	½ cup skim milk and ½ cup evaporated skim milk
1 cup heavy cream	1 cup evaporated skim milk
for thickening: 2 tablespoons flour	1 tablespoon cornstarch
1 cup part-skim ricotta	1 cup lowfat cottage cheese blended with 1–2 tablespoons skim milk until smooth
1 cup margarine	¾ cup vegetable oil
bacon	lean Canadian bacon or lean ham
ice cream	ice milk, sherbert, frozen yogurt, sorbet
jelly, jam	fruit cooked and thickened with cornstarch (2 tablespoons cornstarch for every cup of fruit)

SUGGESTED MENUS

Breakfast:

1 cup cooked rolled oats	132
1 teaspoon ground cinnamon	
½ cup unsweetened applesauce	50
1 bran muffin	39
Total calories	221

1 ounce ready-to-eat whole grain cereal	110
½ cup skim milk	45
¼ cup sliced strawberries	27
Total calories	221

Breakfast taco	142
½ kiwi, sliced	24
¼ cup pico de gallo	13
½ cup skim milk	45
Total calories	224

Huevos con papas	146
¼ cantaloupe, sliced	41
Total calories	187

Migas	204
Herbal tea/coffee	0
Total calories	204

Spinach omelet	170
½ orange, sliced	32
Herbal tea/coffee	0
Total calories	202

Banana Strawberry Smoothie	153
2 blueberry mini-muffins	66
Total calories	219

Breakfast: (cont.)

2 brown rice muffins	167
½ cup skim milk	45
Total calories	212

Cheese topped French toast	116
Strawberry butter (2 T.)	36
½ cup skim milk	45
Total calories	197

Cottage cheese pancakes (2)	156
Fresh fruit sauce (¼ cup)	52
Total calories	208

Whole wheat pancakes (2)	124
Cinnamon yogurt sauce (¼ cup)	44
½ cup strawberries, sliced	28
Total calories	196

Low-cal peanut butter (2 T.)	44
Apple carrot muffins (2)	150
Herbal tea	
Total calories	194

Lunch/Dinner:

Carrot raisin salad	84
Chicken and artichokes	214
Carrot cookie	39
Total calories	337

Tossed raw vegetable salad with buttermilk dressing	50
Chicken and dumplings	208
Fruit cup	50
Total calories	308

Lunch/Dinner: (cont.)

Vemicelli soup	53
Soft turkey taco	187
½ cup chopped lettuce and ¼ cup chopped tomato	15
½ orange, sliced	32
Total calories	287

Chicken salad sandwich with raw vegetables	141
2 slices whole wheat bread	150
Lettuce, tomato slice	8
½ cup sliced cucumbers and carrots	20
Total calories	319

Creamy vegetable soup	25
Turkey salad dijonnaise	299
Fruit cake	71
Total calories	395

Artichoke and green bean salad	82
Salmon dill loaf	175
Baked apple	57
Total calories	314

Marinated sliced cucumbers (1 cup, use low-cal Italian dressing, 2 T.)	24
Tuna cakes (3)	159
Tartar sauce (2 T.)	30
Steamed carrots with dill (¾ cup)	36
Fresh fruit (1 serving)	50
Total calories	299

Apple Waldorf salad	62
Tuna rice salad	149
Strawberry cheesecake	97
Total calories	381

Lunch/Dinner: (cont.)

Hot madrilene soup	36
Tuna stuffed potato	255
Pear cobbler	90
Total calories	381

Egg drop soup	61
Chow mein with brown rice	153
Ginger cookie	56
Total calories	270

Basil tomato quiche	91
Bean and pea salad	86
Ambrosia pie	114
Total calories	291

Tomato herb soup	44
Pasta cannelini	231
Rum souffle	109
Total calories	384

Lettuce and tomato salad with 2 T. creamy garlic dressing	50
Fettuccini	295
Peach with Amaretto	38
Total calories	383

Jicama and orange salad	89
Red snapper Veracruzano	153
Spanish rice	72
Frozen peach yogurt	60
Total calories	374

Apple cabbage slaw	59
Southern baked catfish	253
Tomato provençal	40
Blueberries in yogurt	48
Total calories	400

Lunch/Dinner: (cont.)

Chicken Parmesan	261
Herbed carrots and zucchini	56
Pineapple sherbert	67
Total calories	384

Curried spinach salad	44
Chicken dijon	200
Herb potatoes	78
Oranges poached in red wine	89
Total calories	411

Spinach strawberry salad	44
Chicken Kiev	251
Steamed asparagus (6 spears)	18
Refrigerator yogurt cheesecake	108
Total calories	421

Marinated grilled chicken	196
Corn on the cob (5")	70
Sliced tomato	27
Chocolate mousse	65
Total calories	358

Tossed salad with green goddess dressing (2 T.)	50
Pizza	273
Carob cookie	46
Total calories	369

Basil and bean salad	94
Eggplant Parmesan	152
Banana bran bar	80
Total calories	326

Ensalada de naranjas	49
Tamale pie	285
Strawberry sherbert	51
Total calories	385

Lunch/Dinner: (cont.)

Lettuce and tomato with guacamole surprise	43
Cheese enchiladas	161
Spanish rice	72
Gingersnap baked pear	92
Total calories	368

Lettuce and tomato with guacamole surprise	43
Cheese chalupa	215
Peach crumb bake	75
Total calories	333

Pineapple orange salad	66
Rice and bean casserole	289
Carrot cookie	39
Total calories	394

Lentil burgers (2)	112
½ whole wheat pita pocket	63
½ cup lettuce	5
¼ cup chopped tomato	8
2 tablespoons Dijon mustard	10
1 apple	80
Total calories	278

Stir-fried ginger chicken	193
Wilted Oriental salad	116
Gingered fruit	69
Total calories	378

HERBS: "THE SPICE OF LIFE"

by Trisha Shirey

I. Introduction

Imagine how dull food would be without herbs and spices! Cooking low-calorie, low-sodium "diet" foods need not be boring. Herbs and spices should accent and enhance flavors and not mask them. Beginning cooks should be careful not to over-season or use too many herbs or too much of one herb at any meal. The way to learn how to use herbs is to experiment with them. Begin with small amounts and increase as needed.

Become familiar with individual herbs and their characters, then experiment with blending herb flavors. Keep in mind when combining herbs that one herb will usually predominate. The other herbs should compliment and not fight the primary herb. For example, basil blends well with garlic, chives or parsley but would clash with rosemary in most foods. The classic French cuisine mix "fine herbes" is three or four herbs, usually parsley, chervil, chives and tarragon.

If it is not possible to grow your own fresh herbs in a garden or in containers, look for fresh herbs in your local supermarket, natural foods store or farmers market. Fresh herbs will stay crisp for several days stored in sealed plastic bags in the refrigerator. Parsley keeps up to 2 weeks with stems submerged in water in a jar in the refrigerator. Mince herbs as you need them for best flavor. Add herbs to hot dishes near the end of cooking for most recipes.

Generally you will use twice as much fresh herb as dried. The loss of water in dried leaves reduces the volume greatly. If you must use dried herbs, avoid purchasing containers larger than you will use in 6 months. Many natural foods stores sell bulk herbs so you can buy the amounts you need and get fresher herbs. Store herbs in a cool dark place in tightly sealed, labelled containers. Don't keep your herbs near the stove near excessive heat. Also, avoid powdered herbs. Buy whole leaves when possible and crush them between your fingers or with a mortar and pestle before adding them to foods.

Herbs truly are "the spice of life," so start living!!

II. Planning and Planting an Herb Garden

What's the easiest way to beautify your yard, reduce your salt intake, and enhance the flavor of low-calorie foods? Planting an herb garden will do all of these and provide hours of enjoyment and relaxation.

When selecting a site for your herb garden, find one that will receive at least six to eight hours of sun per day. Some herbs will tolerate more shade, but most need full sun. Most herbs require well-drained soil, so raised beds are ideal. A drip system for watering conserves water and promotes healthy growth. Especially important is that the garden is convenient to your kitchen, so you'll be apt to snip herbs frequently as you cook.

Deciding on which herbs to plant may be the most difficult part of your project. Depending on the space you have available, determine which herbs you like best and will use the most. For instance, if you don't like licorice flavor, don't waste valuable space with fennel. Herbs that I feel no garden should be without are dill, thyme, parsley, sage, basil, mint, and oregano. If you like Mexican food, you will want to add cilantro and Mexican oregano. Those enjoying Oriental food might want lemon grass, chervil, and lovage. Italian parsley, rosemary, chives, and garlic chives enhance Italian dishes.

Study the sizes of the herbs before planting. Parsely, chives, and thyme are relatively small, eight to ten inches tall. Basil, sage, and rosemary can be large, shrub-like plants. Dill and fennel often tower to five feet. Place the smaller plants toward the front of the bed or use them as a border on your flower beds or rose gardens. Thyme makes a very attractive edging plant and comes in many varieties and colors: yellow, gray, and many shades of green. The botanical garden centers of many cities now feature herb gardens so that you can see the size and look of each herb. You can also visit our herb garden at Lake Austin Resort to help plan your garden.

No garden should be without mint, but choosing one from the many varieties—apple, lime, orange, pineapple, spearmint, peppermint, and more—can be difficult. Mints are very invasive and will take over your garden quickly. It's best to confine mint with a metal or wooden barrier, at least twelve inches deep, or keep it in its own planter or bed. Its many uses make mint worth the trouble.

To start a garden, first remove all grass in the area. If you have a bermuda grass lawn, be sure to provide some type of edging to keep weeding to a minimum. Build the soil with organic materials like compost, bone and blood meal, rock phosphate, and peat moss. Depending upon your soil you may need to adjust the pH of your soil with sulfur or lime. Most Texas soils are highly alkaline and need sulfur to bring the pH to a neutral level which herbs appreciate. A soil test prior to preparing your garden is invaluable for assessing the soils' nutrient requirement.

Herbs can be attractively mixed in with your other flowers, and they have the added benefit of helping to repel insects. Salad burnet, prostrate rosemary, thyme, scented geraniums, and basils (particularly globe, opal, and lettuce leaf) are beautiful plants.

Herbs are pest-free, hardy, vigorous, and very forgiving of occasional neglect. They need infrequent, light feedings of organic fertilizer, fish emulsion, or seaweed. Too much fertilizer produces leafy plants without flavor.

Snip outside leaves on the plants and allow the young, inner leaves to provide nourishment for the plant. Don't be reluctant to pick them; regular pruning by harvesting produces healthy, bushy plants. Be sure to keep seed heads clipped off, as they rob the plant of the oils that give them flavor and make the plant less vigorous.

As your collection of herbs flourishes, you'll add more herbs and find many uses for them besides cooking teas, potpourris, crafts, herbal baths, and cosmetics!

III. Herbal Vinegars

Herbal vinegars are an easy and delicious way to spice up your diet and utilize the bounty of your herb garden. They also make appreciated gifts. An assortment of colorful and tasty herbal vinegars will establish you as a gourmet cook!

Start with clean, glass jars with tight-fitting lids. It is not necessary for the jars to have a vacuum seal. Plastic or enamel-coated lids are preferable. If you use metal lids, be careful not to fill the jars too full as the vinegar will have a corrosive action on the metal. Old hot-sauce jars, instant-coffee jars, mayonnaise jars all make good vinegar jars. Wine bottles with new, tight-fitting corks are especially nice. Use your imagination! Use clear glass to allow the lovely herb colors to show through.

You may use a white vinegar, wine vinegar, malt or cider vinegar or any combination of vinegars. White vinegar allows the more delicate herb flavors to show through, while wine vinegars make strong, zesty vinegars.

Heat the vinegar just to a *simmer* in a glass measuring cup in the microwave or in a stainless steel pot on the range. DO NOT use aluminum, cast aluminum or soft enamelled pots as the hot vinegar will react with the soft metal. If the vinegar is boiled it will release all the volatile oils in the herbs which give the vinegar its flavor.

Fill your clean, glass jars one-third to one-half full with fresh, clean herbs. Strong herbs like savory and rosemary require less herbs, while dill or thyme will require more herbs for full-flavored vinegar. Pour the heated vinegar over the herbs, wipe the mouth of the jar, seal immediately and allow to cool. The vinegar will reach its full flavor in 24-48 hours.

You can make wonderful delicately flavored vinegars with fruit. For citrus vinegar, squeeze 2 lemons or 2 oranges and the zest of one fruit and add to one quart of white vinegar. To make strawberry, blueberry or raspberry vinegars blend in a blender one cup of fruit with 2 cups of white vinegar. Add 2 more cups of vinegar to make one quart. Let the mixture sit for 3-4 weeks. Strain before using. For even more interesting flavors, add stick cinnamon, whole cloves, fennel seed, anise seed, whole peppercorns in desired combinations after blending. Fruit vinegars are especially good in cole slaws and fruit salads.

Use your herbal vinegars in any recipe calling for vinegar. Make salad dressings with it, use it for marinade for fish or meat cooked outdoors on the grill, for vegetable marinade or vinagrette or as a low-calorie vegetable dip. Mix the vinegars with nonfat yogurt for a delicious accompaniment to raw vegetables.

Some of my favorite herb combinations in vinegars are:

Basil, garlic cloves, chive flowers in red wine vinegar
Dill and salad burnet in white vinegar

Lemon thyme, lemon grass, lemon verbena, lemon balm and zest of lemon in
  white vinegar
Oregano, thyme, and parsley in red and white vinegar mixed
Marjoram, clove, stick cinnamon in red wine
Blueberry, stick cinnamon
Blueberry, strawberry
Strawberry, mint
Raspberry, clove
Ginger, lemon
Basil, thyme, bell pepper, green onion, black peppercorns

IV. Recipes

HERBED MARGARINE

Flavored margarine adds a special flair to breads, vegetables, pasta, fish and
baked potatoes. You use less margarine per serving because the herbs add so
much flavor.

Any herb can be added to reduced-calorie margarine to make a delicious
herbed "butter." You may use a single herb or a combination of herbs whose
flavors combine well.

As a general rule, use two tablespoons minced, fresh herbs for each half cup of
softened margarine. You'll use less of strong herbs like sage or savory and more
of the milder tasting herbs like parsley and chives. You may also want to add a
few teaspoons of fresh lemon juice to create a fresher flavor. (You may use
dried herbs—cut herb amounts used in half and allow to sit overnight.)

Place the herbed "butter" in a tightly covered container and chill for several
hours until firm. This allows the flavors to develop. Keeps well in refrigerator
and may also be frozen.

HERBED YOGURT

Nonfat yogurt can be dressed up with herbs to make a zesty potato topping,
salad dressing or vegetable topping. Follow directions for herbed margarine,
omitting the lemon juice. Chill for several hours before using or overnight if
you used dried herbs.

√ HERBED YOGURT CHEESE

Follow directions on page 14 for making yogurt cheese. Stir one or two tablespoons fresh herbs into ½ cup firm yogurt cheese and chill until firm. This

makes a tasty spread for crackers, a dip for vegetables or chips, and a low-calorie potato topping.

Garnish the cheese with a sprig or two of the herbs used for a decorative party dip. Top with cracked black pepper for added flavor. This will keep for several days in the refrigerator.

Suggested Herb Combinations—use more or less according to your taste.

MINT "BUTTER"

½ cup reduced-calorie margarine
2 tablespoons chopped fresh mint
2 teaspoons lemon juice

Mix well and chill. Makes an excellent topping for new potatoes, carrots, peas or asparagus.

CHIVE "BUTTER"

½ cup reduce-calorie margarine
1 tablespoon chopped chives
1 tablespoon chopped parsley

A great baked potato topper!

LEMON PARSLEY "BUTTER"

½ cup reduced-calorie margarine
2 tablespoons minced, fresh parsley
1 teaspoon chopped chives
1 teaspoon lemon juice

Good on all vegetables and broiled fish.

SAGE "BUTTER"

½ cup reduced-calorie margarine

1 tablespoon finely minced fresh sage

¼ teaspoon freshly ground black pepper

1 teaspoon lemon juice

1 small garlic clove, minced finely, optional

Blend thoroughly and add to steamed onions, breads or spread on broiled chicken just before it's done to increase browning and add flavor.

BASIL—GARLIC "BUTTER"

½ cup reduced-calorie margarine

2 tablespoons fresh basil, minced

1 small minced garlic clove

2 teaspoons minced, fresh parsley

1 teaspoon lemon juice

Combine well and chill until firm. Great on pasta.

DILL "BUTTER"

½ cup reduced-calorie margarine

2 tablespoons minced, fresh dill

1 tablespoon minced, fresh parsley

¼ teaspoon freshly ground black pepper, optional

1 small garlic clove, minced, optional

Combine well and chill until firm.

For Herbed Yogurt and Cheese recipes, substitute ½ cup yogurt or yogurt cheese for margarine and omit lemon juice if included.

NUTRIENT SUMMARY
(Per Serving)

% of protein, carbohydrate, fat and alcohol calories per serving

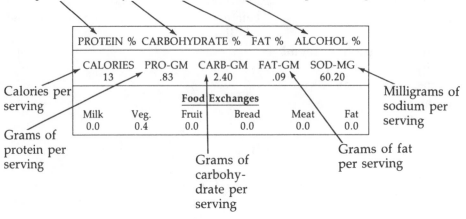

Calories per serving

Grams of protein per serving

Grams of carbohy- drate per serving

Grams of fat per serving

Milligrams of sodium per serving

PROTEIN %	CARBOHYDRATE %	FAT % ALCOHOL %

CALORIES	PRO-GM	CARB-GM	FAT-GM	SOD-MG
13	.83	2.40	.09	60.20

Food Exchanges

Milk	Veg.	Fruit	Bread	Meat	Fat
0.0	0.4	0.0	0.0	0.0	0.0

PROTEIN: Required for growth and maintenance of all tissues. Important in regulating the body's water balance. 15-20% of total daily calories should come from protein.

CARBOHYDRATE: Major source of energy. Provides fiber, vitamins, and minerals. 50-60% of total daily calories should come from carbohydrates (primarily complex).
FOOD SOURCES:
Simple Carbohydrate—sugars, jams, syrups, molasses, honey, sweetened soft drinks.
Complex Carbohydrate—whole grain bread, cereals, vegetables, fruits, potatoes, pasta, whole grains, brown rice.

FAT: Energy source, provides satiety, supplies essential fatty acids, carry fat soluble vitamin A, D, E and K. No more than 30% of total daily calories should come from fat. No more than 10% from saturated fats, up to 10% from polyunsaturated and balance in monounsaturated.
FOOD SOURCES:
Saturated fats—meats, poultry, whole milk dairy products, butter, eggs, coconut oil, palm oil.
Monounsaturated fats—olives, olive oil, avocados, peanut oil.
Polyunsaturated fats—safflower, corn, cottonseed, sunflower, sesame, and soybean oils.

SODIUM: Maintain fluid balance and volume in body, major
                            role in nerve impulse condition. 1100-3300 milli-
                            grams are considered safe sodium consumption for
                            the average healthy adult.
                            FOOD SOURCES: table salt, lemon pepper, garlic
                            salt, condiments—barbeque sauce, soy sauce, MSG,
                            ketchup, mustard, steak sauce, Worcestershire sauce,
                            processed meats, pickles, olives, cheese, chips and
                            crackers, tomato juice, canned vegetables.

The American Heart Association recommends a diet that provides 50-60% of
the daily calories from carbohydrates (primarily complex), 15-20% from protein, and 30% or less from fat.

The following chart lists the grams of protein, carbohydrate, and fat needed to
comply with the Heart Association recommendations for different calorie diets.

	Calories Per Day			
	1000	1200	1500	2000
GRAMS-PROTEIN 15-20% protein (4 calories/gm)	38-50	45-60	56-75	75-100
GRAMS-FAT 25-30% fat (9 calories/gm)	27-33	33-40	42-50	55-66
GRAMS-CARBOHYDRATE 50-60% carbohydrate (4 calories/gm)	125-150	150-180	188-225	250-300

APPETIZERS & BEVERAGES

BEAN DIP

¾ **cup kidney beans, drained**
2 **tablespoons pico de gallo or picante**
½ **teaspoon lime juice**

Put all ingredients in blender. Process until smooth. Chill and serve with crackers or tostados.

Servings: 14 (1 tablespoon serving)

NUTRIENT VALUES					
PROTEIN 24%	CARBOHYDRATE 70%		FAT 6%		ALCOHOL 0%
CALORIES 13.00	PRO-GM 0.826	CARB-GM 2.402	FAT-GM 0.089		SOD-MG 60.20
FOOD EXCHANGES					
MILK 0.0	VEG. 0.4	FRUIT 0.0	BREAD 0.0	MEAT 0.0	FAT 0.0

CUCUMBER DIP

½ **cup lowfat cottage cheese**
½ **cup diced cucumbers, seeds removed**
2 **teaspoons chopped green onion**
1 **teaspoon lemon juice**
½ **teaspoon dried dill weed or 1 teaspoon fresh minced**

Combine all ingredients in blender or food processor. Process until smooth. Chill before serving. Great with raw vegetables.

Yields: ¾ cup (1 tablespoon serving)

NUTRIENT VALUES					
PROTEIN 58%	CARBOHYDRATE 23%		FAT 19%		ALCOHOL 0%
CALORIES 9.309	PRO-GM 1.333	CARB-GM 0.530	FAT-GM 0.191		SOD-MG 38.50
FOOD EXCHANGES					
MILK 0.0	VEG. 0.0	FRUIT 0.0	BREAD 0.0	MEAT 0.2	FAT 0.0

DILLY DIP

1 cup yogurt cheese (see p. 14)
2 tablespoons dill seed
3 tablespoons fresh dill or 2 tablespoons dried

Mix all ingredients and chill for 4 hours or overnight until flavors blend.

Yields: 1 cup (1 tablespoon serving)

Trisha Shirey

NUTRIENT VALUES					
PROTEIN 35%	CARBOHYDRATE 58%		FAT 7%		ALCOHOL 0%
CALORIES 17.10	PRO-GM 1.578	CARB-GM 2.645		FAT-GM 0.133	SOD-MG 20.80
FOOD EXCHANGES					
MILK 0.2	VEG. 0.0	FRUIT 0.0	BREAD 0.1	MEAT 0.0	FAT 0.0

EGGPLANT DIP

¾ pound eggplant
2 tablespoons vegetable stock
1 clove garlic, minced
½ onion, sliced
½ bell pepper, sliced
¼ teaspoon black pepper
¼ teaspoon paprika
1 teaspoon dried basil or 2 teaspoons fresh
½ cup nonfat yogurt

Peel eggplant and dice. Set aside. Saute garlic and onion in stock until onion is clear. Add eggplant and bell pepper. Saute until vegetables are tender. Season vegetables with spices and stir. Remove from heat. Allow to cool.

After vegetables have cooled, puree in batches in a blender. Add yogurt and mix. Serve chilled.

Yields: 1½ cups (1 tablespoon serving)

NUTRIENT VALUES					
PROTEIN 22%	CARBOHYDRATE 73%		FAT 5%		ALCOHOL 0%
CALORIES 7.675	PRO-GM 0.466	CARB-GM 1.566		FAT-GM 0.048	SOD-MG 3.488
FOOD EXCHANGES					
MILK 0.0	VEG. 0.2	FRUIT 0.0	BREAD 0.0	MEAT 0.0	FAT 0.0

ONION DIP

1 **cup nonfat yogurt**
3 **tablespoons minced onion**
2 **teaspoons low-sodium beef bouillon**

In a small bowl, combine all ingredients. Chill. Serve with raw vegetables.

Yields: 1 cup (1 tablespoon serving)

NUTRIENT VALUES					
PROTEIN 38%	CARBOHYDRATE 61%		FAT 1%		ALCOHOL 0%
CALORIES 7.594	PRO-GM 0.718	CARB-GM 1.146	FAT-GM 0.007		SOD-MG 12.10
FOOD EXCHANGES					
MILK 0.1	VEG. 0.0	FRUIT 0.0	BREAD 0.0	MEAT 0.0	FAT 0.0

HERB DIP

½ **cup nonfat yogurt**
1½ **teaspoons lemon juice**
1 **cup lowfat cottage cheese**
2 **teaspoons onion, grated**
1 **teaspoon minced fresh thyme or ¼ teaspoon dried thyme**
1 **teaspoon minced fresh basil or ¼ teaspoon dried basil**
1 **teaspoon minced fresh oregano or ¼ teaspoon dried oregano**
1 **teaspoon minced fresh marjoram or ¼ teaspoon dried marjoram**
¼ **teaspoon salt**

Combine ingredients in the container of an electric blender; process until smooth. Cover and chill. Serve with raw vegetables or whole grain crackers.

Servings: 24 (1 tablespoon serving)

NUTRIENT VALUES					
PROTEIN 57%	CARBOHYDRATE 28%		FAT 16%		ALCOHOL 0%
CALORIES 11.10	PRO-GM 1.536	CARB-GM 0.749	FAT-GM 0.187		SOD-MG 62.00
FOOD EXCHANGES					
MILK 0.0	VEG. 0.0	FRUIT 0.0	BREAD 0.0	MEAT 0.2	FAT 0.0

QUESO CON SALSA

1 **cup yogurt cheese (see p. 14)**
1 **teaspoon ground cumin**
1 **teaspoon garlic powder**
¼ **teaspoon ground oregano**
½ **teaspoon white pepper**
½ **cup picante sauce**

Mix cumin, garlic, oregano, pepper and yogurt cheese. Place in serving dish and pour picante sauce over cheese mixture. Serve with whole grain crackers or tostado chips.

Yields: 1 cup (1 tablespoon serving)

NUTRIENT VALUES					
PROTEIN 33%	CARBOHYDRATE 60%		FAT 7%		ALCOHOL 0%
CALORIES 16.90	PRO-GM 1.490	CARB-GM 2.669	FAT-GM 0.130	SOD-MG 74.60	
FOOD EXCHANGES					
MILK 0.2	VEG. 0.0	FRUIT 0.0	BREAD 0.0	MEAT 0.0	FAT 0.0

CEVICHE

1 **pound firm white fish**
1 **cup fresh lime or lemon juice**
1½ **cups chopped tomato**
1 **cup chopped onion**
15 **olives, chopped**
2 **teaspoons vegetable oil**
1 **tablespoon fresh chopped parsley**
1 **tablespoon fresh chopped cilantro**
¼ **teaspoon dried marjoram or ½ teaspoon fresh**
¼ **teaspoon dried thyme or ½ teaspoon fresh**
½ **teaspoon dried sage or 1 teaspoon fresh**
3 **tablespoons canned chopped green chiles**

Cut fish into bite-size pieces, cover with lime or lemon juice. Add remaining ingredients, stir gently to mix. Refrigerate overnight or a minimum of 4–6 hours. Serve well-chilled with melba rounds or tortilla chips.

Servings: 17 (¼ cup serving)

NUTRIENT VALUES					
PROTEIN 50%	CARBOHYDRATE 24%		FAT 26%		ALCOHOL 0%
CALORIES 43.80	PRO-GM 5.654	CARB-GM 2.717	FAT-GM 1.329	SOD-MG 126.0	
FOOD EXCHANGES					
MILK 0.0	VEG. 0.3	FRUIT 0.1	BREAD 0.0	MEAT 0.6	FAT 0.2

CLAM DIP

1 cup nonfat yogurt
4 ounce can minced clams, drained
2 tablespoons minced onion
¼ teaspoon salt
Dash of pepper
½ clove garlic, minced
1½ teaspoons Worcester-shire sauce

In a small bowl, combine all ingredients. Chill.

Makes: 1 cup (1 tablespoon serving)

NUTRIENT VALUES					
PROTEIN	CARBOHYDRATE		FAT		ALCOHOL
46%	48%		7%		0%
CALORIES	PRO-GM	CARB-GM	FAT-GM		SOD-MG
11.40	1.294	1.348	0.087		48.80
FOOD EXCHANGES					
MILK	VEG.	FRUIT	BREAD	MEAT	FAT
0.1	0.0	0.0	0.0	0.1	0.0

CRAB DIP

1 cup canned crabmeat
1 cup nonfat yogurt
2 green onions, chopped
1 tablespoon fresh chopped dill weed
1 clove garlic, minced

Mix all ingredients together in a small bowl. Serve cold with herb crackers.

Servings: 35 (1 tablespoon serving)

NUTRIENT VALUES					
PROTEIN	CARBOHYDRATE		FAT		ALCOHOL
58%	31%		11%		0%
CALORIES	PRO-GM	CARB-GM	FAT-GM		SOD-MG
7.186	1.010	0.530	0.087		23.90
FOOD EXCHANGES					
MILK	VEG.	FRUIT	BREAD	MEAT	FAT
0.0	0.0	0.0	0.0	0.1	0.0

SEAFOOD DIP

1   teaspoon minced fresh
    dill or ½ teaspoon dried
1   teaspoon Tabasco sauce
1   green onion, chopped
    fine
½   cup nonfat yogurt cheese
    (or "light" sour cream)
¼   cup nonfat yogurt
¼   cup sealegs or crab,
    chopped fine
¼   cup shrimp, chopped
    fine (may use frozen
    precooked popcorn
    shrimp)
¼   cup chopped celery
28 melba rounds

Mix all ingredients and chill. Serve one heaping tablespoon per melba round.

Servings: 28 (1 heaping tablespoon)

NUTRIENT VALUES			
PROTEIN	CARBOHYDRATE	FAT	ALCOHOL
27%	63%	10%	0%
CALORIES	PRO-GM	CARB-GM	FAT-GM	SOD-MG
22.60	1.492	3.480	0.241	14.10
FOOD EXCHANGES					
MILK	VEG.	FRUIT	BREAD	MEAT	FAT
0.1	0.0	0.0	0.0	0.1	0.0

EGGPLANT CAPONATA

2 cups eggplant, chopped, with peel on
4 cups water
¾ cup chopped green pepper
1 cup chopped onion
1 cup chopped tomatoes
1 tablespoon olive oil
2 garlic cloves, minced
2 tablespoons red wine vinegar
2 tablespoons drained capers
¼ teaspoon Italian seasoning
Pinch of cayenne pepper
⅓ cup fresh parsley, chopped

Soak the cubes of eggplant in cold water for 10 minutes. Drain, rinse, drain again, and pat dry.

Heat the olive oil in a nonstick skillet. Add the onions and garlic and saute until they are clear. Add the chopped peppers and eggplant and saute, stirring often, for 10 minutes. Add the vinegar, capers, Italian seasoning and pepper and cook for 5 minutes. Add tomatoes and cook for 5 minutes longer. Stir in the parsley. Serve warm or cold. Serve on whole grain crackers or as a filling in miniature tarts.

Servings: 24 (2 tablespoon serving)

NUTRIENT VALUES			
PROTEIN	CARBOHYDRATE	FAT	ALCOHOL
10%	53%	37%	0%
CALORIES	PRO-GM	CARB-GM	FAT-GM	SOD-MG
14.00	0.389	2.057	0.641	1.103

FOOD EXCHANGES					
MILK	VEG.	FRUIT	BREAD	MEAT	FAT
0.0	0.3	0.0	0.0	0.0	0.1

✓ CRAB AND CHEESE BALL

1   **cup firm yogurt cheese, made from nonfat yogurt (see p. 75)**
4   **ounces crabmeat**
1   **tablespoon lemon juice**
1   **teaspoon prepared horseradish**
1   **teaspoon minced onion**
1   **teaspoon finely chopped fresh chives**
¼   **teaspoon Worcestershire sauce**

Squeeze excess water from crab. Chop crabmeat coarsely and blot well with paper towel. Combine all ingredients in a bowl. Blend well with a fork. Spoon mixture into serving dish. Refrigerate an hour.

To serve, spread on toast, crackers or serve with vegetables. If yogurt thins, serve as a dip with crackers or pita bread triangles.

Yields: 1½ cup (1 tablespoon serving)

NUTRIENT VALUES			
PROTEIN	CARBOHYDRATE	FAT	ALCOHOL
51%	42%	7%	0%
CALORIES	PRO-GM	CARB-GM	FAT-GM	SOD-MG
14.20	1.765	1.452	0.107	39.90

FOOD EXCHANGES					
MILK	VEG.	FRUIT	BREAD	MEAT	FAT
0.1	0.0	0.0	0.0	0.1	0.0

HERB CHEESE BALL

½ pound Neufchatel cheese, room temperature
5 parsley sprigs, no stems
2-3 basil sprigs, or oregano or marjoram (fresh)
1 medium garlic clove
⅛ teaspoon salt
Freshly ground whole black pepper

This is a wonderful party hors d'oeuvre. It freezes well too. Stem the herbs and mince finly. Mince the garlic. Add the herbs, garlic, and salt to Neufchatel cheese and blend well. Cover tightly with plastic wrap and refrigerate or freeze until firm. Form into a ball and roll in black pepper to cover. Wrap again and refrigerate until served. Will keep 2-3 days in refrigerator.

Variation: Omit basil, add 2 tablespoons chopped fresh dill, 1 teaspoon chopped chives.

Servings: 17 (1 tablespoon serving)

Trisha Shirey

NUTRIENT VALUES					
PROTEIN	CARBOHYDRATE			FAT	ALCOHOL
15%	7%			78%	0%
CALORIES	PRO-GM	CARB-GM		FAT-GM	SOD-MG
36.30	1.408	0.634		3.174	69.00
FOOD EXCHANGES					
MILK	VEG.	FRUIT	BREAD	MEAT	FAT
0.0	0.0	0.0	0.0	0.2	0.6

CRAB STUFFED CHERRY TOMATOES

18 cherry tomatoes
2 tablespoons 1½%–2% cottage cheese
1 teaspoon minced onion
¾ teaspoon lemon juice
¼ teaspoon horseradish
1 clove garlic
4 ounces crabmeat, fresh or canned (drained)
2 tablespoons celery, minced
2 teaspoons green pepper, finely chopped

Cut top off each tomato; scoop out pulp and discard. Place hollowed tomatoes upside down on paper towels to drain. Place cottage cheese and garlic in container of electric blender and process until smooth. Place in small bowl and add remaining ingredients. Mix well. Spoon mixture into hollowed cherry tomatoes. Chill before serving.

Servings: 18 (1 tomato per serving)

NUTRIENT VALUES					
PROTEIN 60%	CARBOHYDRATE 22%		FAT 18%		ALCOHOL 0%
CALORIES 9.562	PRO-GM 1.417	CARB-GM 0.517		FAT-GM 0.189	SOD-MG 40.00
FOOD EXCHANGES					
MILK 0.0	VEG. 0.1	FRUIT 0.0	BREAD 0.0	MEAT 0.2	FAT 0.0

BROILED MUSHROOMS

1 pound raw mushrooms
1 ounce part-skim mozzarella, grated
1 slice whole wheat bread, made into crumbs
½ teaspoon minced lemon thyme

Clean mushrooms and remove stem from caps. Pat dry and place on baking sheet.

Mix grated cheese, breadcrumbs, and thyme. Fill mushroom caps. Broil until cheese melts. Serve immediately.

Servings: 18–20

NUTRIENT VALUES					
PROTEIN 27%	CARBOHYDRATE 48%		FAT 25%		ALCOHOL 0%
CALORIES 12.50	PRO-GM 0.942	CARB-GM 1.661		FAT-GM 0.380	SOD-MG 15.30
FOOD EXCHANGES					
MILK 0.0	VEG. 0.2	FRUIT 0.0	BREAD 0.1	MEAT 0.1	FAT 0.0

MUSHROOM DELIGHTS

1 **pound medium-sized mushrooms (approx. 20 per pound)**
1 **clove garlic, minced**
½ **cup chopped onion**
¼ **cup Parmesan cheese**
1 **teaspoon lemon juice**
Pepper to taste

Rinse mushrooms, pat dry and remove stems. In a small pan, saute chopped mushroom stems, garlic and onion until lightly brown. Combine with cheese, lemon juice and seasonings. Pile into caps and place in shallow baking pan with about ¼ cup water in the bottom. Bake in 350° oven, for 15 minutes.

Servings: 20 (1 mushroom each)

NUTRIENT VALUES					
PROTEIN	CARBOHYDRATE		FAT		ALCOHOL
29%	41%		30%		0%
CALORIES	PRO-GM	CARB-GM		FAT-GM	SOD-MG
13.20	1.054	1.484		0.484	24.10
FOOD EXCHANGES					
MILK	VEG.	FRUIT	BREAD	MEAT	FAT
0.0	0.3	0.0	0.0	0.1	0.0

PESTO STUFFED MUSHROOMS

1 **pound fresh mushrooms (approximately 20 per pound)**
7 **tablespoons basil pesto (see page 66)**

Wash mushrooms. Remove stems. Place mushroom caps on serving plate. Place 1 teaspoon pesto in each mushroom. Serve cold.

Servings: 20 (1 mushroom per serving)

NUTRIENT VALUES					
PROTEIN	CARBOHYDRATE		FAT		ALCOHOL
23%	35%		42%		0%
CALORIES	PRO-GM	CARB-GM		FAT-GM	SOD-MG
14.90	0.963	1.424		0.762	16.20
FOOD EXCHANGES					
MILK	VEG.	FRUIT	BREAD	MEAT	FAT
0.0	0.2	0.0	0.1	0.1	0.1

CHINESE STUFFED PEPPERS

1 **pound medium-sized mushrooms (approximately 20 per pound)**
1 **clove garlic, minced**
1 **small onion, diced**
¼ **cup Parmesan cheese**
1 **teaspoon lemon juice**
½ **teaspoon pepper**
10 **banana peppers, stemmed, seeded and halved**
¼ **teaspoon ground ginger**

Rinse mushrooms, pat dry and remove stems. In a small pan, saute chopped mushrooms stems, garlic and onion until lightly brown. Combine with cheese, lemon juice and seasonings.

Stuff in banana pepper halves.

Servings: 20 (½ pepper each)

NUTRIENT VALUES					
PROTEIN	CARBOHYDRATE		FAT		ALCOHOL
25%	51%		23%		0%
CALORIES	PRO-GM	CARB-GM		FAT-GM	SOD-MG
17.80	1.260	2.540		0.513	24.70
FOOD EXCHANGES					
MILK	VEG.	FRUIT	BREAD	MEAT	FAT
0.0	0.5	0.0	0.0	0.1	0.0

CHEESE TOASTIES

6 **slices whole wheat bread**
1 **egg white, beaten**
⅓ **cup nonfat yogurt**
½ **teaspoon Worcestershire sauce**
⅛ **teaspoon dry mustard**
Dash of cayenne pepper
½ **cup grated farmer's cheese (2 ounces)**

Trim crust from bread which has been lightly toasted. Mix remaining ingredients and chill. Spread 1 tablespoon cheese mixture on each slice; cut into four triangles or squares. Garnish with pimiento or paprika prior to baking. Bake at 350° for 10 minutes.

Servings: 24

NUTRIENT VALUES					
PROTEIN	CARBOHYDRATE		FAT		ALCOHOL
23%	46%		31%		0%
CALORIES	PRO-GM	CARB-GM		FAT-GM	SOD-MG
28.80	1.530	3.121		0.948	53.50
FOOD EXCHANGES					
MILK	VEG.	FRUIT	BREAD	MEAT	FAT
0.1	0.0	0.0	0.2	0.0	0.1

ARTICHOKE SQUARES

14 ounces artichoke hearts, drain, reserving liquid (8½ ounces drained weight)
½ cup chopped onion
1 clove garlic, chopped
¼ cup water
1 large egg and 2 egg whites
¼ cup whole wheat breadcrumbs (½ slice whole wheat bread)
¼ teaspoon black pepper
¼ teaspoon ground oregano
½ teaspoon Tabasco sauce
2 tablespoon fresh parsley, chopped
¾ cup part skim mozzarella cheese
½ cup grated zucchini
Vegetable coating spray

Chop the artichoke hearts and set aside.

Saute the onions and garlic in water until soft. Set aside.

Beat the eggs in a small bowl until frothy. Add the breadcrumbs, pepper, oregano, Tabasco, parsley, and zucchini. Stir in the cheese, artichokes and sauteed onion. Turn the mixture into a 8 × 8 pan coated with vegetable coating spray. Bake at 350° for 30 minutes. Cut into 1 inch squares and serve warm or at room temperature.

Servings: 32

NUTRIENT VALUES			
PROTEIN	CARBOHYDRATE	FAT	ALCOHOL
32%	34%	34%	0%
CALORIES	PRO-GM	CARB-GM	FAT-GM	SOD-MG
17.60	1.496	1.579	0.713	20.90
FOOD EXCHANGES					
MILK	VEG.	FRUIT	BREAD	MEAT	FAT
0.0	0.2	0.0	0.0	0.2	0.0

HOT CHEESE SQUARES

5   egg whites lightly
    beaten
1   cup lowfat cottage
    cheese
1   cup grated part-skim
    mozzarella
1   can (4 oz.) diced green
    chiles
¼   cup whole wheat flour
½   teaspoon baking powder
Vegetable coating spray

Combine egg whites, cottage cheese, mozzarella and chiles. Mix flour and baking powder and add to cheese mixture. Spray 8 × 8 baking dish with vegetable coating spray. Pour in batter. Bake at 350° for 40 minutes. Allow to cool slightly before serving.

Servings: 25

NUTRIENT VALUES					
PROTEIN	CARBOHYDRATE		FAT		ALCOHOL
34%	44%		21%		0%
CALORIES	PRO-GM	CARB-GM		FAT-GM	SOD-MG
42.70	3.589	4.633		0.978	74.70
FOOD EXCHANGES					
MILK	VEG.	FRUIT	BREAD	MEAT	FAT
0.0	0.0	0.0	0.2	0.4	0.1

BEAN PATE

1½ cup cooked fava beans
    (or white navy beans)
1   cup yogurt cheese,
    nonfat (see p. 14)
Freshly ground black pepper
Sprigs of mint

Combine beans, yogurt cheese, and pepper in a food processor. Blend into a smooth paste. Place in a small serving dish and garnish with mint. Serve with tortilla chips or whole grain crackers.

Yields: 2½ cups (1 tablespoon serving)

NUTRIENT VALUES					
PROTEIN	CARBOHYDRATE		FAT		ALCOHOL
32%	66%		2%		0%
CALORIES	PRO-GM	CARB-GM		FAT-GM	SOD-MG
13.90	1.113	2.300		0.038	8.488
FOOD EXCHANGES					
MILK	VEG.	FRUIT	BREAD	MEAT	FAT
0.1	0.0	0.0	0.1	0.1	0.0

SALMON PATE

1 7¾-ounce can pink salmon
½ cup canned water-packed artichoke hearts, drained
½ cup cooked green beans
⅓ cup lowfat cottage cheese
3 tablespoons diced pimiento
2 tablespoons chopped onion
1 clove garlic, minced
1½ teaspoon dill weed or 1 tablespoon minced fresh dill
¼ teaspoon Tabasco

Place drained salmon in blender with all other ingredients; blend well. Pour into serving bowl or mold and chill for several hours. Serve with raw vegetables or crackers.

Yields: 2 cups (1 tablespoon serving)

NUTRIENT VALUES			
PROTEIN	CARBOHYDRATE	FAT	ALCOHOL
51%	20%	30%	0%
CALORIES	PRO-GM	CARB-GM	FAT-GM	SOD-MG
14.80	1.859	0.719	0.481	45.50
FOOD EXCHANGES					
MILK	VEG.	FRUIT	BREAD	MEAT	FAT
0.0	0.1	0.0	0.0	0.2	0.0

PINEAPPLE BANANA SHAKE

8 ounce can unsweetened crushed pineapple, undrained
1 cup skim milk
1 banana, cut into chunks
½ teaspoon vanilla
2–3 ice cubes
2 teaspoons fresh mint leaves (optional)

Drain pineapple, reserving ¼ cup juice and set aside. Combine pineapple, ¼ cup juice, milk, banana and vanilla in container of an electric blender. Process until frothy. Pour into glasses and serve immediately.

Servings: 2 (1 cup serving)

NUTRIENT VALUES			
PROTEIN	CARBOHYDRATE	FAT	ALCOHOL
15%	81%	4%	0%
CALORIES	PRO-GM	CARB-GM	FAT-GM	SOD-MG
136.0	5.479	29.50	0.697	67.00
FOOD EXCHANGES					
MILK	VEG.	FRUIT	BREAD	MEAT	FAT
0.5	0.0	1.8	0.0	0.0	0.0

STRAWBERRY SHAKE

1 **cup skim milk**
1 **cup nonfat yogurt**
1 **tablespoon honey**
2 **teaspoons vanilla**
2 **cups frozen strawberries**

Combine first four ingredients in a blender, gradually add strawberries and blend until smooth.

Servings: 4 (1 cup serving)

NUTRIENT VALUES					
PROTEIN	CARBOHYDRATE		FAT		ALCOHOL
22%	76%		2%		0%
CALORIES	PRO-GM	CARB-GM		FAT-GM	SOD-MG
92.30	5.253	18.10		0.233	74.30
FOOD EXCHANGES					
MILK	VEG.	FRUIT	BREAD	MEAT	FAT
0.6	0.0	0.5	0.3	0.0	0.0

BANANA-PEANUT BUTTER SMOOTHIE

⅔ **cup nonfat milk**
¼ **cup nonfat dry milk or yogurt**
1 **banana**
1 **tablespoon peanut butter**
3–4 **ice cubes**

Combine all ingredients in blender container. Process until smooth.

Servings: 2 (1 cup serving)

NUTRIENT VALUES					
PROTEIN	CARBOHYDRATE		FAT		ALCOHOL
20%	55%		24%		0%
CALORIES	PRO-GM	CARB-GM		FAT-GM	SOD-MG
163.0	8.796	23.70		4.640	128.0
FOOD EXCHANGES					
MILK	VEG.	FRUIT	BREAD	MEAT	FAT
0.5	0.0	1.0	0.0	0.3	0.8

BANANA PINEAPPLE SMOOTHIE

1   cup skim milk
½   cup nonfat dry milk or
    yogurt
1   ripe banana
1   cup pineapple chunks
3–4 ice cubes
Dash cinnamon

Place all ingredients into a blender container and process until smooth.

Servings: 2 (1½ cup serving)

NUTRIENT VALUES				
PROTEIN	CARBOHYDRATE		FAT	ALCOHOL
22%	74%		4%	0%
CALORIES	PRO-GM	CARB-GM	FAT-GM	SOD-MG
199.0	11.30	38.60	1.043	159.0
FOOD EXCHANGES					
MILK	VEG.	FRUIT	BREAD	MEAT	FAT
1.3	0.0	1.8	0.0	0.0	0.0

BANANA STRAWBERRY SMOOTHIE

1   cup skim milk
¼   cup nonfat dry milk or
    yogurt
1   ripe banana
1   cup strawberries
3–4 ice cubes
Dash cinnamon

Place all ingredients into a blender container and process until smooth.

Servings: 2 (1½ cup serving)

NUTRIENT VALUES				
PROTEIN	CARBOHYDRATE		FAT	ALCOHOL
21%	74%		5%	0%
CALORIES	PRO-GM	CARB-GM	FAT-GM	SOD-MG
153.0	8.433	29.80	0.927	113.0
FOOD EXCHANGES					
MILK	VEG.	FRUIT	BREAD	MEAT	FAT
0.8	0.0	1.5	0.0	0.0	0.0

STRAWBERRY PINEAPPLE SMOOTHIE

⅔ cup skim milk
¼ cup nonfat dry milk or
    nonfat yogurt
1   cup strawberries
1   cup pineapple chunks
3–4 ice cubes
Dash cinnamon

Place all ingredients into a blender container and process until smooth.

Servings: 2 (1½ cup serving)

NUTRIENT VALUES					
PROTEIN	CARBOHYDRATE			FAT	ALCOHOL
21%	73%			6%	0%
CALORIES	PRO-GM		CARB-GM	FAT-GM	SOD-MG
122.0	6.656		23.40	0.869	91.40
FOOD EXCHANGES					
MILK	VEG.	FRUIT	BREAD	MEAT	FAT
0.5	0.0	1.3	0.0	0.0	0.0

TROPICAL SMOOTHIE

1   cup skim milk
¼ cup nonfat dry milk
1   orange, peeled and
    sectioned
1   ripe banana
1   cup pineapple chunks
1   teaspoon coconut extract
3–4 ice cubes

Combine all ingredients in blender container. Process until smooth.

Servings: 3 (generous 1 cup serving)

NUTRIENT VALUES					
PROTEIN	CARBOHYDRATE			FAT	ALCOHOL
17%	79%			4%	0%
CALORIES	PRO-GM		CARB-GM	FAT-GM	SOD-MG
133.0	5.928		27.90	0.708	75.10
FOOD EXCHANGES					
MILK	VEG.	FRUIT	BREAD	MEAT	FAT
0.5	0.0	1.5	0.0	0.0	0.0

GRAPE SPRITZER

4 lime slices
2½ cups club soda, chilled
   or sparkling mineral
   water
1½ cups unsweetened grape
   juice, chilled

Place 1 lime slice in each of 4 glasses. Combine club soda and grape juice; mix well. Pour 1 cup mixture over lime slice in each glass.

Makes: 4 (1 cup serving)

NUTRIENT VALUES					
PROTEIN 4%	CARBOHYDRATE 95%		FAT 1%		ALCOHOL 0%
CALORIES 63.10	PRO-GM 0.646	CARB-GM 16.00		FAT-GM 0.104	SOD-MG 32.90
FOOD EXCHANGES					
MILK 0.0	VEG. 0.0	FRUIT 1.1	BREAD 0.0	MEAT 0.0	FAT 0.0

HONEYDEW SPLASH

1 cup ripe honeydew
  melon, cubed
1 cup white grape juice
2 mint leaves
¼ teaspoon lemon extract
2 cups sparkling water

Place the melon cubes, grape juice, mint and lemon extract in a blender and process until smooth.

Divide the mixture between four glasses. Fill glass with sparkling water and stir. Garnish with lime slice or strawberry.

Servings: 4

NUTRIENT VALUES					
PROTEIN 4%	CARBOHYDRATE 95%		FAT 1%		ALCOHOL 0%
CALORIES 53.80	PRO-GM 0.545	CARB-GM 13.40		FAT-GM 0.090	SOD-MG 8.500
FOOD EXCHANGES					
MILK 0.0	VEG. 0.0	FRUIT 0.9	BREAD 0.0	MEAT 0.0	FAT 0.0

KIWI SPLASH

2 ripe kiwi fruits
⅓ cup white grape juice
2 teaspoons honey
1½ cup sparkling mineral
   water

Peel the kiwi fruits and place in a blender with the juice and honey. Process until smooth.

Divide the mixture between two glasses. Pour in sparkling mineral water and stir. Garnish with strawberry and kiwi slice.

Servings: 2 (1¼ cup serving)

NUTRIENT VALUES			
PROTEIN	CARBOHYDRATE	FAT	ALCOHOL
4%	93%	3%	0%
CALORIES	PRO-GM	CARB-GM	FAT-GM	SOD-MG
93.50	0.985	23.30	0.372	9.249
FOOD EXCHANGES					
MILK	VEG.	FRUIT	BREAD	MEAT	FAT
0.0	0.0	1.3	0.3	0.0	0.0

ORANGE FIZZ

1 (10-ounce) bottle
   sparkling water
1 quart orange juice
Orange slices

Mix sparkling water and orange juice and pour over crushed ice and orange slices in a pitcher.

Servings: 7 (6 ounce serving)

NUTRIENT VALUES			
PROTEIN	CARBOHYDRATE	FAT	ALCOHOL
6%	93%	1%	0%
CALORIES	PRO-GM	CARB-GM	FAT-GM	SOD-MG
64.00	0.960	15.30	0.080	2.001
FOOD EXCHANGES					
MILK	VEG.	FRUIT	BREAD	MEAT	FAT
0.0	0.0	1.1	0.0	0.0	0.0

WATERMELON COOLER

4 ounces very ripe watermelon, cut into cubes, seeds removed
1 teaspoon lemon juice
4 ounces naturally sparkling water or pure seltzer water
3 ice cubes

In the food processor fitted with the steel blade or in a blender, shave the ice cubes. Puree the watermelon until it is liquid. Add the lemon juice and water and blend. Pour into a glass over the shaved ice. Garnish with a mint leaf or lemon slice.

Servings: 1

NUTRIENT VALUES			
PROTEIN 7%	CARBOHYDRATE 82%	FAT 11%	ALCOHOL 0%
CALORIES 36.50	PRO-GM 0.722	CARB-GM 8.480	FAT-GM 0.497	SOD-MG 27.20
FOOD EXCHANGES					
MILK 0.0	VEG. 0.0	FRUIT 0.5	BREAD 0.0	MEAT 0.0	FAT 0.0

SPICED TOMATO JUICE

5½ ounces low-sodium tomato juice
⅛ teaspoon oregano or ¼ teaspoon fresh minced
¼ teaspoon parsley or ½ teaspoon fresh minced
Dash of garlic powder or ½ minced garlic clove
½ teaspoon Mrs. Dash or salt substitute
1 teaspoon fresh lime juice
Dash black pepper

Put tomato juice in blender. Add remaining ingredients. Blend briefly and pour over ice cubes.

Servings: 1

NUTRIENT VALUES			
PROTEIN 15%	CARBOHYDRATE 82%	FAT 3%	ALCOHOL 0%
CALORIES 27.50	PRO-GM 1.214	CARB-GM 6.715	FAT-GM 0.109	SOD-MG 15.70
FOOD EXCHANGES					
MILK 0.0	VEG. 1.0	FRUIT 0.0	BREAD 0.0	MEAT 0.0	FAT 0.0

Specific Dressings . . .

SAUCES &
CONDIMENTS

BAKED POTATO TOPPERS

Sprouts
Lowfat or nonfat yogurt
Grated lowfat cheese
Yogurt cheese (page 14)
Chopped broccoli
Toasted sesame seeds
Chives
Sliced raw mushrooms
Herbal seasoning to taste
Mock sour cream (page 74)
Spaghetti sauce
Chopped cauliflower
Diced green onions
Guacamole Surprise (page 71)
Grated zucchini
Grated carrots
Chicken salad
Grated squash
Diced bell pepper
Tofu
Picante sauce
Horseradish topping (page 71)
Buttermilk cream sauce (page 80)
Water packed tuna

PICO DE GALLO

8   medium tomatoes, chopped
1   medium red onion, chopped
2   cloves garlic, chopped
3   oranges
6   limes
12 hot peppers, seeded and chopped

Chop up tomatoes, onions, garlic and peppers. Squeeze juice of limes and oranges over mixture to cover.

Yields: 2 quarts (¼ cup serving)

Lucy Curb

NUTRIENT VALUES				
PROTEIN 12%	CARBOHYDRATE 82%		FAT 6%	ALCOHOL 0%
CALORIES 13.30	PRO-GM 0.464	CARB-GM 3.150	FAT-GM 0.106	SOD-MG 3.041
FOOD EXCHANGES					
MILK 0.0	VEG. 0.3	FRUIT 0.1	BREAD 0.0	MEAT 0.0	FAT 0.0

SALSA VERDE (GREEN SAUCE)

1   small onion
1   medium jalapeno, stemmed and chopped
1   tablespoon cilantro, chopped
1   small garlic clove, chopped
1   pound fresh tomatillos

Combine onion, jalapeno, cilantro and garlic in blender.

Blanch fresh tomatillos in boiling water to cover to soften slightly, 2 minutes; drain. Add to blender container. Process all ingredients until smooth.

Yields: 2 cups (1 tablespoon serving)

NUTRIENT VALUES					
PROTEIN	CARBOHYDRATE		FAT		ALCOHOL
4%	94%		2%		0%
CALORIES	PRO-GM	CARB-GM	FAT-GM		SOD-MG
5.930	0.055	1.432	0.013		7.926
FOOD EXCHANGES					
MILK	VEG.	FRUIT	BREAD	MEAT	FAT
0.0	0.2	0.0	0.0	0.0	0.0

BASIL PESTO

3   cups fresh basil (leaves only)
4   cloves garlic
2   tablespoons pine nuts or walnuts
4   tablespoons Parmesan cheese
2   tablespoons Romano cheese
1   tablespoon olive oil
3   tablespoons water

Add all ingredients together in a blender container. Process until a smooth paste. Use spatula and off/on motions to help processing.

Yields: 1¼ cups (1 tablespoon serving)

Great for chicken salads, pasta or spread on Melba toast. Before basil freezes in winter, make extra pesto in the fall and freeze for pesto all year.

NUTRIENT VALUES					
PROTEIN	CARBOHYDRATE		FAT		ALCOHOL
21%	16%		64%		0%
CALORIES	PRO-GM	CARB-GM	FAT-GM		SOD-MG
25.70	1.416	1.054	1.911		44.50
FOOD EXCHANGES					
MILK	VEG.	FRUIT	BREAD	MEAT	FAT
0.0	0.0	0.0	0.1	0.2	0.3

CILANTRO PESTO

6 tablespoons water
2 cloves garlic, peeled
4 tablespoons Parmesan
   cheese
2½ cups cilantro sprigs
¼ cup walnut halves or
   pine nuts
1 tablespoons safflower oil
¼ teaspoon salt
1 cup chopped fresh
   parsley

Combine all ingredients in blender or food processor and puree. Pulse for a few seconds then stop. Use a spatula to fold in ingredients from sides back into bowl to help blend. Will refrigerate up to one week.

Yields: 1 cup (1 tablespoon serving)

Wonderful tossed with hot pasta, used as a sandwich spread, or as a potato topper.

NUTRIENT VALUES			
PROTEIN	CARBOHYDRATE	FAT	ALCOHOL
17%	16%	66%	0%
CALORIES	PRO-GM	CARB-GM	FAT-GM	SOD-MG
31.20	1.457	1.384	2.470	65.40

FOOD EXCHANGES					
MILK	VEG.	FRUIT	BREAD	MEAT	FAT
0.0	0.0	0.0	0.1	0.2	0.4

GREEN CHILE PESTO

2 cloves garlic, peeled
⅓ cup grated Parmesan cheese
2 4-ounce cans green chiles
½ cup walnut pieces or pine nuts
½ cup chopped fresh parsley
1 tablespoon safflower oil
1 whole jalapeno, pickled or to taste
2 teaspoons jalapeno juice
¼ teaspoon salt

Place all ingredients in container of electric blender or food processor. Puree using off/on motions to blend. Mixture will be thick. Use spatula down sides of container to help blend. Will refrigerate for one week.

Yields: 1½ cups (1 tablespoon serving)

NUTRIENT VALUES					
PROTEIN	CARBOHYDRATE		FAT		ALCOHOL
17%	11%		72%		0%
CALORIES	PRO-GM	CARB-GM	FAT-GM		SOD-MG
29.00	1.280	0.835	2.465		56.50
FOOD EXCHANGES					
MILK	VEG.	FRUIT	BREAD	MEAT	FAT
0.0	0.1	0.0	0.6	0.1	0.5

RED BASIL PESTO

1½ cups fresh opal basil
   leaves
5 sun-dried tomatoes, (not
   oil packed)
2 garlic cloves
2 tablespoons Romano
   cheese, freshly grated
6 tablespoons Parmesan
   cheese, freshly grated
2 tablespoons pine nuts or
   walnuts
1 tablespoon olive oil
¼ cup water
Freshly ground pepper

Combine the opal basil, sun-dried tomatoes, garlic, cheeses and pine nuts in a food processor or blender. Mix together. With the machine running slowly add the olive oil and water. Season to taste with pepper and process to the desired consistency. Let stand 5 minutes before serving.

Makes: 1¼ cups (1 tablespoon serving)

Use tossed with hot pasta, as a spread on corn on the cob, or in chicken salad.

NUTRIENT VALUES					
PROTEIN	CARBOHYDRATE		FAT		ALCOHOL
22%	24%		55%		0%
CALORIES	PRO-GM	CARB-GM		FAT-GM	SOD-MG
33.40	1.901	2.097		2.133	55.20
FOOD EXCHANGES					
MILK	VEG.	FRUIT	BREAD	MEAT	FAT
0.0	0.0	0.0	0.1	0.2	0.3

BARBECUE SAUCE

½   cup water
¼   cup white wine
3   tablespoons lemon juice
1   tablespoon Dijon
     mustard
½   teaspoon pepper
½   teaspoon paprika
¼   cup catsup
2   tablespoons tomato paste
2   tablespoons
     Worcestershire

Combine all ingredients in a large saucepan. Bring to a boil, then reduce heat and simmer 20 minutes, stirring occasionally.

Yields: 1 cup (1 tablespoon serving)

NUTRIENT VALUES			
PROTEIN	CARBOHYDRATE	FAT	ALCOHOL
6%	91%	3%	0%
CALORIES	PRO-GM	CARB-GM	FAT-GM	SOD-MG
9.078	0.143	2.076	0.029	71.20
FOOD EXCHANGES					
MILK	VEG.	FRUIT	BREAD	MEAT	FAT
0.0	0.1	0.0	0.1	0.0	0.0

COCKTAIL SAUCE

½   cup catsup
5   teaspoons prepared
     horseradish, drained
3   teaspoons lemon juice
¼   teaspoon Worcestershire
¼   teaspoon Tabasco sauce

Mix all ingredients in a mixing bowl. Refrigerate until ready to serve.

Yields: ⅔ cup (1 tablespoon serving)

NUTRIENT VALUES			
PROTEIN	CARBOHYDRATE	FAT	ALCOHOL
1%	99%	0%	0%
CALORIES	PRO-GM	CARB-GM	FAT-GM	SOD-MG
13.50	0.044	3.590	0.000	154.0
FOOD EXCHANGES					
MILK	VEG.	FRUIT	BREAD	MEAT	FAT
0.0	0.0	0.0	0.2	0.0	0.0

HORSERADISH TOPPING

¾ cup lowfat cottage
  cheese
2 tablespoons horseradish
¼ cup nonfat yogurt
1 teaspoon Worcestershire
1 tablespoon fresh chives

Combine all ingredients in blender and process until smooth. Refrigerate. Excellent potato topper.

Yields: 1⅓ cups (1 tablespoon serving)

NUTRIENT VALUES					
PROTEIN	CARBOHYDRATE		FAT		ALCOHOL
60%	31%		10%		0%
CALORIES	PRO-GM	CARB-GM		FAT-GM	SOD-MG
7.976	1.159	0.592		0.083	52.70
FOOD EXCHANGES					
MILK	VEG.	FRUIT	BREAD	MEAT	FAT
0.0	0.0	0.0	0.0	0.1	0.0

GUACAMOLE SURPRISE

10 ounce package asparagus
   spears, steamed
½ cup pico de gallo or
   picante sauce
1 tablespoon fresh lemon
  juice
1 teaspoon fresh minced
  oregano
1 clove garlic, minced
¾ teaspoon cumin
Cilantro to taste
2 tablespoons nonfat
  yogurt
2 tablespoons reduced-
  calorie mayonnaise

Combine all ingredients in a blender and process until smooth. Serve chilled.

Yields: 2 cups (¼ cup serving)

NUTRIENT VALUES					
PROTEIN	CARBOHYDRATE		FAT		ALCOHOL
17%	44%		39%		0%
CALORIES	PRO-GM	CARB-GM		FAT-GM	SOD-MG
27.70	1.419	3.586		1.420	113.0
FOOD EXCHANGES					
MILK	VEG.	FRUIT	BREAD	MEAT	FAT
0.0	0.4	0.0	0.1	0.0	0.3

LEMON BUTTER

½ cup reduced-calorie margarine
¼ cup fresh lemon juice
1 tablespoon fresh parsley, minced
¼ teaspoon white pepper

Place all ingredients in a saucepan. Cook over medium heat until margarine is melted. Serve with fish or steamed vegetables.

Yields: 10 tablespoons (1 tablespoon serving)

NUTRIENT VALUES					
PROTEIN 0%	CARBOHYDRATE 5%		FAT 94%		ALCOHOL 0%
CALORIES 41.80	PRO-GM 0.038	CARB-GM 0.596		FAT-GM 4.562	SOD-MG 104.0
FOOD EXCHANGES					
MILK 0.0	VEG. 0.0	FRUIT 0.1	BREAD 0.0	MEAT 0.0	FAT 0.9

CURRY MAYONNAISE

¼ cup nonfat yogurt
¼ cup reduced-calorie mayonnaise
1½ teaspoons curry powder
1½ teaspoons Dijon mustard
Dash of ground ginger
½ teaspoon lemon juice
½ clove minced garlic
½ scallion, finely chopped
1½ teaspoons pickle relish

Mix all ingredients together and chill.

Yields: ½ cup (1 tablespoon serving)

Excellent as a spread on sandwiches or for a little zing in potato salad.

NUTRIENT VALUES					
PROTEIN 6%	CARBOHYDRATE 25%		FAT 69%		ALCOHOL 0%
CALORIES 27.25	PRO-GM .0412	CARB-GM 1.657		FAT-GM 2.056	SOD-MG 25.20
FOOD EXCHANGES					
MILK 0.05	VEG. 0.0	FRUIT 0.0	BREAD 0.0	MEAT 0.0	FAT 0.5

LOW-CALORIE MAYONNAISE

⅔ **cup nonfat yogurt**
⅓ **cup reduced-calorie mayonnaise**

Combine ingredients and refrigerate.

Yields: 1 cup (1 tablespoon serving)

Great way to reduce calories and fat and still retain taste.

NUTRIENT VALUES			
PROTEIN	CARBOHYDRATE	FAT	ALCOHOL
10%	23%	67%	0%
CALORIES	PRO-GM	CARB-GM	FAT-GM	SOD-MG
17.80	0.459	0.997	1.320	6.670
FOOD EXCHANGES					
MILK	VEG.	FRUIT	BREAD	MEAT	FAT
0.1	0.0	0.0	0.0	0.0	0.3

MOCK MAYONNAISE

½ **cup lowfat buttermilk**
1 **cup lowfat cottage cheese**
1 **cup nonfat yogurt**
½ **teaspoon garlic powder or 1 clove garlic, minced**
½ **teaspoon oregano**

Place all ingredients in a blender and process until smooth. Chill. Will keep in refrigerator 1–2 weeks.

Makes: 2½ cups (1 tablespoon serving)

Great to use as a mayonnaise substitute in dressings, salads, and dips.

NUTRIENT VALUES			
PROTEIN	CARBOHYDRATE	FAT	ALCOHOL
54%	37%	9%	0%
CALORIES	PRO-GM	CARB-GM	FAT-GM	SOD-MG
8.400	1.096	0.754	0.085	30.70
FOOD EXCHANGES					
MILK	VEG.	FRUIT	BREAD	MEAT	FAT
0.1	0.0	0.0	0.0	0.1	0.0

TOFU MAYONNAISE

6 ounces tofu, drained
1 tablespoon lemon juice
2 teaspoons soy sauce
⅛ teaspoon pepper
¼ teaspoon dry mustard

Combine all ingredients in a blender and process until smooth.

Yields: ½ cup (1 tablespoon serving)

NUTRIENT VALUES			
PROTEIN	CARBOHYDRATE	FAT	ALCOHOL
39%	17%	43%	0%
CALORIES	PRO-GM	CARB-GM	FAT-GM	SOD-MG
16.60	1.803	0.804	0.886	87.20

FOOD EXCHANGES					
MILK	VEG.	FRUIT	BREAD	MEAT	FAT
0.0	0.2	0.0	0.0	0.0	0.3

MOCK SOUR CREAM

¼ cup skim milk
1 cup lowfat cottage cheese
1 tablespoon lemon juice

Put all the ingredients into a blender. Process until smooth. Refrigerate.

Yields: 1¼ cups (1 tablespoon serving)

NUTRIENT VALUES			
PROTEIN	CARBOHYDRATE	FAT	ALCOHOL
65%	23%	12%	0%
CALORIES	PRO-GM	CARB-GM	FAT-GM	SOD-MG
9.513	1.512	0.527	0.123	47.50

FOOD EXCHANGES					
MILK	VEG.	FRUIT	BREAD	MEAT	FAT
0.0	0.0	0.0	0.0	0.2	0.0

NONFAT YOGURT

1 quart nonfat (skim) milk
⅓ cup nonfat dry milk
(powder)
1 tablespoon plain nonfat
or lowfat yogurt (must
have live culture,
example—Dannon)

Combine the milk with dry milk, stirring to dissolve. Heat to 120° and place in a glass or stainless steel container. Allow to cool to 110°. Remove ½ cup of the warm milk and blend in the yogurt. Add this mixture back to the remaining milk.

Cover the container with a dish towel and place in an oven that has been preheated to 200°, then turn off heat. Let the yogurt stand for about 12 hours. If you are using an electric oven, leave light on for heat. In a gas oven, the pilot light will provide heat.

Refrigerate yogurt. Will keep for about a week.

Makes: 1 quart

NUTRIENT VALUES			
PROTEIN	CARBOHYDRATE	FAT	ALCOHOL
39%	56%	5%	0%
CALORIES	PRO-GM	CARB-GM	FAT-GM	SOD-MG
112.0	10.90	15.50	0.650	163.0
FOOD EXCHANGES					
MILK	VEG.	FRUIT	BREAD	MEAT	FAT
1.4	0.0	0.0	0.0	0.0	0.0

TARTAR SAUCE

½ cup nonfat yogurt
2 hard cooked egg whites, chopped
2 tablespoons minced celery
¼ cup reduced-calorie mayonnaise
2 teaspoons dill pickle relish
2 teaspoons capers, drained
¼ teaspoon white pepper
1 tablespoon chopped parsley
2 tablespoons minced onion
1 tablespoon pimientos, minced

In a small bowl, mix all ingredients. Chill.

Yields: 1 cup plus 2 tablespoons (1 tablespoon serving)

NUTRIENT VALUES				
PROTEIN	CARBOHYDRATE		FAT	ALCOHOL
19%	29%		53%	0%
CALORIES	PRO-GM	CARB-GM	FAT-GM	SOD-MG
15.40	0.713	1.098	0.898	15.40
FOOD EXCHANGES					
MILK	VEG.	FRUIT	BREAD	MEAT	FAT
0.0	0.0	0.0	0.0	0.1	0.2

CHEESE SAUCE

½ cup lowfat cottage
cheese
2 tablespoons grated
Parmesan cheese
1 tablespoon reduced-
calorie margarine
1 tablespon cornstarch
mixed with 2
tablespoons water
¾ cup skim milk
½ teaspoon oregano,
thyme, basil, or
marjoram

Mix Parmesan and cottage cheese. Melt the margarine in a saucepan over low heat. Stir in the cornstarch mix and cook until mixture begins to thicken. Slowly add the skim milk and herbs. Stir constantly over medium heat until sauce is smooth. Add cheese mixture and stir until the mixture melts. Simmer additional 2–3 minutes.

Yields: 1¾ cup (1 tablespoon serving)

Excellent on potatoes, rice, or steamed vegetables.

NUTRIENT VALUES					
PROTEIN	CARBOHYDRATE		FAT		ALCOHOL
37%	28%		35%		0%
CALORIES	PRO-GM	CARB-GM		FAT-GM	SOD-MG
10.20	0.921	0.706		0.395	32.80
FOOD EXCHANGES					
MILK	VEG.	FRUIT	BREAD	MEAT	FAT
0.0	0.0	0.0	0.0	0.1	0.0

DILL LEMON SAUCE

¼ cup fresh dill, finely minced
2 tablespoons fresh parsley, finely minced
1 tablespoon reduced-calorie mayonnaise
2 tablespoons nonfat yogurt
2 tablespoons lowfat buttermilk
2 tablespoons lemon juice
¼ teaspoon black pepper

Mix ingredients together and chill.

Yields: 10 tablespoons (1 tablespoon serving)

Excellent over fish, especially baked or grilled salmon.

NUTRIENT VALUES				
PROTEIN	CARBOHYDRATE		FAT	ALCOHOL
14%	39%		47%	0%
CALORIES	PRO-GM	CARB-GM	FAT-GM	SOD-MG
7.865	0.285	0.815	0.429	6.120
FOOD EXCHANGES					
MILK	VEG.	FRUIT	BREAD	MEAT	FAT
0.0	0.0	0.0	0.0	0.0	0.1

LEMON SAUCE

1 tablespoon reduced-calorie margarine
1 tablespoon cornstarch
2 tablespoons water
½ cup chicken broth, defatted or 2 teaspoons low-sodium bouillon and ½ cup water
¼ cup fresh lemon juice
¼ teaspoon white pepper
1 lemon, sliced into thin rounds
½ teaspoon minced lemon thyme

In a medium saucepan, melt margarine over low heat. Mix cornstarch and water to make a smooth paste. Add to margarine, stirring constantly to prevent lumping. Add broth, lemon juice, water, pepper, thyme, lemon slices. Simmer 5 minutes. Serve warm.

Yields: ¾ cup (1 tablespoon serving)

Serve over fresh steamed vegetables, fish, or as a potato topper.

NUTRIENT VALUES				
PROTEIN	CARBOHYDRATE		FAT	ALCOHOL
6%	60%		34%	0%
CALORIES	PRO-GM	CARB-GM	FAT-GM	SOD-MG
10.20	0.202	2.010	0.514	11.10
FOOD EXCHANGES					
MILK	VEG.	FRUIT	BREAD	MEAT	FAT
0.0	0.0	0.1	0.0	0.0	0.1

LOWFAT CREAM SAUCE

2 tablespoons reduced-
   calorie margarine
1 tablespoon cornstarch
1 tablespoon water
½ cup lowfat buttermilk
¼ teaspoon dried oregano
   or ½ teaspoon fresh
2 tablespoons grated
   Parmesan cheese
¾ cup skim milk
¼ teaspoon white pepper

Melt the margarine in a saucepan. Mix corn-starch with 1 tablespoon water until smooth. Stir in cornstarch and cook for 3–4 minutes. Slowly add ¼ cup of the buttermilk. Stir well over medium heat until the sauce is smooth. Add oregano, cheese, milk and remaining buttermilk and stir until the mixture is smooth. Add white pepper. Excellent potato topper.

Yields: 1 cup (1 tablespoon serving)

NUTRIENT VALUES			
PROTEIN	CARBOHYDRATE	FAT	ALCOHOL
21%	31%	48%	0%
CALORIES	PRO-GM	CARB-GM	FAT-GM	SOD-MG
19.50	1.025	1.490	1.041	46.30

FOOD EXCHANGES					
MILK	VEG.	FRUIT	BREAD	MEAT	FAT
0.1	0.0	0.0	0.0	0.0	0.2

MARINARA SAUCE

1 (46-ounce) can tomato
   juice, low sodium
½ pound fresh mushrooms,
   sliced
½ cup chopped green
   pepper
¼ cup chopped red pepper
¼ cup chopped onion
1 teaspoon dried whole
   basil or 2 teaspoons
   fresh
½ teaspoon dried whole
   oregano or 1 teaspoon
   fresh
1 clove garlic, chopped
1 bay leaf
1 teaspoon sugar

Combine all ingredients in a large Dutch oven; simmer, uncovered for 45 minutes. Remove bay leaf.

Yields: 3½ cups (½ cup serving)

Serve over spaghetti, rice, or noodles, or as a potato topper.

NUTRIENT VALUES					
PROTEIN	CARBOHYDRATE		FAT	ALCOHOL	
16%	79%		5%	0%	
CALORIES	PRO-GM	CARB-GM	FAT-GM	SOD-MG	
48.00	2.303	11.10	0.319	20.10	
FOOD EXCHANGES					
MILK	VEG.	FRUIT	BREAD	MEAT	FAT
0.0	1.9	0.0	0.0	0.0	0.0

ITALIAN SAUCE

4-5 ripe tomatoes (fresh or canned)
1 clove garlic
2 tablespoons minced onion
1 tablespoon fresh basil
1 tablespoon fresh oregano
1 tablespoon olive oil

Skin and finely dice tomatoes. Then mince onion and garlic. Chop basil and oregano. Heat olive oil in nonstick skillet; add onion and garlic. Saute until onion is clear, then add tomatoes, basil, oregano and ½ cup water. Simmer for 5 minutes.

Yields: 2 cups
Servings: 4 (½ cup serving)

NUTRIENT VALUES					
PROTEIN 6%	CARBOHYDRATE 30%		FAT 63%		ALCOHOL 0%
CALORIES 47.80	PRO-GM 0.809	CARB-GM 3.893		FAT-GM 3.620	SOD-MG 97.90
FOOD EXCHANGES					
MILK 0.0	VEG. 0.6	FRUIT 0.0	BREAD 0.0	MEAT 0.0	FAT 0.6

MUSHROOM SAUCE

2 tablespoons reduced-calorie margarine
2 tablespoons all purpose flour
1 cup skim milk
4 ounces canned mushrooms, drained

Melt margarine in saucepan then remove from heat. Mix flour with ¼ cup milk to make a smooth paste. Stir flour into melted margarine until smooth. Return saucepan to stove over low heat. Gradually add remaining milk, stirring constantly until thickened. Add drained mushrooms.

Yields: 1½ cups (1 tablespoon serving)

"Good served over broiled chicken, or fish, or steamed vegetables."

NUTRIENT VALUES					
PROTEIN 18%	CARBOHYDRATE 42%		FAT 41%		ALCOHOL 0%
CALORIES 11.30	PRO-GM 0.514	CARB-GM 1.207		FAT-GM 0.521	SOD-MG 16.30
FOOD EXCHANGES					
MILK 0.0	VEG. 0.0	FRUIT 0.0	BREAD 0.0	MEAT 0.0	FAT 0.1

SWEET AND SOUR SAUCE I

1 tablespoon reduced-
  calorie margarine
1 tablespoon cornstarch
1 cup skim milk
1 teaspoon dry mustard
1 teaspoon brown sugar
2 teaspoons white wine
  vinegar

In a medium saucepan melt margarine over medium heat. Mix cornstarch with 2 table-spoons skim milk until smooth. Add corn-starch mixture to saucepan, stirring until bubbly. Add remaining milk and other ingre-dients and cook stirring constantly with wire whisk until smooth and creamy.

Yields: 1 cup (1 tablespoon serving)

Excellent way to prepare sweet & sour chicken or shrimp, or a Chinese potato.

NUTRIENT VALUES				
PROTEIN	CARBOHYDRATE		FAT	ALCOHOL
19%	51%		30%	0%
CALORIES	PRO-GM	CARB-GM	FAT-GM	SOD-MG
11.70	0.548	1.514	0.394	16.30
FOOD EXCHANGES					
MILK	VEG.	FRUIT	BREAD	MEAT	FAT
0.1	0.0	0.0	0.0	0.0	0.1

SWEET AND SOUR SAUCE II

2 tablespoons light brown
  sugar, not packed
1 tablespoon cornstarch
2 tablespoons white wine
  vinegar
½ cup chicken stock,
  defatted
1 tablespoon soy sauce
¼ teaspoon garlic powder
¼ teaspoon ground ginger
3 tablespoons blueberry or
  strawberry vinegar

Mix all ingredients together in a medium saucepan. Stir well to dissolve cornstarch and brown sugar. Place over medium heat, stirring until slightly thick and smooth.

Yields: ⅞ cup (1 tablespoon serving)

Excellent over hot rice or vegetables.

NUTRIENT VALUES				
PROTEIN	CARBOHYDRATE		FAT	ALCOHOL
7%	92%		1%	0%
CALORIES	PRO-GM	CARB-GM	FAT-GM	SOD-MG
9.688	0.187	2.372	0.013	74.00
FOOD EXCHANGES					
MILK	VEG.	FRUIT	BREAD	MEAT	FAT
0.0	0.0	0.0	0.1	0.0	0.0

TOMATO GINGER SAUCE

½ onion, thinly sliced
2 tablespoons cornstarch
¼ cup water
2½ cups vegetable stock, divided
¼ cup tomato paste
½ teaspoon freshly grated ginger root
1½ teaspoons soy sauce

Saute onion in ½ cup stock until soft. Mix cornstarch and water to make a paste. Add to onions. Slowly add the remaining stock and tomato paste, stirring constantly. Add ginger and simmer over low heat for about 15 minutes. Add soy sauce and serve warm. Good over pasta, grains, and vegetables.

Yields: 1¾ cup (1 tablespoon serving)

NUTRIENT VALUES					
PROTEIN	CARBOHYDRATE		FAT		ALCOHOL
12%	84%		4%		0%
CALORIES	PRO-GM	CARB-GM		FAT-GM	SOD-MG
6.142	0.190	1.372		0.029	20.00
FOOD EXCHANGES					
MILK	VEG.	FRUIT	BREAD	MEAT	FAT
0.0	0.1	0.0	0.0	0.0	0.0

WHITE SAUCE

2 tablespoons reduced-calorie margarine
2 tablespoons cornstarch
2 cups skim milk
¼ teaspoon freshly grated white pepper (optional)

Melt margarine in saucepan, then remove from heat. Mix cornstarch with ¼ cup milk to make a smooth paste (this will prevent lumping). Stir cornstarch into melted margarine until smooth. Return saucepan to stove over low heat. Gradually add remaining milk, stirring constantly until thickened.

Yields: 1 cup (1 tablespoon serving)

NUTRIENT VALUES					
PROTEIN	CARBOHYDRATE		FAT		ALCOHOL
21%	46%		34%		0%
CALORIES	PRO-GM	CARB-GM		FAT-GM	SOD-MG
21.10	1.097	2.413		0.789	32.50
FOOD EXCHANGES					
MILK	VEG.	FRUIT	BREAD	MEAT	FAT
0.1	0.0	0.0	0.1	0.0	0.2

GINGER/CILANTRO MARINADE

2–3 cloves fresh garlic, minced
⅓ teaspoon crushed red pepper (or more)
2 tablespoons cilantro, chopped
1 1-inch piece ginger root, grated
1 tablespoon white wine (optional)
2 tablespoons fresh lime juice
1 cup grapefruit juice

Mix all ingredients together and marinade fish, poultry, or vegetables in a glass bowl a minimum of four hours.

Yields: 1¼ cups (1 tablespoon serving)

NUTRIENT VALUES					
PROTEIN	CARBOHYDRATE		FAT		ALCOHOL
7%	82%		4%		6%
CALORIES	PRO-GM	CARB-GM		FAT-GM	SOD-MG
6.800	0.126	1.520		0.036	0.595
FOOD EXCHANGES					
MILK	VEG.	FRUIT	BREAD	MEAT	FAT
0.0	0.0	0.1	0.0	0.0	0.0

HONEY AND ORANGE MARINADE

1 cup fresh orange juice
1 tablespoon peanut oil
¼ cup white wine vinegar
3 tablespoons low-sodium soy sauce
1 tablespoon honey
½ teaspoon white pepper

Combine all the ingredients in a bowl. Marinate poultry from 1 to 4 hours before grilling or baking.

Makes: 1½ cups (1 tablespoon serving)

NUTRIENT VALUES					
PROTEIN	CARBOHYDRATE		FAT		ALCOHOL
7%	57%		36%		0%
CALORIES	PRO-GM	CARB-GM		FAT-GM	SOD-MG
13.80	0.261	2.076		0.579	129.0
FOOD EXCHANGES					
MILK	VEG.	FRUIT	BREAD	MEAT	FAT
0.0	0.0	0.1	0.1	0.0	0.1

PINEAPPLE/SOY MARINADE

1   cup unsweetened
    pineapple juice
3   tablespoons low-sodium
    soy sauce
1   teaspoon ground ginger
1   clove garlic, minced
¼   cup Italian reduced-
    calorie salad dressing

Combine all ingredients, stirring well. Use to marinate chicken or vegetables. Baste meat with remaining marinade during cooking.

Yields: 1⅓ cups (1 tablespoon serving)

NUTRIENT VALUES					
PROTEIN	CARBOHYDRATE		FAT		ALCOHOL
10%	67%		23%		0%
CALORIES	PRO-GM	CARB-GM	FAT-GM		SOD-MG
11.20	0.287	1.974	0.296		170.0
FOOD EXCHANGES					
MILK	VEG.	FRUIT	BREAD	MEAT	FAT
0.0	0.0	0.1	0.0	0.0	0.1

ORANGE MARINADE

½   cup fresh orange juice
½   cup fresh grapefruit
     juice
2–3 clove fresh garlic,
     minced
1   1 inch piece ginger root,
     grated
¼   teaspoon white pepper
1   tablespoon vegetable oil
2   tablespoons soy sauce

Mix all ingredients together and marinade fish, poultry, or vegetables in a glass bowl a minimum of 4 hours.

Yields: 1¼ cup (1 tablespoon serving)

NUTRIENT VALUES					
PROTEIN	CARBOHYDRATE		FAT		ALCOHOL
8%	45%		47%		0%
CALORIES	PRO-GM	CARB-GM	FAT-GM		SOD-MG
12.90	0.261	1.526	0.702		103.0
FOOD EXCHANGES					
MILK	VEG.	FRUIT	BREAD	MEAT	FAT
0.0	0.0	0.1	0.0	0.0	0.1

APPLE DESSERT SAUCE

2 **cups unsweetened apple juice**
½ **teaspoon ground cinnamon**
2 **tablespoons cornstarch**
¼ **cup plus 2 tablespoons water**

Combine apple juice and cinnamon in a saucepan. Bring to a boil; reduce heat to low. Combine cornstarch and water; gradually add to apple juice mixture, stirring constantly. Cook until smooth and thickened, stirring constantly.

Makes: 2 cups (1 tablepoon serving)

Serve sauce warm over pancakes, waffles, or french toast. Great over ice milk or nonfat yogurt.

NUTRIENT VALUES					
PROTEIN 1%		CARBOHYDRATE 98%		FAT 2%	ALCOHOL 0%
CALORIES 9.152	PRO-GM 0.012		CARB-GM 2.279	FAT-GM 0.019	SOD-MG 0.453
FOOD EXCHANGES					
MILK 0.0	VEG. 0.0	FRUIT 0.1	BREAD 0.0	MEAT 0.0	FAT 0.0

APRICOT SAUCE

1 **cup apricots (fresh or softened dried)**
3 **tablespoons honey**
1 **cup nonfat yogurt**
2 **teaspoons lemon juice**

Combine all ingredients in blender container and puree until smooth.

Yields: 1¾ cups (1 tablespoon serving)

NUTRIENT VALUES					
PROTEIN 13%		CARBOHYDRATE 86%		FAT 1%	ALCOHOL 0%
CALORIES 13.30	PRO-GM 0.456		CARB-GM 2.978	FAT-GM 0.014	SOD-MG 6.074
FOOD EXCHANGES					
MILK 0.1	VEG. 0.0	FRUIT 0.0	BREAD 0.1	MEAT 0.0	FAT 0.0

BLUEBERRY SAUCE

2 tablespoons sugar
1 tablespoon cornstarch
½ cup water
1 tablespoon fresh lemon juice
2 cups frozen blueberries

Combine sugar and cornstarch in a small saucepan; stir in water and lemon juice. Add blueberries; bring to a boil. Reduce heat and simmer 10 minutes, stirring constantly, until clear and thickened. Serve sauce warm over pancakes.

Makes: 2 cups (1 tablespoon serving)

NUTRIENT VALUES			
PROTEIN	CARBOHYDRATE	FAT	ALCOHOL
2%	92%	6%	0%
CALORIES	PRO-GM	CARB-GM	FAT-GM	SOD-MG
8.709	0.043	2.191	0.062	0.074
FOOD EXCHANGES					
MILK	VEG.	FRUIT	BREAD	MEAT	FAT
0.0	0.0	0.1	0.1	0.0	0.0

CINNAMON YOGURT SAUCE

1 cup nonfat yogurt
1 teaspoon ground cinnamon
1 teaspoon vanilla extract
2 tablespoons pineapple juice or apple juice concentrate

In a blender container, combine all ingredients, blend until smooth. Chill.

Makes: 1 cup (1 tablespoon serving)

Delicious over baked apples, cooked winter squash, pancakes, or waffles.

NUTRIENT VALUES			
PROTEIN	CARBOHYDRATE	FAT	ALCOHOL
25%	74%	0%	0%
CALORIES	PRO-GM	CARB-GM	FAT-GM	SOD-MG
11.00	0.693	2.027	0.004	10.70
FOOD EXCHANGES					
MILK	VEG.	FRUIT	BREAD	MEAT	FAT
0.1	0.0	0.1	0.0	0.0	0.0

FRESH FRUIT SAUCE

3 ripe bananas
1 orange, peeled
2 tablespoons lemon juice
¼ cup raisins
¼ cup boiling water

Pour boiling water over raisins and let stand until raisins are plump. Combine all ingredients in blender and puree until smooth. Substitute 1 cup whole strawberries, blueberries, or raspberries in place of orange for a new flavor.

Yields: 2½ cups (1 tablespoon serving)

Best to use sauce immediately. Serve over pancakes, waffles, or French toast.

NUTRIENT VALUES					
PROTEIN	CARBOHYDRATE		FAT		ALCOHOL
4%	92%		3%		0%
CALORIES	PRO-GM	CARB-GM		FAT-GM	SOD-MG
12.60	0.155	3.262		0.051	0.202
FOOD EXCHANGES					
MILK	VEG.	FRUIT	BREAD	MEAT	FAT
0.0	0.0	0.2	0.0	0.0	0.0

FRUIT FLAVORED YOGURT CHEESE SPREAD

½ cup yogurt cheese
¼ cup thawed undiluted frozen orange juice, pineapple or apple
¼ teaspoon vanilla

Combine ingredients and mix well. Serve on whole grain pancakes, waffles, fruit salad or use as a spread for toast or crackers.

Yields: ⅔ cup (1 tablespoon serving)

NUTRIENT VALUES					
PROTEIN	CARBOHYDRATE		FAT		ALCOHOL
25%	75%		1%		0%
CALORIES	PRO-GM	CARB-GM		FAT-GM	SOD-MG
18.20	1.123	3.422		0.011	14.70
FOOD EXCHANGES					
MILK	VEG.	FRUIT	BREAD	MEAT	FAT
0.1	0.0	0.1	0.0	0.0	0.0

HONEY APPLE TOPPING

2　tart apples, chopped
⅓　cup apple juice or cider
1　tablespoon honey
⅛　teaspoon cinnamon

Place all of the ingredients in a blender and process until smooth. Topping may be served warm or cold.

Yields: 1¼ cup (1 tablespoon serving)

Good over fresh fruit, poultry, or vanilla ice milk.

NUTRIENT VALUES				
PROTEIN	CARBOHYDRATE		FAT	ALCOHOL
1%	96%		3%	0%
CALORIES	PRO-GM	CARB-GM	FAT-GM	SOD-MG
12.40	0.021	3.229	0.045	0.166
FOOD EXCHANGES					
MILK	VEG.	FRUIT	BREAD	MEAT	FAT
0.0	0.0	0.2	0.1	0.0	0.0

ORANGE SAUCE

1　cup nonfat yogurt
1　tablespoon orange juice
　　concentrate
2　tablespoons honey
2　tablespoons orange rind

Beat with an egg beater or wire whisk until smooth.

Makes: 1¼ cups (1 tablespoon serving)

NUTRIENT VALUES				
PROTEIN	CARBOHYDRATE		FAT	ALCOHOL
17%	83%		0%	0%
CALORIES	PRO-GM	CARB-GM	FAT-GM	SOD-MG
13.10	0.568	2.787	0.002	8.123
FOOD EXCHANGES					
MILK	VEG.	FRUIT	BREAD	MEAT	FAT
0.1	0.0	0.0	0.1	0.0	0.0

RICOTTA ALMOND CREAM

1 cup part skim ricotta
½ teaspoon almond extract
1 tablespoon grated orange zest
1 teaspoon grated lemon zest
¼ teaspoon grated nutmeg
¼ teaspoon vanilla
1½ teaspoons honey
⅛ teaspoon cinnamon
⅛ cup slivered almonds

Combine all ingredients and chill.

Excellent served with sliced apple or pear.

Yields: 1¼ cups (1 tablespoon serving)

NUTRIENT VALUES			
PROTEIN	CARBOHYDRATE	FAT	ALCOHOL
26%	22%	52%	0%
CALORIES	PRO-GM	CARB-GM	FAT-GM	SOD-MG
23.00	1.553	1.282	1.360	15.50
FOOD EXCHANGES					
MILK	VEG.	FRUIT	BREAD	MEAT	FAT
0.0	0.0	0.0	0.0	0.3	0.2

STRAWBERRY YOGURT SAUCE

1 cup nonfat yogurt
1 cup strawberries, fresh or frozen (unsweetened)
1 teaspoon vanilla extract
2 tablespoons pineapple juice concentrate

In a blender container, combine all ingredients. Blend until smooth. Chill.

Makes: 2 cups (1 tablespoon serving)

Great with fruit salad, cottage cheese, pancakes, waffles or waffles with fresh fruit.

NUTRIENT VALUES			
PROTEIN	CARBOHYDRATE	FAT	ALCOHOL
22%	76%	2%	0%
CALORIES	PRO-GM	CARB-GM	FAT-GM	SOD-MG
6.719	0.372	1.284	0.017	5.375
FOOD EXCHANGES					
MILK	VEG.	FRUIT	BREAD	MEAT	FAT
0.0	0.0	0.1	0.0	0.0	0.0

BERRY SYRUP

2 **cups berries (blueberries, strawberries, raspberries)**
2 **tablespoons pineapple juice concentrate**
½ **teaspoon vanilla**

Crush berries with a fork or potato masher; add pineapple juice concentrate and simmer gently 5 minutes. Stir in vanilla. Serve warm.

Makes: 2 cups (1 tablespoon serving)

NUTRIENT VALUES			
PROTEIN	CARBOHYDRATE	FAT	ALCOHOL
3%	93%	4%	0%
CALORIES	PRO-GM	CARB-GM	FAT-GM	SOD-MG
7.000	0.061	1.738	0.034	0.875
FOOD EXCHANGES					
MILK	VEG.	FRUIT	BREAD	MEAT	FAT
0.0	0.0	0.1	0.0	0.0	0.0

STRAWBERRY SYRUP

2 **cups strawberries, fresh**
⅓ **cup maple syrup**

Place the strawberries and maple syrup in a blender. Process until smooth. Simmer over low heat for 10 minutes or until thickened.

To serve warm, place the sauce in a small saucepan over low heat. Stir frequently until heated through.

Makes: 1 cup (1 tablespoon serving)

Great over pancakes, waffles, or fruit.

NUTRIENT VALUES			
PROTEIN	CARBOHYDRATE	FAT	ALCOHOL
2%	95%	3%	0%
CALORIES	PRO-GM	CARB-GM	FAT-GM	SOD-MG
22.30	0.114	5.642	0.069	1.249
FOOD EXCHANGES					
MILK	VEG.	FRUIT	BREAD	MEAT	FAT
0.0	0.0	0.1	0.2	0.1	0.0

YOGURT TOPPING

¼ cup nonfat yogurt
1 teaspoon lime juice
½ teaspoon honey

Mix ingredients and chill. Serve on sliced kiwi or fruit of your choice.

Servings: 2 (2 tablespoon serving)

NUTRIENT VALUES					
PROTEIN	CARBOHYDRATE		FAT		ALCOHOL
27%	72%		0%		0%
CALORIES	PRO-GM	CARB-GM	FAT-GM		SOD-MG
19.90	1.386	3.648	0.003		21.10
FOOD EXCHANGES					
MILK	VEG.	FRUIT	BREAD	MEAT	FAT
0.3	0.0	0.0	0.0	0.0	0.0

APPLE BUTTER

4 Golden Delicious apples, cored and sliced
¼ cup water
1 tablespoon lemon juice
¾ teaspoon cinnamon
¼ teaspoon ground cloves
⅛ teaspoon nutmeg
4 tablespoons frozen apple juice concentrate

In a 2-quart saucepan, combine apples, water and lemon juice. Cover and simmer until the fruit is soft, about 30 minutes. Cool mixture, then process in blender until smooth. Return puree to pan and add remaining ingredients. Simmer puree mixture uncovered, stirring occasionally as it thickens, about 1 hour.

Yields: 2 cups (1 tablespoon serving)

NUTRIENT VALUES					
PROTEIN	CARBOHYDRATE		FAT		ALCOHOL
1%	96%		4%		0%
CALORIES	PRO-GM	CARB-GM	FAT-GM		SOD-MG
13.10	0.029	3.386	0.058		0.695
FOOD EXCHANGES					
MILK	VEG.	FRUIT	BREAD	MEAT	FAT
0.0	0.0	0.2	0.0	0.0	0.0

APRICOT BUTTER

1 (11-ounce) package dried
  apricots
1 cup water
(May also use dried peaches,
  apples or figs.)

Combine apricots and water in a small saucepan. Bring mixture to a boil; cover, reduce heat, and simmer 15 minutes or until apricots are tender. Cool slightly.

Process apricot mixture in a container of an electric blender or food processor until smooth. Store in refrigerator.

Yields: 2 cups (1 tablespoon serving)

Wonderful on toast, crackers or peanut butter sandwiches.

NUTRIENT VALUES			
PROTEIN	CARBOHYDRATE	FAT	ALCOHOL
5%	93%	2%	0%
CALORIES	PRO-GM	CARB-GM	FAT-GM	SOD-MG
23.20	0.356	6.020	0.045	0.975
FOOD EXCHANGES					
MILK	VEG.	FRUIT	BREAD	MEAT	FAT
0.0	0.0	0.4	0.0	0.0	0.0

CRANBERRY APPLESAUCE

3 medium-size apples,
  unpeeled and sliced
1 cup cranberries
¼ cup apple juice
2 tablespoons honey
¼ cup water

Place all ingredients in a food processor or blender; process until smooth. Pour into a medium-size saucepan and simmer for 10 minutes. Cool.

Yields: 2 cups (1 tablespoon serving)

Serve with pancakes, yogurt, blintzes, ice milk, or fresh fruit.

NUTRIENT VALUES			
PROTEIN	CARBOHYDRATE	FAT	ALCOHOL
1%	96%	4%	0%
CALORIES	PRO-GM	CARB-GM	FAT-GM	SOD-MG
12.90	0.029	3.345	0.057	0.170
FOOD EXCHANGES					
MILK	VEG.	FRUIT	BREAD	MEAT	FAT
0.0	0.0	0.2	0.1	0.0	0.0

STRAWBERRY BUTTER

8 cups fresh or frozen
   whole strawberries
1 tablespoon lemon juice
12 ounces frozen pineapple
   juice concentrate

Wash and stem strawberries. Puree berries in a blender until smooth. Pour puree into a 3-quart saucepan and add remaining ingredients. Simmer uncovered, stirring occasionally about 2½ to 3 hours.

Yields: 2½ cups (1 tablespoon serving)

NUTRIENT VALUES			
PROTEIN	CARBOHYDRATE	FAT	ALCOHOL
3%	96%	1%	0%
CALORIES	PRO-GM	CARB-GM	FAT-GM	SOD-MG
18.20	0.127	4.617	0.032	1.880
FOOD EXCHANGES					
MILK	VEG.	FRUIT	BREAD	MEAT	FAT
0.0	0.0	0.3	0.0	0.0	0.0

LOW-CALORIE PEANUT BUTTER

1 cup cooked carrots
2 tablespoons peanut
   butter

Puree carrots in food processor or blender. Add peanut butter and continue to blend until smooth. Mixture will be very thick; use spatula if necessary or on/off motions to blend mixture.

Yields: ¾ cup (1 tablespoon serving)

NUTRIENT VALUES			
PROTEIN	CARBOHYDRATE	FAT	ALCOHOL
16%	31%	54%	0%
CALORIES	PRO-GM	CARB-GM	FAT-GM	SOD-MG
21.70	0.902	1.780	1.392	21.20
FOOD EXCHANGES					
MILK	VEG.	FRUIT	BREAD	MEAT	FAT
0.0	0.2	0.0	0.0	0.1	0.3

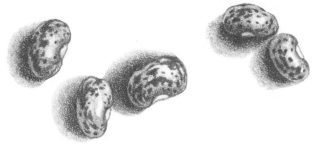

Special Risings . . .

BREAD & GRAINS

APPLE CARROT MUFFINS

¼ cup nonfat dry milk
  powder
1½ teaspoons baking
  powder
¼ teaspoon allspice
¼ nutmeg
½ teaspoon cinnamon
1¼ cups whole wheat flour
1 tablespoon honey
1 tablespoon safflower oil
2 egg whites
½ cup plus 2 tablespoons
  water
½ teaspoon vanilla
½ cup grated unpeeled
  apple
½ cup grated carrot
Vegetable coating spray

Preheat oven to 400°. In a large bowl, combine dry milk, baking powder, allspice, nutmeg, cinnamon, and flour. In a separate bowl, combine honey, oil, egg whites, water and vanilla, and stir into dry ingredients. Fold in apple and carrot. Spoon into muffin tins that have been sprayed with vegetable coating spray. Fill one half full. Bake 20–25 minutes or until brown.

Yields: 12 medium muffins (1 muffin per serving)

NUTRIENT VALUES			
PROTEIN	CARBOHYDRATE	FAT	ALCOHOL
13%	71%	16%	0%
CALORIES	PRO-GM	CARB-GM	FAT-GM	SOD-MG
74.70	2.375	13.20	1.366	59.00
FOOD EXCHANGES					
MILK	VEG.	FRUIT	BREAD	MEAT	FAT
0.0	0.0	0.0	0.5	0.0	0.0

BLUEBERRY MUFFINS

1 cup all-purpose flour
1⅓ cups whole wheat flour
2 tablespoons sugar
1 tablespoon baking powder
½ teaspoon ground cinnamon
1 cup skim milk
¼ cup reduced-calorie margarine, melted
2 egg whites, beaten
1 teaspoon vanilla extract
1½ cups blueberries (fresh or frozen)
Vegetable coating spray

Combine first 5 ingredients in a large bowl; make a well in center of mixture. Combine milk, margarine, egg whites, and vanilla; add to dry ingredients stirring just until moistened. Fold blueberries.

Spoon batter into muffin pans coated with coating spray. Use 2 tablespoons batter per muffin.

Bake at 350° for 15 minutes or until knife inserted comes out clean.

Yields: 48 miniature muffins (1 muffin per serving)

NUTRIENT VALUES			
PROTEIN	CARBOHYDRATE	FAT	ALCOHOL
12%	73%	16%	0%
CALORIES	PRO-GM	CARB-GM	FAT-GM	SOD-MG
32.80	0.956	5.913	0.569	36.50
FOOD EXCHANGES					
MILK	VEG.	FRUIT	BREAD	MEAT	FAT
0.0	0.0	0.0	0.3	0.0	0.1

BRAN MUFFINS

2 cups raw wheat bran
1 cup rolled oats (not instant)
¼ cup whole wheat flour
2 teaspoons cinnamon
1 teaspoon baking soda
2 egg whites
1 cup lowfat buttermilk
¼ cup molasses, light
2 apples, cored, chopped, (unpeeled)
Vegetable coating spray

Combine bran, oats, wheat flour, cinnamon, and 1 chopped apple in a large mixing bowl and mix well.

In a blender combine soda, egg whites, buttermilk, molasses and 1 apple.

Pour blended ingredients into dry ingredients and mix. Shape into balls and place in muffin tin that has been sprayed with vegetable coating spray. Bake at 400° for 25 minutes or until done. (35 minutes for regular muffins)

Yields: 36 miniature or 12 regular muffins

NUTRIENT VALUES			
PROTEIN	CARBOHYDRATE	FAT	ALCOHOL
16%	75%	9%	0%
CALORIES	PRO-GM	CARB-GM	FAT-GM	SOD-MG
38.90	1.963	9.114	0.495	34.40
FOOD EXCHANGES					
MILK	VEG.	FRUIT	BREAD	MEAT	FAT
0.0	0.0	0.0	0.5	0.0	0.0

BROWN RICE MUFFINS

1 cup cold cooked brown rice
1 cup skim milk
4 egg whites, beaten
2 tablespoons honey
1 teaspoon vanilla
1 teaspoon cinnamon
1¼ cups whole wheat flour
1 tablespoon baking powder
Vegetable coating spray

Combine rice, milk, egg whites, honey and vanilla. Add dry ingredients and stir just enough to moisten. Pour into muffin tins that have been sprayed with vegetable coating spray. Bake at 400° for 25–30 minutes. (Use ¼ cup batter per muffin)

Yields: 12 muffins (1 muffin per serving)

NUTRIENT VALUES			
PROTEIN	CARBOHYDRATE	FAT	ALCOHOL
17%	80%	3%	0%
CALORIES	PRO-GM	CARB-GM	FAT-GM	SOD-MG
83.60	3.396	16.50	0.290	110.0
FOOD EXCHANGES					
MILK	VEG.	FRUIT	BREAD	MEAT	FAT
0.1	0.0	0.0	1.0	0.1	0.0

OATMEAL BRAN MUFFINS

1 cup rolled oats (not instant or quick)
¾ cup whole wheat flour
¼ cup wheat bran
¼ cup raisins
1 teaspoon baking soda
1⅓ cups lowfat buttermilk
1 tablespoon vegetable oil
1 tablespoon honey
1 teaspoon vanilla
Vegetable coating spray

Mix all dry ingredients together. In another bowl, mix liquid ingredients. Stir together gently, just until dry ingredients are moistened. Spray muffin tins with coating spray. Fill tins ⅔ full and bake at 325° for 20–25 minutes until browned.

Yields: 12 muffins (1 muffin per serving)

Trisha Shirey

NUTRIENT VALUES					
PROTEIN	CARBOHYDRATE		FAT		ALCOHOL
13%	68%		19%		0%
CALORIES	PRO-GM	CARB-GM		FAT-GM	SOD-MG
94.50	3.214	16.80		2.069	103.0
FOOD EXCHANGES					
MILK	VEG.	FRUIT	BREAD	MEAT	FAT
0.1	0.0	0.2	0.9	0.0	0.4

PINEAPPLE BRAN MUFFINS

1 cup whole wheat flour
1 cup wheat bran
1 tablespoon baking powder
½ teaspoon cinnamon
¼ cup raisins
2 egg whites
¼ cup honey
2 tablespoons vegetable oil
½ cup skim milk
1 8-oz. can crushed pineapple packed in juice (undrained)
Vegetable coating spray

Mix all dry ingredients in a large bowl. Add raisins. Mix egg whites, oil, honey, milk and pineapple and whisk together. Stir into dry ingredients until just moistened. Don't overmix. Use heaping ¼ cup batter per muffin. Pour into muffin tins sprayed with coating spray. Bake at 400° for 20 minutes.

Servings: 12 muffins (1 muffin per serving)

Trisha Shirey

NUTRIENT VALUES					
PROTEIN	CARBOHYDRATE		FAT		ALCOHOL
10%	72%		18%		0%
CALORIES	PRO-GM	CARB-GM		FAT-GM	SOD-MG
123.0	3.413	25.10		2.782	91.60
FOOD EXCHANGES					
MILK	VEG.	FRUIT	BREAD	MEAT	FAT
0.0	0.0	0.4	1.2	0.1	0.5

DROP BISCUITS

1 cup whole wheat flour
½ teaspoon salt
1 teaspoon baking powder
2 beaten egg whites
2 tablespoons safflower oil
½ cup skim milk
Vegetable coating spray
Option: 1 teaspoon dried
    sage (not powdered) or 2
    teaspoons fresh
    marjoram

Mix dry ingredients. In a separate bowl, mix oil, milk and egg whites. Add to dry ingredients and mix lightly. Spray baking sheet with coating spray or oil lightly. Drop by tablespoonfuls onto baking sheet. Bake at 400° for 15–20 minutes or until browned.

Servings: 12 biscuits (1 per serving)

NUTRIENT VALUES					
PROTEIN	CARBOHYDRATE		FAT		ALCOHOL
12%	52%		36%		0%
CALORIES	PRO-GM	CARB-GM	FAT-GM		SOD-MG
62.40	1.923	7.998	2.440		123.0
FOOD EXCHANGES					
MILK	VEG.	FRUIT	BREAD	MEAT	FAT
0.0	0.0	0.0	0.5	0.1	0.5

BUTTERMILK CORNBREAD

1½ cups cornmeal
1 cup whole wheat flour
1½ teaspoons baking
    powder
¾ teaspoon baking soda
½ teaspoon sugar
½ teaspoon salt
2 egg whites lightly
    beaten
1½ cups lowfat buttermilk
Vegetable coating spray

Combine cornmeal, flour, baking powder, soda, sugar, and salt in a large bowl. Combine egg whites and buttermilk in a bowl, beating well; add to cornmeal mixture and stir just until combined. Spray nonstick muffin pan with vegetable coating spray. Pour in batter filling ¾ full. Bake at 400° for 25 minutes.

Yields: 17 muffins (1 per serving)

NUTRIENT VALUES					
PROTEIN	CARBOHYDRATE		FAT		ALCOHOL
14%	81%		5%		0%
CALORIES	PRO-GM	CARB-GM	FAT-GM		SOD-MG
81.60	2.865	16.10	0.454		119.0
FOOD EXCHANGES					
MILK	VEG.	FRUIT	BREAD	MEAT	FAT
0.0	0.0	0.0	1.0	0.0	0.0

FRENCH TOAST

2 slices flax seed bread or
  whole wheat bread
2 egg whites
2 tablespoons skim milk
½ teaspoon vanilla extract
¼ teaspoon cinnamon

In a mixing bowl, combine the egg whites, milk, vanilla and cinnamon. Beat lightly. Heat a nonstick griddle or heavy skillet until hot. Dip bread slices in the egg white mixture and brown on both sides until golden and crisp. Serve with fruit sauce.

Servings: 2

Wonderful topped with fresh fruit, fruit puree, lowfat cottage cheese, or mock sour cream.

NUTRIENT VALUES			
PROTEIN	CARBOHYDRATE	FAT	ALCOHOL
29%	59%	12%	0%
CALORIES	PRO-GM	CARB-GM	FAT-GM	SOD-MG
83.70	6.318	12.70	1.137	217.0
FOOD EXCHANGES					
MILK	VEG.	FRUIT	BREAD	MEAT	FAT
0.0	0.0	0.0	0.8	0.5	0.3

CHEESE TOPPED FRENCH TOAST

3 egg whites, beaten
2 tablespoons skim milk
1 teaspoon sugar
½ teaspoon cinnamon
4 slices whole grain bread
Vegetable coating spray

Combine first four ingredients in a bowl and stir until blended. Dip bread slices into egg mixture, coating well. Spray a nonstick skillet with vegetable coating spray and place over low heat. Arrange bread in single layer and cook until browned. Repeat with all bread slices. Spoon 2 tablespoons topping over each bread slice. Top with fresh fruit.

TOPPING
½ cup lowfat cottage
  cheese
1 tablespoon brown sugar
1 teaspoon vanilla
½ teaspoon lemon juice

Combine all ingredients in container of blender. Process until smooth.

Servings: 4

NUTRIENT VALUES			
PROTEIN	CARBOHYDRATE	FAT	ALCOHOL
29%	52%	19%	0%
CALORIES	PRO-GM	CARB-GM	FAT-GM	SOD-MG
116.0	8.819	15.60	2.538	316.0
FOOD EXCHANGES					
MILK	VEG.	FRUIT	BREAD	MEAT	FAT
0.0	0.0	0.0	0.9	0.8	0.4

APPLE PANCAKES

½ cup all-purpose flour
½ cup whole wheat flour
1½ teaspoons baking
    powder
1½ teaspoons brown sugar
1 medium apple
2 egg whites
¾ cup skim milk
Vegetable coating spray

Mix flours, baking powder and brown sugar together. Peel and core apple and cut into thin slices. Then cut slices into ½-inch pieces. Beat the egg whites and milk together in blender for 30 seconds. Add to dry ingredients. Mix well. Fold in the apple pieces. Bake on a nonstick skillet that has been sprayed with vegetable coating spray. Cook until browned on both sides. (Apples will remain crisp.) Use ¼ cup batter per pancake.

Yields: 8 pancakes

2–3 pancakes topped with warmed applesauce and cinnamon, apple butter, or yogurt makes a filling breakfast.

NUTRIENT VALUES					
PROTEIN 19%	CARBOHYDRATE 77%		FAT 4%		ALCOHOL 0%
CALORIES 68.80	PRO-GM 3.220	CARB-GM 12.90		FAT-GM 0.272	SOD-MG 240.0
FOOD EXCHANGES					
MILK 0.1	VEG. 0.0	FRUIT 0.0	BREAD 0.8	MEAT 0.1	FAT 0.0

BLUEBERRY PANCAKES

½ cup lowfat buttermilk
2 egg whites
1½ teaspoons safflower oil
6 tablespoons whole wheat
    flour
2 tablespoons raw wheat
    bran
1½ teaspoons honey
½ teaspoon baking powder
¼ teaspoon baking soda
½ cup blueberries, fresh or
    frozen

Beat together buttermilk, egg whites, honey and oil. Mix dry ingredients and add to milk mixture, blending well. Stir blueberries in gently. Cook on medium-hot nonstick griddle until brown on both sides and firm to touch.

Servings: 6 (1 pancake per serving)

NUTRIENT VALUES					
PROTEIN 17%	CARBOHYDRATE 64%		FAT 19%		ALCOHOL 0%
CALORIES 68.50	PRO-GM 3.114	CARB-GM 11.40		FAT-GM 1.494	SOD-MG 104.0
FOOD EXCHANGES					
MILK 0.1	VEG. 0.0	FRUIT 0.1	BREAD 0.5	MEAT 0.2	FAT 0.3

BUCKWHEAT PANCAKES

½ cup buckwheat flour
½ cup whole wheat flour
1½ teaspoons brown sugar
1   teaspoon baking powder
1   teaspoon safflower oil
1   egg white, slightly
    beaten
1   cup skim milk
Vegetable coating spray

Sift the buckwheat flour (it tends to be lumpy) and stir the other dry ingredients in lightly with a fork. Add the milk, egg white and oil and mix briefly. Cook the pancakes on a hot nonstick griddle. Use ¼ cup batter per pancake. Turn when bubbles appear. Use vegetable coating spray on griddle if neccessary.

Servings: 7 (1 pancake per serving)

If pancakes are to dry for your taste, use all purpose flour in place of whole wheat.

NUTRIENT VALUES			
PROTEIN	CARBOHYDRATE	FAT	ALCOHOL
15%	75%	10%	0%
CALORIES	PRO-GM	CARB-GM	FAT-GM	SOD-MG
79.50	3.014	14.80	0.879	73.00
FOOD EXCHANGES					
MILK	VEG.	FRUIT	BREAD	MEAT	FAT
0.0	0.0	0.0	1.0	0.0	0.0

COTTAGE CHEESE PANCAKES

1   cup lowfat cottage
    cheese
4   egg whites, lightly
    beaten
2   tablespoons whole wheat
    flour
¼   cup wheat bran
1   tablespoon safflower oil
Vegetable coating spray
Fresh fruit

Mix cottage cheese, egg whites, flour, bran and oil together until blended. Cook on a nonstick skillet sprayed with vegetable coating spray over medium heat. Brown, then turn and brown other side. Serve with fresh fruit, strawberries, peaches, or blueberries.

Servings: 6 (1 pancake per serving)

NUTRIENT VALUES			
PROTEIN	CARBOHYDRATE	FAT	ALCOHOL
38%	29%	32%	0%
CALORIES	PRO-GM	CARB-GM	FAT-GM	SOD-MG
77.80	7.983	6.132	2.962	186.0
FOOD EXCHANGES					
MILK	VEG.	FRUIT	BREAD	MEAT	FAT
0.0	0.0	0.0	0.0	1.0	0.5

OATMEAL PANCAKES

1 cup + 2 tablespoons
   skim milk
1 cup rolled oats
2 egg whites, slightly
   beaten
½ cup whole wheat flour
1 tablespoon brown sugar
1 teaspoon baking powder
Vegetable coating spray

Combine the milk and oats in a bowl and let stand 5 minutes.

Stir in the egg whites, flour, sugar and baking powder. Stir just until the dry ingredients are moistened. Bake on a nonstick griddle, sprayed with vegetable coating spray. Turn when bubbles appear.

Servings: 8 (1 pancake per serving)

NUTRIENT VALUES					
PROTEIN	CARBOHYDRATE		FAT		ALCOHOL
19%	71%		10%		0%
CALORIES	PRO-GM	CARB-GM	FAT-GM		SOD-MG
89.70	4.243	15.90	0.976		72.70
FOOD EXCHANGES					
MILK	VEG.	FRUIT	BREAD	MEAT	FAT
0.1	0.0	0.0	0.9	0.1	0.1

ORANGE WHOLE WHEAT PANCAKES

1 teaspoon cinnamon
1 cup whole wheat pastry
   flour
1 teaspoon baking powder
1 teaspoon oil
2 egg whites, slightly
   beaten
1 cup orange juice
   (unsweetened)
1 tablespoon honey
½ teaspoon vanilla
Vegetable coating spray

Sift dry ingredients together and add liquid ingredients, stirring just until moistened. Cook on nonstick skillet or griddle sprayed with vegetable coating spray. Cook over medium heat, using ¼ cup batter per pancake.

Servings: 7 (1 pancake per serving)

NUTRIENT VALUES					
PROTEIN	CARBOHYDRATE		FAT		ALCOHOL
10%	80%		10%		0%
CALORIES	PRO-GM	CARB-GM	FAT-GM		SOD-MG
86.00	2.166	17.00	0.946		62.30
FOOD EXCHANGES					
MILK	VEG.	FRUIT	BREAD	MEAT	FAT
0.0	0.0	0.5	0.5	0.0	0.0

WHOLE WHEAT PANCAKES

1 cup lowfat buttermilk
¼ cup rolled oats
⅔ cup wheat bran
2 eggs whites
¼ cup whole wheat flour
1 teaspoon apple juice concentrate, undiluted
⅛ teaspoon salt
¾ teaspoon baking soda

Combine buttermilk, oats and bran in large mixing bowl. Let stand 5 minutes. Add egg whites and beat until blended. Mix whole wheat flour, apple juice concentrate, salt and baking soda until blended. Add to bran mixture and blend until all flour is moistened. Pour ¼ cup batter on nonstick griddle. Cook until bubbles form and the edge is dry. Turn and cook until brown.

Serve with fruit sauce or fresh fruit.

Servings: 8 (1 pancake per serving)

NUTRIENT VALUES			
PROTEIN	CARBOHYDRATE	FAT	ALCOHOL
23%	67%	10%	0%
CALORIES	PRO-GM	CARB-GM	FAT-GM	SOD-MG
61.90	4.361	12.50	0.799	158.0

FOOD EXCHANGES					
MILK	VEG.	FRUIT	BREAD	MEAT	FAT
0.1	0.0	0.0	0.8	0.1	0.1

PUMPKIN SPICE WAFFLES

1 teaspoon cinnamon
1 large egg or egg
   substitute
2 egg whites
2 tablespoons brown sugar
1 cup skim evaporated
   milk
2 tablespoons safflower oil
½ cup all-purpose flour
½ cup whole wheat flour
1½ teaspoons baking
   powder
½ teaspoon salt
½ teaspoon pumpkin pie
   spice
½ cup canned pumpkin
½ Granny Smith apple,
   pared, cored, and diced
Vegetable coating spray

Whisk cinnamon, eggs, and brown sugar together in mixing bowl. Add evaporated milk and oil, and whisk until blended.

Mix flour, baking powder, salt, and pumpkin pie spice in a separate bowl. Add to egg mixture and stir just until blended. Stir in pumpkin, then fold in apple. Spray waffle iron with vegetable coating spray. Heat waffle iron as directed by manufacturer and make waffles using ½ cup batter for each waffle.

Yields: 10 (1 waffle per serving)

NUTRIENT VALUES			
PROTEIN	CARBOHYDRATE	FAT	ALCOHOL
15%	58%	27%	0%
CALORIES	PRO-GM	CARB-GM	FAT-GM	SOD-MG
118.0	4.477	16.90	3.448	196.0
FOOD EXCHANGES					
MILK	VEG.	FRUIT	BREAD	MEAT	FAT
0.0	0.0	0.0	1.0	0.0	0.5

DOUBLE DILL BREAD

1 package baking yeast
¼ cup warm, not hot, water
1 cup lowfat cottage cheese (small curd)
1 tablespoon sugar
1 tablespoon reduced-calorie margarine
1 teaspoon dill seed, crushed slightly
2 teaspoons minced fresh dill weed
1 teaspoon dried onion flakes
½ teaspoon salt
½ teaspoon baking soda
2 egg whites
2–2¼ cups whole wheat flour
Vegetable coating spray

Dissolve yeast in warm water. Heat cottage cheese until lukewarm. Remove from heat and add sugar, herbs, margarine, onion, salt, soda, egg whites, and yeast/water. Mix. Add flour gradually to form a stiff dough.

Spray a 1½-quart casserole dish with vegetable coating spray. Turn dough into casserole dish and allow to rise in a warm place for 30–40 minutes. (Should double in size.) Bake at 350° for 40–45 minutes. Serve warm.

Yields: 16 slices (1 slice per serving)

Trisha Shirey

NUTRIENT VALUES					
PROTEIN 20%	CARBOHYDRATE 68%		FAT 12%		ALCOHOL 0%
CALORIES 82.40	PRO-GM 4.065	CARB-GM 13.80	FAT-GM 1.061		SOD-MG 160.0
FOOD EXCHANGES					
MILK 0.0	VEG. 0.0	FRUIT 0.0	BREAD 1.8	MEAT 0.5	FAT 0.3

HERB CHEDDAR BREAD

1   package baking yeast
¼   cup warm water
½   cup skim milk
2   tablespoons reduced-
    calorie margarine
1   tablespoon sugar
1   egg
2   egg whites
1   teaspoon oregano,
    crushed*
1   teaspoon marjoram*
1   teaspoon thyme*
2–2½ cups whole wheat
    flour
1½ cups grated cheddar
    cheese
Vegetable coating spray
*Use 2 teaspoons minced if
    using fresh herbs

Dissolve yeast in warm water. Heat milk and margarine until margarine is melted. Add sugar and allow to cool slightly. Add eggs and herbs, beat until smooth. Add half of the flour and the cheese and mix well. Mix in remaining flour with wooden spoon. Add a little more flour if dough is sticky. Turn out on a lightly floured board and knead four minutes until smooth. Place in a 1½-quart glass baking dish that has been coated with vegetable coating spray. Let rise until doubled. (About 30 minutes.) Bake at 350° for 30 minutes. Spray top with vegetable coating spray and bake five minutes more to brown. Let cool slightly. Serve warm.

Yields: 16 slices (1 slice per serving)

Trisha Shirey

NUTRIENT VALUES			
PROTEIN	CARBOHYDRATE	FAT	ALCOHOL
18%	48%	34%	0%
CALORIES	PRO-GM	CARB-GM	FAT-GM	SOD-MG
129.0	5.792	15.40	4.815	97.10
FOOD EXCHANGES					
MILK	VEG.	FRUIT	BREAD	MEAT	FAT
0.0	0.0	0.0	0.9	0.5	0.7

TOMATO BREAD

1⅓ cup low-sodium tomato juice
1 tablespoon vegetable margarine
1 tablespoon sugar
½ teaspoon basil, dried or 1 teaspoon minced fresh
½ teaspoon oregano, dried or 1 teaspoon minced fresh
⅓ cup freshly grated Parmesan cheese
1 package active dry yeast
¼ cup warm water
2¾–3 cups whole wheat flour
Vegetable coating spray

Heat juice and margarine until margarine melts. Add sugar, herbs and cheese. Stir yeast and water together. Add to tomato mixture. Stir in half the flour using a large, wooden spoon for about two minutes. Gradually mix in remaining flour to make a soft dough that clings together in a ball and leaves sides of bowl. Knead on a lightly floured board until smooth and elastic, 5–8 minutes. Spray a 4 × 8 loaf pan with vegetable coating spray. Place dough in pan and spray top of dough. Let rise in a warm place until doubled in size (about 30 minutes). Bake at 375° about 25 minutes. Spray top again with vegetable coating spray and bake another 5 minutes to brown loaf.

Yields: 1 loaf—18 slices (1 slice per serving)

Trisha Shirey

NUTRIENT VALUES			
PROTEIN	CARBOHYDRATE	FAT	ALCOHOL
14%	72%	14%	0%
CALORIES	PRO-GM	CARB-GM	FAT-GM	SOD-MG
91.40	3.084	16.40	1.411	45.10

FOOD EXCHANGES					
MILK	VEG.	FRUIT	BREAD	MEAT	FAT
0.0	0.1	0.0	1.0	0.1	0.2

PUMPKIN SPICE BREAD

1	cup wheat bran
1	cup all-purpose flour
2	cups whole wheat flour
2	teaspoons baking soda
½	teaspoon salt
2	teaspoons cinnamon
1	teaspoon nutmeg
⅓	cup molasses
2	tablespoons vegetable oil
4	egg whites
1	cup water
2	cups canned pumpkin
1	teaspoon vanilla extract
⅓	cup chopped pecans
Vegetable coating spray	
1	teaspoon butter extract

Sift together the flour, bran, soda, salt, cinnamon and nutmeg. Make a well in the center of the dry ingredients and add all at once the molasses, vanilla, oil, egg whites, water, pumpkin and butter extract. Mix well and add the nuts. Pour batter into a 9 × 5 inch loaf pan that has been sprayed with vegetable coating spray. Bake at 325° for 45 minutes or until knife inserted in the center of loaf comes out clean.

Servings: 16 (1 slice serving)

NUTRIENT VALUES				
PROTEIN	CARBOHYDRATE		FAT	ALCOHOL
12%	68%		21%	0%
CALORIES	PRO-GM	CARB-GM	FAT-GM	SOD-MG
156.0	4.867	28.60	3.838	179.0
FOOD EXCHANGES					
MILK	VEG.	FRUIT	BREAD	MEAT	FAT
0.0	0.0	0.0	1.7	0.2	0.8

BASIC BEANS (FRIJOLES)

1   pound pinto beans
Water or broth to cover
    about 2 inches above
    beans
1   tablespoon olive oil
1   whole onion, quartered
4–6 garlic cloves, whole
½   teaspoon comino
    ("cumin") seeds
1–2 whole dried red peppers
1   teaspoon crumbled
    oregano
1   teaspoon chili powder
2   whole cloves

Wash beans well to remove stones and dirt. Remove any beans that "float." In a large pot, cover with cold water or broth. Bring to a boil. Turn off heat, cover pot, and let sit one hour. Drain. Rinse well. Refill with fresh water. Add remaining ingredients. Bring to a boil; immediately reduce to simmer and cover. Cook 2–2½ hours. Add hot water to beans as needed as they simmer. Beans should be covered with water as they cook. (Adding cold water causes beans to split and become mushy).

For black beans, add 1 bay leaf or 1 tablespoon epazote (last half hour). Also, usually cook ½ hour more.

Yields: 8 cups (1 cup serving)

NUTRIENT VALUES					
PROTEIN	CARBOHYDRATE		FAT		ALCOHOL
23%	67%		10%		0%
CALORIES	PRO-GM	CARB-GM		FAT-GM	SOD-MG
225.0	13.50	38.80		2.583	10.40
FOOD EXCHANGES					
MILK	VEG.	FRUIT	BREAD	MEAT	FAT
0.0	0.3	0.0	2.8	0.0	0.3

KASHA (BUCKWHEAT GROATS)

1   cup buckwheat groats
1½ cups water or defatted
    chicken stock

Spread the buckwheat groats on an ungreased cookie sheet and place in the oven for 15 minutes at 350°. Bring water or stock to a boil and add baked groats. Cover, reduce heat and simmer for 20–25 minutes.

Servings: 4 (½ cup serving)

NUTRIENT VALUES					
PROTEIN	CARBOHYDRATE		FAT		ALCOHOL
17%	78%		5%		0%
CALORIES	PRO-GM	CARB-GM		FAT-GM	SOD-MG
147.0	6.656	30.90		0.863	1.500
FOOD EXCHANGES					
MILK	VEG.	FRUIT	BREAD	MEAT	FAT
0.0	0.0	0.0	2.1	0.0	0.0

LONG-GRAIN BROWN RICE

1   cup brown rice, raw
2¼ cups water

Bring water to boil in a 2-quart saucepan. Add rice to water, bring to boil, cover. Reduce heat until only light steam escapes from under the lid. Cook for 45 minutes. Don't stir and don't peek. A defatted stock may be used instead of water for added flavor.

For rice with a fluffier texture, toast it on a baking sheet in a 350° oven for 10 minutes, before adding to water, turning occasionally to toast evenly. Follow directions above.

Servings: 6 (½ cup serving)

NUTRIENT VALUES			
PROTEIN	CARBOHYDRATE	FAT	ALCOHOL
8%	87%	5%	0%
CALORIES	PRO-GM	CARB-GM	FAT-GM	SOD-MG
111.0	2.317	23.80	0.583	2.833
FOOD EXCHANGES					
MILK	VEG.	FRUIT	BREAD	MEAT	FAT
0.0	0.0	0.0	1.4	0.0	0.3

CHEESE GRITS

2   cups water
½ cup hominy grits
1   cup grated farmers cheese or part-skim mozzarella
1   tablespoon reduced-calorie margarine
2   egg whites, beaten slightly
¼ teaspoon cayenne pepper
¼ teaspoon paprika
Vegetable coating spray

In a large saucepan, heat water to boiling, add grits. Reduce heat and cook until grits are very thick, remove from heat. Spray an 8 × 8 inch baking dish with vegetable coating spray. Stir together grits and remaining ingredients; pour into prepared dish, sprinkle with additional paprika. Bake for 30–35 minutes at 350°.

Servings: 6

NUTRIENT VALUES			
PROTEIN	CARBOHYDRATE	FAT	ALCOHOL
22%	33%	45%	0%
CALORIES	PRO-GM	CARB-GM	FAT-GM	SOD-MG
153.0	7.360	10.90	6.603	106.0
FOOD EXCHANGES					
MILK	VEG.	FRUIT	BREAD	MEAT	FAT
0.4	0.0	0.0	0.7	0.2	0.6

CHINESE FRIED RICE

2   **cups cooked brown rice, cold**
1   **tablespoon reduced-calorie margarine**
¼   **cup mushrooms, thinly sliced**
2   **tablespoons green onions, chopped**
4   **teaspoons soy sauce**

In a large, nonstick skillet, melt margarine over medium heat. Stir in rice, mushrooms, onions, and soy sauce. Reduce heat and cook uncovered 10–15 minutes, stirring occasionally or until well browned.

Servings: 4

NUTRIENT VALUES					
PROTEIN 9%	CARBOHYDRATE 74%		FAT 16%		ALCOHOL 0%
CALORIES 104.0	PRO-GM 2.433	CARB-GM 19.30		FAT-GM 1.896	SOD-MG 376.0
FOOD EXCHANGES					
MILK 0.0	VEG. 0.0	FRUIT 0.0	BREAD 1.1	MEAT 0.0	FAT 0.3

CURRIED RICE

¾   **cup raw, long-grain brown rice**
1   **tablespoon reduced-calorie margarine**
½   **cup chopped onion**
3   **cups chicken stock, defatted**
2   **tablespoons raisins**
¾   **teaspoon curry powder**

In a 2-quart saucepan, melt margarine over medium heat. Add onion and rice. Saute several minutes, until rice begins to brown. Add stock, raisins, and curry powder. Bring to a boil, then reduce heat. Cover and simmer 35–40 minutes. Remove from heat and serve.

Servings: 4

NUTRIENT VALUES					
PROTEIN 10%	CARBOHYDRATE 77%		FAT 13%		ALCOHOL 0%
CALORIES 168.0	PRO-GM 4.363	CARB-GM 32.50		FAT-GM 2.435	SOD-MG 36.80
FOOD EXCHANGES					
MILK 0.0	VEG. 0.3	FRUIT 0.3	BREAD 1.6	MEAT 0.0	FAT 0.6

LEMON RICE

1½ teaspoons vegetable oil
½ cup raw long grain
   brown rice
¼ cup diced celery
½ carrot, chopped
½ onion, minced
½ cup chicken broth,
   defatted
1 teaspoon fresh lemon
   juice
¼ cup parsley or dill
1 bay leaf
Dash of ground pepper
Lemon slices for garnish
1 teaspoon minced lemon
   basil or lemon thyme

Heat oil, saute rice until golden. Add onion, celery, carrots, bay leaf and cook another 3–4 minutes. Add broth, lemon juice, parsley, pepper and lemon herb. Bring to a boil, reduce to simmer. Place lemon slices on top and cook covered, on low. Simmer until tender, about 20 minutes.

Servings: 4

NUTRIENT VALUES			
PROTEIN	CARBOHYDRATE	FAT	ALCOHOL
9%	74%	18%	0%
CALORIES	PRO-GM	CARB-GM	FAT-GM	SOD-MG
114.0	2.457	21.20	2.275	17.30
FOOD EXCHANGES					
MILK	VEG.	FRUIT	BREAD	MEAT	FAT
0.0	0.4	0.0	1.0	0.0	0.6

QUICK SPANISH RICE

3   green onions, chopped
2   cloves garlic, chopped
3   ounces tomato paste
2½ cups chicken stock,
     defatted
1   teaspoon low sodium soy
     sauce
1   stalk celery, chopped
1   carrot, chopped
¼   teaspoon chili powder
1   bay leaf
2½ cups cooked brown rice,
     cold

Combine all ingredients except rice. Bring to a boil, lower heat and cover. Simmer 15 minutes. Add cooked rice. Cover, and continue to cook 10–15 minutes. Remove bay leaf before serving.

Servings: 6 (½ cup serving)

NUTRIENT VALUES			
PROTEIN	CARBOHYDRATE	FAT	ALCOHOL
13%	81%	6%	0%
CALORIES	PRO-GM	CARB-GM	FAT-GM	SOD-MG
99.00	3.193	20.50	0.697	82.40

FOOD EXCHANGES					
MILK	VEG.	FRUIT	BREAD	MEAT	FAT
0.0	0.7	0.0	1.0	0.0	0.1

SPANISH RICE

½ cup long-grain brown
    rice, raw
1½ cups green onions,
    chopped
1   clove garlic, chopped
2   ounces tomato sauce
1¼ cups chicken stock,
    defatted
1   tablespoon picante sauce
½ stalk celery, chopped
1   carrot, chopped
¼ teaspoon chili powder
1   bay leaf
¼ green pepper, diced
Vegetable cooking spray

Spray heavy or nonstick skillet with vegetable coating spray. Place over medium heat and add rice, onions, and garlic. Stir over medium heat until rice browns slightly. Add tomato sauce, stock, picante sauce, celery, carrots, chili powder, green pepper, and bay leaf and stir. Bring to a boil, lower heat and cover. Simmer 40 minutes or until liquid is absorbed. Do not lift lid while rice is cooking. Remove bay leaf before serving.

Servings: 6 (¾ cup serving)

NUTRIENT VALUES			
PROTEIN	CARBOHYDRATE	FAT	ALCOHOL
11%	82%	7%	0%
CALORIES	PRO-GM	CARB-GM	FAT-GM	SOD-MG
72.00	1.962	15.10	0.596	34.40
FOOD EXCHANGES					
MILK	VEG.	FRUIT	BREAD	MEAT	FAT
0.0	0.4	0.0	0.7	0.0	0.2

LAKE AUSTIN RESORT GRANOLA

3   cups wheat germ
2   cups rolled oats
1   cup wheat bran
½ cup sesame seeds
1   cup sunflower seeds
½ cup soy flour
¼ cup brown sugar
1   cup raisins

Combine ingredients except raisins and seeds. Place in shallow baking dish. Toast for 45 minutes, stirring every 15 minutes in a 325° oven. Add toasted seeds and raisins. Store in refrigerator.

Servings: 36 (¼ cup serving)

NUTRIENT VALUES			
PROTEIN	CARBOHYDRATE	FAT	ALCOHOL
18%	53%	29%	0%
CALORIES	PRO-GM	CARB-GM	FAT-GM	SOD-MG
101.0	4.780	14.40	3.470	1.833
FOOD EXCHANGES					
MILK	VEG.	FRUIT	BREAD	MEAT	FAT
0.0	0.0	0.2	0.8	0.1	0.9

BLUEBERRY RICE SALAD

1 cup fresh blueberries
1 cup cooked brown rice
   or wheatberries, chilled
2 tablespoons chopped
   walnuts
½ cup minced celery
¼ cup minced red onion
1 tablespoon minced fresh
   dill or 1 teaspoon dried
Spinach leaves

Combine the blueberries, rice, walnuts, celery, onions and dill in a medium bowl. Toss with lime dressing. Serve on a bed of spinach leaves.

LIME DRESSING
3 tablespoons lime juice
1 tablespoon honey
½ teaspoon dry mustard
¼ teaspoon paprika
1 egg white
2 teaspoons safflower oil

Place all ingredients in a blender and process until well mixed.

Servings: 3 (¾ cup serving)

NUTRIENT VALUES				
PROTEIN	CARBOHYDRATE		FAT	ALCOHOL
9%	60%		31%	0%
CALORIES	PRO-GM	CARB-GM	FAT-GM	SOD-MG
183.0	4.301	28.80	6.555	38.20
FOOD EXCHANGES					
MILK	VEG.	FRUIT	BREAD	MEAT	FAT
0.0	0.2	0.7	1.2	0.3	1.3

Especially Warming...
SOUPS

BEEF STOCK

4 pounds beef or veal bones
4 quarts cold water or as needed
1 onion, quartered
2 stalks celery chopped
1 carrot, cut into large chunks
6 sprigs parsley
½ teaspoon thyme
1 bay leaf
10 black peppercorns
5 whole cloves

Place bones in a 5-quart saucepan. Cover with cold water. Slowly bring to a boil. Remove foam. Add onion, celery, carrot, parsley, thyme, bay leaf, peppercorns and cloves. Reduce heat and simmer for 2–3 hours. Add water as stock cooks down, if necessary. Cool stock to room temperature. Remove beef bones and vegetables and discard. Place in refrigerator overnight. Fat will rise to the top and harden and can easily be removed. Use within 2–3 days or freeze.

Yields: 1 quart

Calories: 11 per cup

CHICKEN STOCK OR TURKEY STOCK

3 pounds chicken backs skinned or turkey bones
3 quarts water or as needed
2 carrots, scraped and cut in pieces
2 stalks celery, without leaves
1 onion, cut in half
2 garlic buds
1 bay leaf
½ teaspoon thyme
10 black peppercorns
Cold water to cover by 1 inch

Put the chicken or turkey parts, vegetables and spices in a 4-quart pot. Add cold water to cover by 1 inch. Bring slowly to a boil. Cover, leaving lid ajar about 1 inch to allow steam to escape. Simmer very slowly for 2 hours, add water as necessary. Cool stock to room temperature. Remove chicken or turkey and vegetables and discard. Place in refrigerator overnight. Fat will rise to the top and harden and can easily be removed. Use within 2–3 days or freeze.

If stock is too weak, can reheat and continue cooking to evaporate the liquid and concentrate flavor.

Yields: 2 quarts

Calories: 13 per cup

VEGETABLE STOCK

2   large onions, chopped
3   large carrots, chopped
½   cup chopped green beans
4   stalks celery, chopped
3   medium-size tomatoes, cubed
1   potato, cubed
½   pound spinach or greens
2   cloves garlic, minced
2   quarts water
10 peppercorns
1   bay leaf
6   sprigs of parsley
1   teaspoon dried thyme leaves or 2 teaspoons fresh
1   teaspoon dried rosemary or 2 teaspoons fresh

Combine all ingredients in a large saucepan. Bring to a boil. Reduce heat and simmer for 2 hours. Add water as necessary to keep vegetables covered. Discard vegetables and strain liquid.

Yields: 5–6 cups

Calories: 12 per cup

CREAM OF ASPARAGUS SOUP

2   cups fresh asparagus, washed, trimmed and sliced
1   cup water
1   tablespoon reduced-calorie margarine
2   tablespoons water
2   tablespoons cornstarch
2   cups skim milk
¼   teaspoon white pepper

Bring water to boil in a large saucepan. Add asparagus and reduce heat. Cover and simmer 10 minutes or until asparagus is tender. Mix cornstarch and water to make a smooth paste. In a small saucepan, melt margarine over medium heat. Add cornstarch stirring constantly to prevent lumping. Continue stirring while adding milk. Cook over low heat, stirring occasionally until mixture begins to thicken. Remove from heat and allow to cool. Combine milk mixture and asparagus in blender. Puree until smooth. Serve warm. Reheat if necessary.

Servings: 8 (½ cup serving)

NUTRIENT VALUES			
PROTEIN	CARBOHYDRATE	FAT	ALCOHOL
27%	55%	18%	0%
CALORIES	PRO-GM	CARB-GM	FAT-GM	SOD-MG
47.20	3.367	6.857	1.007	50.80

FOOD EXCHANGES					
MILK	VEG.	FRUIT	BREAD	MEAT	FAT
0.3	0.5	0.0	0.1	0.0	0.1

CREAM OF BROCCOLI SOUP

2 cups chopped broccoli
1 cup water
¼ cup chopped onion
¼ cup chopped green
   pepper
1 bay leaf
1 cup evaporated skim
   milk
¼ teaspoon black pepper
⅛ teaspoon allspice
¼ teaspoon thyme

Combine first 5 ingredients in a medium saucepan, cover and cook over medium heat about 10 minutes or until broccoli is tender. Remove and discard bay leaf. Pour broccoli mixture into blender. Allow to cool. Process, adding milk gradually until smooth. Return mixture to saucepan. Add remaining ingredients, cook over low heat for 15 additional minutes.

Servings: 4 (½ cup serving)

NUTRIENT VALUES			
PROTEIN	CARBOHYDRATE	FAT	ALCOHOL
35%	62%	3%	0%
CALORIES	PRO-GM	CARB-GM	FAT-GM	SOD-MG
67.50	6.001	10.50	0.214	87.50
FOOD EXCHANGES					
MILK	VEG.	FRUIT	BREAD	MEAT	FAT
0.6	0.6	0.0	0.0	0.0	0.0

CREAM OF CAULIFLOWER SOUP

4 cups fresh cauliflower,
   washed and cut into
   small florets
¼ cup water
3 tablespoons flour
3 cups skim milk
½ teaspoon white pepper
½ teaspoon onion powder

In a 3-quart saucepan, steam cauliflower until tender. Set aside. In a separate saucepan, mix flour and water, stirring over low heat until bubbly. Add milk, stirring constantly until smooth. Add pepper and onion powder. Remove from heat and allow mixture to cool. Mix sauce and cauliflower and puree in blender until smooth. Return to saucepan and reheat.

Servings: 6 (½ cup serving)

NUTRIENT VALUES			
PROTEIN	CARBOHYDRATE	FAT	ALCOHOL
31%	64%	5%	0%
CALORIES	PRO-GM	CARB-GM	FAT-GM	SOD-MG
76.40	6.146	12.70	0.462	75.20
FOOD EXCHANGES					
MILK	VEG.	FRUIT	BREAD	MEAT	FAT
0.5	0.7	0.0	0.2	0.0	0.0

EGG DROP SOUP

4 cups chicken broth,
   defatted
3 tablespoons cold water
1 tablespoon cornstarch
2 green onions with tops,
   chopped
4 egg whites, beaten until
   frothy
1 teaspoon coarse ground
   pepper
1 teaspoon soy sauce
1 teaspoon dry cooking
   sherry

In a 3-quart saucepan, bring broth to a boil. In a small mixing bowl, add water and cornstarch. Mix until smooth. Add to boiling broth, stirring constantly until slightly thick and smooth. Add onions. Drizzle in beaten egg whites, stirring constantly. Remove from heat. Add pepper, soy sauce and sherry. Serve immediately.

Servings: 4 (1 cup serving)

NUTRIENT VALUES			
PROTEIN	CARBOHYDRATE	FAT	ALCOHOL
38%	31%	5%	26%
CALORIES	PRO-GM	CARB-GM	FAT-GM	SOD-MG
60.90	5.647	4.714	0.321	308.0

FOOD EXCHANGES					
MILK	VEG.	FRUIT	BREAD	MEAT	FAT
0.0	0.0	0.0	0.3	0.4	0.0

LEEK SOUP

1½ cups minced fresh leeks
   with greens
1 cup chopped onion
1 clove garlic, minced
1 quart chicken stock,
   defatted
2 cups diced raw potatoes
1 cup skim evaporated
   milk
½ teaspoon white pepper

Saute leeks, onion and garlic in 1 cup stock for 5 minutes. Add remaining stock and potatoes. Bring to a boil, reduce heat and simmer 20 minutes. Add milk. Remove from heat and allow mixture to cool. Puree half of soup in blender and return to saucepan. Serve warm. Garnish with chopped green onion.

Servings: 10 (½ cup serving)

NUTRIENT VALUES			
PROTEIN	CARBOHYDRATE	FAT	ALCOHOL
20%	77%	3%	0%
CALORIES	PRO-GM	CARB-GM	FAT-GM	SOD-MG
78.10	3.952	15.10	0.300	38.30

FOOD EXCHANGES					
MILK	VEG.	FRUIT	BREAD	MEAT	FAT
0.3	1.0	0.0	0.3	0.0	0.0

MUSHROOM SOUP

1 tablespoon reduced-
   calorie margarine
1 pound fresh mushrooms,
   washed, drained and
   sliced
½ cup minced onion
½ cup minced celery
1 garlic clove, minced
5 cups beef or chicken
   broth, defatted
1 teaspoon white pepper
1 tablespoon dry cooking
   sherry

In a 3-quart saucepan, melt margarine over medium heat. Add mushrooms, onion, celery and garlic. Saute 3 to 5 minutes or until brown. Add broth and pepper. Bring to a boil. Reduce heat, cover and simmer 15 minutes or until vegetables are tender. Remove from heat and add sherry. Serve warm.

Servings: 5 (1¼ cup serving)

NUTRIENT VALUES			
PROTEIN	CARBOHYDRATE	FAT	ALCOHOL
24%	45%	27%	5%
CALORIES	PRO-GM	CARB-GM	FAT-GM	SOD-MG
58.10	3.771	7.156	1.901	39.90

FOOD EXCHANGES					
MILK	VEG.	FRUIT	BREAD	MEAT	FAT
0.0	1.1	0.0	0.0	0.0	0.2

CREAMY POTATO SOUP

3 medium potatoes (about
   1 pound), peeled and
   thinly sliced
1 medium onion, thinly
   sliced
1 large stalk celery, thinly
   sliced
3 packets low-sodium
   chicken broth or
   bouillon (3 tablespoons)
6 cups water
¼ teaspoon black pepper
Minced chives

Combine all ingredients except chives in a saucepan. Bring to a boil; cover, reduce heat, and simmer 30 minutes or until potatoes are tender. Remove from heat and allow mixture to cool.

Process mixture, ½ batch at a time, in container of an electric blender until smooth. Return to saucepan and cook until thoroughly heated. Garnish with chives.

Servings: 8 (1 cup serving)

NUTRIENT VALUES			
PROTEIN	CARBOHYDRATE	FAT	ALCOHOL
12%	85%	3%	0%
CALORIES	PRO-GM	CARB-GM	FAT-GM	SOD-MG
41.20	1.328	9.080	0.139	6.080

FOOD EXCHANGES					
MILK	VEG.	FRUIT	BREAD	MEAT	FAT
0.0	0.3	0.0	0.4	0.0	0.0

SORRELL SOUP

2 cups chopped sorrell leaves (cut veins from leaves, then chop in large pieces)
2 cups diced raw potatoes
4 cups water or vegetable broth
1 tablespoon reduced-calorie margarine
½ cup nonfat yogurt
Vegetable coating spray

Spray a nonstick pan with vegetable coating spray. Add potatoes and margarine and saute over low heat for 5 minutes. Add sorrell and toss until wilted. Add water and cook for 20 minutes. Cool, then blend until smooth in an electric blender in two batches. Reheat soup but do not boil. Stir in yogurt just before serving.

Yields: 5 (1 cup serving)

Trisha Shirey

NUTRIENT VALUES					
PROTEIN 16%	CARBOHYDRATE 66%		FAT 18%		ALCOHOL 0%
CALORIES 60.50	PRO-GM 2.496	CARB-GM 10.20		FAT-GM 1.236	SOD-MG 45.00
FOOD EXCHANGES					
MILK 0.1	VEG. 0.2	FRUIT 0.0	BREAD 0.4	MEAT 0.0	FAT 0.2

CREAMED SPINACH SOUP

¼ cup vegetable stock
½ cup chopped onion
½ cup raw long-grain brown rice
1 clove garlic, minced
¼ teaspoon ground nutmeg
6 cups vegetable stock
2 pounds fresh spinach
1 cup skim evaporated milk
¼ teaspoon cayenne pepper
2 tablespoons lemon juice

In a 3-quart saucepan, saute onion in ¼ cup stock over low heat until clear. Add the rice, garlic and nutmeg and saute several minutes, then add the remaining stock. Cover and cook 40 minutes or until rice is done. Add the spinach and cook just until the spinach is wilted. Puree the mixture in a blender and then return the puree to the saucepan. Add the milk and pepper and reheat. Just before serving, stir in the lemon juice.

Servings: 8 (1 cup serving)

NUTRIENT VALUES					
PROTEIN 25%	CARBOHYDRATE 70%		FAT 6%		ALCOHOL 0%
CALORIES 106.0	PRO-GM 6.983	CARB-GM 19.70		FAT-GM 0.696	SOD-MG 130.0
FOOD EXCHANGES					
MILK 0.3	VEG. 1.3	FRUIT 0.0	BREAD 0.5	MEAT 0.0	FAT 0.1

CREAM OF SPINACH SOUP

1 10-ounce package fresh
   spinach, cleaned and
   chopped
½ cup water
1½ teaspoons reduced-
   calorie margarine
3 tablespoons water
3 tablespoons cornstarch
2½ cups skim milk
¼ teaspoon nutmeg

Bring water to a boil in a large saucepan.
Add spinach. Return to boil, then reduce
heat. Cover and simmer 10–15 minutes or
until spinach is tender. Drain spinach and set
aside. Mix cornstarch with 3 tablespoons of
water to make smooth paste. In a medium
saucepan, melt margarine over medium heat.
Add cornstarch, stirring to prevent lumping.
Add milk, stirring constantly until smooth
and creamy. Remove from heat and allow to
cool. Puree in a blender with spinach. Add
nutmeg. Serve warm.

Servings: 7 (⅔ cup serving)

NUTRIENT VALUES			
PROTEIN	CARBOHYDRATE	FAT	ALCOHOL
29%	59%	12%	0%
CALORIES	PRO-GM	CARB-GM	FAT-GM	SOD-MG
57.40	4.319	8.875	0.801	88.10

FOOD EXCHANGES					
MILK	VEG.	FRUIT	BREAD	MEAT	FAT
0.4	0.4	0.0	0.1	0.0	0.1

SPINACH AND MUSHROOM SOUP

¼ cup chopped green
   onions
2 cups sliced mushrooms
3 cups chicken stock,
   defatted
10 ounces fresh spinach,
   washed and chopped
2 tablespoons cornstarch
3 tablespoons cold water
½ cup yogurt cheese (see p.
   14)

Heat ½ cup stock in a large saucepan. Saute
onions and mushrooms until tender. Add remaining stock and spinach and bring to a
boil. Reduce heat and simmer several minutes. Meanwhile mix cornstarch and water to
make smooth paste. Add to saucepan. Simmer until thickened. Top each serving with 1
tablespoon yogurt cheese.

Servings: 8 (½ cup serving)

NUTRIENT VALUES			
PROTEIN	CARBOHYDRATE	FAT	ALCOHOL
34%	59%	7%	0%
CALORIES	PRO-GM	CARB-GM	FAT-GM	SOD-MG
38.00	3.455	6.085	0.318	48.90

FOOD EXCHANGES					
MILK	VEG.	FRUIT	BREAD	MEAT	FAT
0.2	0.6	0.0	0.1	0.0	0.0

BUTTERNUT SQUASH SOUP

1 cup diced peeled
  potatoes
¾ cup butternut squash,
  cut in chunks
¼ cup chopped celery
1 garlic clove, minced
1 tablespoon parsley,
  chopped
¼ teaspoon black pepper
1½ cups chicken broth,
  defatted
1½ cups skim milk

In a 3-quart saucepan, combine the first 7 ingredients. Bring to a boil; then reduce heat and simmer for 20 minutes until vegetables are tender. Remove from heat and allow mixture to cool. Blend the soup mixture in a blender or food processor until smooth. Return to the saucepan. Add the milk and heat thoroughly, but do not boil. Serve warm.

Servings: 4 (¾ cup serving)

NUTRIENT VALUES				
PROTEIN	CARBOHYDRATE		FAT	ALCOHOL
23%	73%		4%	0%
CALORIES	PRO-GM	CARB-GM	FAT-GM	SOD-MG
88.90	5.303	16.80	0.434	58.60
FOOD EXCHANGES					
MILK	VEG.	FRUIT	BREAD	MEAT	FAT
0.4	0.0	0.0	0.8	0.0	0.0

SQUASH SOUP

Vegetable coating spray
½ cup chopped onion
2 tablespoons fresh parsley, chopped
2 teaspoons dried whole basil
2 teaspoons dried oregano
½ teaspoon salt
4 cups yellow squash, sliced
1 medium zucchini, cut into ¼-inch slices
2 cloves garlic, minced
1 tablespoon cornstarch
5 cups chicken stock, defatted
1 cup skim milk

Coat a large nonstick saucepan with vegetable coating spray. Add onion and saute over low heat until clear. Add parsley, basil, oregano, salt, yellow and zucchini squash and garlic. Combine cornstarch and 1 cup stock in a small bowl, stirring until well blended; add to vegetable mixture, stirring well. Add stock. Stirring constantly, bring to a boil. Cover, reduce heat, and simmer 30 minutes, stirring often. Remove from heat and allow to cool. Process mixture in blender until smooth. Return to saucepan, add milk and reheat.

Servings: 8 (1 cup serving)

NUTRIENT VALUES					
PROTEIN	CARBOHYDRATE		FAT		ALCOHOL
31%	58%		11%		0%
CALORIES	PRO-GM	CARB-GM		FAT-GM	SOD-MG
42.40	3.553	6.565		0.568	141.0
FOOD EXCHANGES					
MILK	VEG.	FRUIT	BREAD	MEAT	FAT
0.1	0.6	0.0	0.1	0.0	0.0

ZUCCHINI CONSOMME

3 cups chicken broth, defatted
2 cups shredded zucchini
1 tablespoon Mrs. Dash or herbal salt substitute
¼ cup chopped onion

Combine ingredients in saucepan. Bring to a boil. Reduce heat and simmer 20 minutes. Serve hot.

Servings: 4 (¾ cup serving)

NUTRIENT VALUES					
PROTEIN	CARBOHYDRATE		FAT		ALCOHOL
36%	51%		13%		0%
CALORIES	PRO-GM	CARB-GM		FAT-GM	SOD-MG
22.10	2.188	3.040		0.343	1.713
FOOD EXCHANGES					
MILK	VEG.	FRUIT	BREAD	MEAT	FAT
0.0	0.5	0.0	0.0	0.0	0.0

HOT MADRILENE SOUP

1 tablespoon reduced-calorie margarine
¼ cup chopped onion
3 cups tomato juice, low sodium
1 bay leaf
1 cup chicken broth, defatted
½ teaspoon Worcestershire sauce
½ teaspoon celery seed
8 teaspoons grated Parmesan cheese
8 teaspoons minced parsley

In a nonstick skillet, melt margarine and saute onion until tender. Add tomato juice, bay leaf, broth, Worcestershire sauce and celery seed. Heat to just boiling; reduce heat and simmer for 15 minutes. Garnish individual servings with Parmesan and parsley.

Servings: 8 (½ cup serving)

NUTRIENT VALUES					
PROTEIN	CARBOHYDRATE		FAT		ALCOHOL
19%	47%		34%		0%
CALORIES	PRO-GM	CARB-GM		FAT-GM	SOD-MG
36.00	1.904	4.591		1.477	68.10
FOOD EXCHANGES					
MILK	VEG.	FRUIT	BREAD	MEAT	FAT
0.0	0.8	0.0	0.0	0.1	0.1

TOMATO HERB SOUP

4 cups tomato juice, low sodium
1 bay leaf
2 whole cloves
½ teaspoon dill seed
½ teaspoon basil
½ teaspoon marjoram
½ teaspoon oregano
Black pepper to taste
Parsley

Place herbs in tomato juice in a medium saucepan. Let stand one hour to allow flavors to blend. Heat to boiling point. Remove from heat and strain. Garnish with parsley if desired.

Servings: 4 (1 cup serving)

NUTRIENT VALUES					
PROTEIN	CARBOHYDRATE		FAT		ALCOHOL
15%	81%		4%		0%
CALORIES	PRO-GM	CARB-GM		FAT-GM	SOD-MG
44.10	1.959	10.70		0.210	24.50
FOOD EXCHANGES					
MILK	VEG.	FRUIT	BREAD	MEAT	FAT
0.0	1.8	0.0	0.0	0.0	0.0

CREAMY VEGETABLE SOUP

2 cups chicken broth, defatted
1 cup sliced carrots
½ cup squash (summer squash)
¾ cup chopped turnips
2 tablespoons chopped onion
¼ teaspoon white pepper
¼ teaspoon celery seed
½ cup skim milk

In a large saucepan bring the broth to a boil and add the carrot, squash, turnip, onion, and seasonings. Reduce heat and simmer 10–15 minutes or until vegetables are tender. Allow mixture to cool. Puree in a blender. Reheat and add skim milk. Serve warm.

Servings: 6 (½ cup serving)

NUTRIENT VALUES			
PROTEIN	CARBOHYDRATE	FAT	ALCOHOL
27%	65%	8%	0%
CALORIES	PRO-GM	CARB-GM	FAT-GM	SOD-MG
24.90	1.798	4.342	0.243	26.30

FOOD EXCHANGES					
MILK	VEG.	FRUIT	BREAD	MEAT	FAT
0.1	0.6	0.0	0.0	0.0	0.0

HEARTY VEGETABLE SOUP

1½ onion, chopped
5   cloves garlic, minced
1   or more jalapenos,
    chopped
3-4 canned green chilies, cut
    into strips
8   ounce can tomatoes,
    chopped
8   cups chicken broth,
    defatted
1½ cups frozen corn
3   medium zucchini, sliced
1   teaspoon oregano
½   teaspoon thyme
1   teaspoon fresh mint,
    chopped

Saute onions and garlic in water until translucent. Add peppers, tomatoes, oregano, thyme and cook 5 minutes until bubbly. Add warm chicken stock and bring to a boil; reduce heat immediately and simmer for 10 minutes. Add the mint, squash and corn and cook until just tender. Adjust seasonings.

Garnish with fresh mint or cilantro sprig.

Servings: 4 (2½ cup serving)

NUTRIENT VALUES					
PROTEIN	CARBOHYDRATE		FAT		ALCOHOL
22%	70%		7%		0%
CALORIES	PRO-GM	CARB-GM		FAT-GM	SOD-MG
137.0	8.573	27.00		1.248	168.0
FOOD EXCHANGES					
MILK	VEG.	FRUIT	BREAD	MEAT	FAT
0.0	2.1	0.0	0.9	0.5	0.0

VEGETABLE STEW

4 cups chicken stock,
   defatted
2 cloves garlic, minced
1 onion, sliced
2 carrots, sliced
1 potato, sliced
3 cups chopped green
   cabbage
2 cups chopped tomatoes
2 turnips, peeled and
   chopped
1 cup chopped celery
1 teaspoon sage
1 teaspoon basil
1 teaspoon poultry
   seasoning
3 tablespoons cornstarch
¼ cup water

Combine the chicken stock, garlic, onion, carrots, and potato. Cover and cook for 5 minutes over medium heat. Add the cabbage, tomatoes, turnips, celery, and seasonings. Simmer for 10 more minutes. Combine cornstarch and water to make a smooth paste. Add to stew, stirring until thickened. Serve with French bread or cornbread.

Servings: 5 (1⅔ cup serving)

NUTRIENT VALUES				
PROTEIN	CARBOHYDRATE		FAT	ALCOHOL
15%	80%		5%	0%
CALORIES	PRO-GM	CARB-GM	FAT-GM	SOD-MG
145.0	5.603	30.90	0.871	64.80
FOOD EXCHANGES					
MILK	VEG.	FRUIT	BREAD	MEAT	FAT
0.0	2.3	0.0	1.0	0.0	0.0

BARLEY MUSHROOM SOUP

1 tablespoon reduced-
  calorie margarine
½ cup chopped onions
½ cup chopped celery
½ cup chopped carrots
4 cups mushrooms, sliced
7 cups water
½ cup barley
4 cups defatted beef stock
¼ teaspoon black pepper

In a medium saucepan, melt margarine over medium heat. Add onions, celery, carrots and mushrooms. Cook 10 minutes, stirring frequently. Add water if vegetables begin to stick. Add remaining ingredients. Cover, reduce heat to low and simmer 1 hour or until vegetables are tender.

Servings: 8 (1 cup serving)

NUTRIENT VALUES					
PROTEIN	CARBOHYDRATE		FAT	ALCOHOL	
14%	71%		14%	0%	
CALORIES	PRO-GM	CARB-GM	FAT-GM	SOD-MG	
72.00	2.720	13.40	1.188	26.70	
FOOD EXCHANGES					
MILK	VEG.	FRUIT	BREAD	MEAT	FAT
0.0	0.6	0.0	0.6	0.0	0.1

BEAN WITH BARLEY SOUP

¼ cup water
½ cup onion, chopped
1 cup grated carrots
1 cup grated potatoes
6 cups vegetable stock
1 clove garlic, minced
½ teaspoon black pepper
1 cup cooked white beans
¼ cup barley

Saute the onion in water until clear. Add the next five ingredients. Bring to a boil and then reduce the heat. Simmer until the vegetables are tender. Allow to cool. Then puree in a blender. Return the puree to the saucepan. Add the beans and barley. Simmer 45–50 minutes. Stir occasionally, adding more stock if necessary.

Servings: 4 (1 cup serving)

NUTRIENT VALUES					
PROTEIN	CARBOHYDRATE		FAT	ALCOHOL	
15%	83%		2%	0%	
CALORIES	PRO-GM	CARB-GM	FAT-GM	SOD-MG	
200.0	7.632	42.40	0.569	16.20	
FOOD EXCHANGES					
MILK	VEG.	FRUIT	BREAD	MEAT	FAT
0.0	0.8	0.0	2.4	0.3	0.0

LENTIL SOUP

2	quarts vegetable stock
1	cup dried lentils
½	cup chopped onion
¼	cup chopped celery
1	bay leaf
½	teaspoon dried oregano
3	tablespoons tomato paste
2	tablespoons white wine vinegar or herbal vinegar

Bring the stock to a boil in a large saucepan. Rinse the lentils and add to boiling stock. Add all the remaining ingredients except the vinegar. Reduce the heat, cover and simmer, until the lentils are very soft, about 1½ hours. Remove the soup from the heat and add the vinegar. Discard the bay leaf. Puree half of the soup. Return the puree back to the saucepan and reheat.

Servings: 5 (1½ cup serving)

NUTRIENT VALUES					
PROTEIN	CARBOHYDRATE		FAT		ALCOHOL
25%	70%		4%		0%
CALORIES	PRO-GM	CARB-GM	FAT-GM		SOD-MG
159.0	10.20	28.30.	0.754		18.10
FOOD EXCHANGES					
MILK	VEG.	FRUIT	BREAD	MEAT	FAT
0.0	0.5	0.0	1.7	0.0	0.1

LIMA BEAN SOUP

2	cups dried lima beans
½	cup finely chopped onion
1	carrot, peeled and thinly sliced
4	cloves garlic, chopped
1	stalk celery, thinly sliced
8	ounces crushed tomatoes with puree
¼	cup chopped, fresh parsley
2	tablespoons low-sodium soy sauce
8	cups water

Place all the ingredients in a 2-quart saucepan and cover. Bring to a boil. Reduce the heat and simmer for 1½ hours or until the beans are tender. Add water if necessary. Puree ½ of bean mixture. Return to saucepan and reheat.

Servings: 7 (1 cup serving)

NUTRIENT VALUES					
PROTEIN	CARBOHYDRATE		FAT		ALCOHOL
23%	73%		4%		0%
CALORIES	PRO-GM	CARB-GM	FAT-GM		SOD-MG
199.0	11.70	37.50	0.983		361.0
FOOD EXCHANGES					
MILK	VEG.	FRUIT	BREAD	MEAT	FAT
0.0	0.6	0.0	2.6	0.0	0.0

MINESTRONE

1   onion, finely chopped
¼   cup vegetable stock
1½ cups chopped celery
14½–16-ounce can tomatoes
      with juice
3   cups vegetable stock
¼   cup chopped parsley
3   cups water
Dash of pepper
2   bay leaves
1   teaspoon oregano
2   teaspoons basil
½   teaspoon rosemary
1   clove garlic, minced
½   cup chopped carrot
½   cup diced zucchini
½   cup diced potato
¼   cup chopped green
      pepper
¼   cup frozen or fresh corn
1   cup sliced mushrooms
1   cup cooked garbanzo
      beans
½   cup broken whole wheat
      spaghetti, uncooked
½   cup cooked barley

Saute onion and celery in stock until soft. Add the tomatoes, 3 cups stock, water, parsley, seasonings and vegetables. Simmer soup 30 minutes. Add spaghetti, garbanzos and cooked barley. Continue cooking over medium heat for 10 minutes.

Servings: 11 (¾ cup serving)

NUTRIENT VALUES			
PROTEIN	CARBOHYDRATE	FAT	ALCOHOL
15%	77%	8%	0%
CALORIES	PRO-GM	CARB-GM	FAT-GM	SOD-MG
80.20	3.130	16.20	0.745	170.0

FOOD EXCHANGES					
MILK	VEG.	FRUIT	BREAD	MEAT	FAT
0.0	0.7	0.0	0.7	0.1	0.0

QUICK BLACK BEAN SOUP

30 ounces canned black beans
2 cups chicken stock, defatted
2 cups water
1 carrot, grated
1 onion, chopped
1 potato, grated
2 stalks celery, chopped
1 teaspoon dried oregano
1 teaspoon cumin
⅛ teaspoon cayenne pepper
¼ cup lemon juice
1 bay leaf
½ teaspoon paprika

Place all ingredients except lemon juice in a 2-quart saucepan. Cook over medium heat for 25 minutes. Cool. Puree half of mixture in a blender or food processor. Add back to pot. Reheat to serve. Add lemon juice just before serving. Garnish each serving with spoonful of nonfat yogurt, chopped green onions, and fresh chopped cilantro.

Servings: 7 (1 cup serving)

NUTRIENT VALUES					
PROTEIN	CARBOHYDRATE		FAT		ALCOHOL
23%	72%		5%		0%
CALORIES	PRO-GM	CARB-GM	FAT-GM		SOD-MG
182.0	10.90	34.00	0.978		23.60
FOOD EXCHANGES					
MILK	VEG.	FRUIT	BREAD	MEAT	FAT
0.0	0.4	0.1	0.2	0.0	0.0

SPLIT PEA SOUP

2 carrots, thinly sliced
1 onion, finely chopped
2 stalks celery, thinly
  sliced
1 bay leaf
2 teaspoons basil
2 teaspoons oregano
4 cloves garlic, minced
½ teaspoon rosemary
6 cups chicken stock,
  defatted
2 cups dry split peas
2 tablespoons low-sodium
  soy sauce

Saute the carrots, onion, celery and herbs in ½ cup chicken stock for 10 minutes over medium heat in a 3-quart saucepan. Add the split peas and remaining chicken stock. Cook over low heat for one hour or until the peas are soft. Remove from heat and add soy sauce. Serve.

Servings: 4 (1¼ cup serving)

NUTRIENT VALUES					
PROTEIN	CARBOHYDRATE		FAT		ALCOHOL
27%	68%		5%		0%
CALORIES	PRO-GM	CARB-GM		FAT-GM	SOD-MG
296.0	20.80	53.00		1.803	555.0
FOOD EXCHANGES					
MILK	VEG.	FRUIT	BREAD	MEAT	FAT
0.0	9.5	0.0	0.3	0.0	0.0

VERMICELLI SOUP

2 garlic cloves, peeled
½ bunch green onions, white part only
1 tablespoon vegetable oil
2½ ounces vermicelli, broken
3 tomatoes, fresh or 16 ounces canned
3 cups chicken stock, defatted
1½ green chiles, whole (canned)
1 tablespoon pimiento

Chop garlic and onion. Heat the oil in a 2-quart saucepan and lightly brown vermicelli. Watch carefully and stir constantly to prevent burning. Add garlic and onion, saute for several minutes. Add tomatoes, stock, chiles and pimiento. Simmer about 8 minutes or until most of the liquid is absorbed. Serve hot.

Servings: 10 (½ cup serving)

NUTRIENT VALUES				
PROTEIN	CARBOHYDRATE		FAT	ALCOHOL
14%	59%		27%	0%
CALORIES	PRO-GM	CARB-GM	FAT-GM	SOD-MG
52.70	1.900	7.929	1.647	3.676
FOOD EXCHANGES					
MILK	VEG.	FRUIT	BREAD	MEAT	FAT
0.0	0.3	0.0	0.3	0.0	0.3

WHITE BEAN SOUP

1   cup navy beans (fresh
    cooked or canned)
1   cup vegetable stock
1½ cups water
½   cup chopped onion
1   clove garlic, chopped
2   carrots, peeled and
    chopped
2   stalks celery, chopped
1   slice fresh lemon
½   cup canned tomatoes
    with juice
2   teaspoons soy sauce
½   teaspoon black pepper

Combine all ingredients in a large saucepan. Cook gently over medium heat 15–20 minutes or until vegetables are tender. Allow to cool. Puree half of mixture in a blender and return to pot. Reheat until warm.

Servings: 4 (1 cup serving)

NUTRIENT VALUES			
PROTEIN	CARBOHYDRATE	FAT	ALCOHOL
21%	74%	4%	0%
CALORIES	PRO-GM	CARB-GM	FAT-GM	SOD-MG
94.30	5.243	18.50	0.488	254.0
FOOD EXCHANGES					
MILK	VEG.	FRUIT	BREAD	MEAT	FAT
0.0	1.1	0.0	0.6	0.3	0.0

BOK CHOY CHICKEN SOUP

1   ounce uncooked, long-
    grain brown rice
2   cups chicken stock,
    defatted
3   cups chopped bok choy
¼   cup chopped green
    onions
1½ ounces skinned and
    boned chicken breast,
    raw
¼   cup fresh bean sprouts
½   teaspoon Vegit or Mrs.
    Dash
Pinch of white pepper

Place the rice and stock in a 4-quart saucepan. Cover and place over high heat. When stock boils, reduce the heat and simmer for 20 minutes. Wash the bok choy and cut into thin diagonal slices. Set aside. Cut the chicken into thin strips across the grain. Combine chicken and chopped onions. After cooking the rice for 20 minutes, add the bok choy to the saucepan. Cover and cook for 4 minutes. Stir in the green onions and chicken strips. Cover the pan and cook for several more minutes. Add the bean sprouts. Cover the pan and cook for one minute. Season with Vegit and pepper. Serve hot.

Servings: 5 (¾ cup serving)

NUTRIENT VALUES				
PROTEIN	CARBOHYDRATE		FAT	ALCOHOL
34%	52%		14%	0%
CALORIES	PRO-GM	CARB-GM	FAT-GM	SOD-MG
44.20	3.883	6.010	0.700	27.90
FOOD EXCHANGES					
MILK	VEG.	FRUIT	BREAD	MEAT	FAT
0.0	0.3	0.0	0.3	0.2	0.3

CHICKEN GUMBO

3   chicken breast halves, skinned
2   cloves garlic, minced
1   tablespoon safflower oil
6   cups water
1   canned jalapeno, chopped (or to taste)
2   cups fresh tomatoes, peeled and chopped
2   cups fresh okra, washed, and sliced
½   cup chopped onion
¼   cup long-grain brown rice, raw
1   tablespoon water
1½ teaspoons gumbo filé
¼   teaspoon coriander

Heat oil in a large nonstick saucepan over medium heat. Add chicken and garlic and brown lightly. Add water and bring to a boil. Reduce heat and cover. Simmer 45 minutes or until chicken is tender. Remove chicken. Reserve broth. Chill and skim off excess fat. Remove meat from bone. Chop into bite-size pieces. In a large saucepan combine cubed chicken, jalapeno, tomatoes, okra, onion, rice and reserved chicken broth. Bring to a boil, then reduce heat. Cover and simmer 30 minutes, adding water if mixture begins to stick. Mix gumbo filé and water to make a smooth paste. Add to saucepan with coriander, stirring constantly. Simmer until slightly thickened. Serve warm.

Servings: 4 (1¼ cup serving)

NUTRIENT VALUES			
PROTEIN	CARBOHYDRATE	FAT	ALCOHOL
37%	34%	29%	0%
CALORIES	PRO-GM	CARB-GM	FAT-GM	SOD-MG
235.0	22.60	20.80	7.750	73.60
FOOD EXCHANGES					
MILK	VEG.	FRUIT	BREAD	MEAT	FAT
0.0	1.8	0.0	0.5	1.6	2.4

CREAM OF CHICKEN SOUP

2 chicken breasts, cleaned, skinned, washed and drained
3 cups water
½ cup celery with leaves, chopped
¼ teaspoon dried tarragon
1 tablespoon reduced-calorie margarine
3 tablespoons cornstarch
2 cups skim milk
2 tablespoons chicken bouillon cubes, low sodium
3 tablespoons water
½ teaspoon white pepper

In a 3-quart saucepan, add chicken breasts, water, celery and tarragon. Bring to a boil then reduce heat. Cover and simmer 45 minutes or until chicken is tender. Remove chicken and set aside. Allow broth to cool then place in freezer to allow fat to rise to top. Skim off congealed fat. Bone chicken when cool and chop. Add chopped chicken to defatted broth and reheat. Mix cornstarch with 3 tablespoons water to make a smooth paste. In a small saucepan, melt margarine over medium heat. Add cornstarch mixture, stirring constantly to prevent lumping. Add milk slowly, stirring constantly until smooth and creamy. Remove from heat and add to chicken broth with bouillon and pepper. Cook over medium heat for 8-10 minutes.

Yields: 4 (1 cup serving)

NUTRIENT VALUES			
PROTEIN	CARBOHYDRATE	FAT	ALCOHOL
51%	23%	26%	0%
CALORIES	PRO-GM	CARB-GM	FAT-GM	SOD-MG
237.0	30.40	13.50	6.811	111.0
FOOD EXCHANGES					
MILK	VEG.	FRUIT	BREAD	MEAT	FAT
0.5	0.0	0.0	0.3	2.1	2.4

LIME SOUP

2 corn tortillas
⅓ large onion, minced
2 cloves garlic, minced
½ jalapeno, minced
¼ teaspoon thyme
1 ripe tomato, peeled and chopped
¼ teaspoon cumin
3 cups chicken stock, defatted
1 lime
⅛ teaspoon oregano
¾ cup cooked chicken, white meat

Cut tortillas into wedges. Bake at 350° on a nonstick baking sheet until crisp, approximately 20 minutes. Saute onion, garlic and jalapenos in a nonstick skillet over low heat. Add thyme, tomato and cumin. Cook 10 minutes. In stainless or enamel pot, simmer chicken stock, add juice and "shells" of lime (check for bitterness) and simmer 5-8 minutes. Remove lime shell and add oregano. Bring to a quick boil. Add tomato mixture and lower heat to simmer, cook 20 minutes. Add cooked chicken and cook until warmed. Serve piping hot!

Servings: 8 (½ cup serving)

Serving Suggestions: Fill bowl with very hot soup. Top with tortilla wedge. Garnish each bowl with a lime section. Have bowls of cilantro, chopped jalapenos or green onions available.

NUTRIENT VALUES			
PROTEIN	CARBOHYDRATE	FAT	ALCOHOL
49%	35%	17%	0%
CALORIES	PRO-GM	CARB-GM	FAT-GM	SOD-MG
65.90	8.143	5.816	1.238	41.20
FOOD EXCHANGES					
MILK	VEG.	FRUIT	BREAD	MEAT	FAT
0.0	0.2	0.1	0.2	0.8	0.1

NEW ENGLAND CLAM CHOWDER

1 cup vegetable stock
1 cup chopped onion
½ cup chopped celery
1 tablespoon cornstarch
¾ teaspoon salt substitute
½ teaspoon seafood seasoning
2 potatoes, peeled and diced (approximately 12 ounces)
1 8-ounce bottle clam juice
3 cups skim milk
1 8-ounce can minced clams, drained
1 teaspoon chopped parsley

In a 2–3-quart saucepan, saute onion and celery in the stock until clear. Remove from heat; add the cornstarch and seasonings. Stir until the vegetables are evenly coated. Return to heat.

Add the potatoes, clam juice, and just enough water to barely cover. Stir well. Bring to a boil, lower the heat, and cover. Simmer for 15 minutes, or until the potatoes are tender.

Add the milk, clams, and parsley and heat through being careful not to boil. Serve warm.

Servings: 4 (1½ cup serving)

NUTRIENT VALUES			
PROTEIN	CARBOHYDRATE	FAT	ALCOHOL
19%	77%	4%	0%
CALORIES	PRO-GM	CARB-GM	FAT-GM	SOD-MG
187.0	8.943	36.50	0.944	48.60
FOOD EXCHANGES					
MILK	VEG.	FRUIT	BREAD	MEAT	FAT
0.0	0.5	0.0	2.0	0.6	0.0

TUNA CHOWDER

2   teaspoons reduced-
    calorie margarine
2   teaspoons flour
¾   cup water
1   teaspoon low-sodium
    chicken bouillon
1   small zucchini,
    julienned
¼   cup chopped green
    onions
½   cup evaporated skim
    milk
8   ounces canned tomatoes,
    drained, and chopped
¼   teaspoon thyme
1   6½-ounce can water-
    packed tuna, drained

Melt margarine in saucepan over low heat. Add flour and stir until mixture is thickened. Slowly stir in water and bouillon. Continue cooking until thickened, stirring constantly. Add zucchini and green onion. Cover and simmer 5 minutes. Stir in remaining ingredients, heat gently.

Servings: 2 (1⅓ cup serving)

NUTRIENT VALUES				
PROTEIN	CARBOHYDRATE		FAT	ALCOHOL
57%	29%		13%	0%
CALORIES	PRO-GM	CARB-GM	FAT-GM	SOD-MG
208.0	30.20	15.30	3.143	615.0
FOOD EXCHANGES					
MILK	VEG.	FRUIT	BREAD	MEAT	FAT
0.5	1.3	0.0	0.3	2.5	0.5

VEGETABLE CLAM SOUP

½ cup vegetable stock
½ cup chopped onion
2 cups zucchini, grated
1 large carrot, peeled and chopped
2 medium potatoes, chopped
2½ cups vegetable stock or bouillon
1 tablespoon ground cumin
1 7-ounce can minced clams, with liquid
½ cup skim evaporated milk
½ teaspoon white pepper

In a large saucepan heat ½ cup stock and saute the onion for 5 minutes. Add the zucchini, carrot, potatoes, stock, and cumin. Bring to a boil, reduce heat and simmer until the vegetables are just tender, about 15 minutes. Cool mixture. Puree the cooled mixture in a blender, then return the puree to the saucepan. Add the clams, milk and pepper and reheat slowly. Serve hot.

Servings: 4 (1¼ cup serving)

NUTRIENT VALUES				
PROTEIN	CARBOHYDRATE		FAT	ALCOHOL
29%	65%		6%	0%
CALORIES	PRO-GM	CARB-GM	FAT-GM	SOD-MG
123.0	9.175	20.20	0.851	73.40
FOOD EXCHANGES					
MILK	VEG.	FRUIT	BREAD	MEAT	FAT
0.3	1.1	0.0	0.5	0.6	0.0

CUCUMBER SOUP

2 medium cucumbers
1½ cups nonfat yogurt
¼ teaspoon white pepper
1 teaspoon fresh lemon juice
¼ teaspoon chopped fresh mint
½ teaspoon chervil

Peel, seed and dice cucumbers. Set aside. Puree half of the cucumbers and mix puree with remaining ingredients. Pour into a bowl. Add remaining cucumbers and mix well. Chill.

Servings: 4 (¾ cup serving)

NUTRIENT VALUES				
PROTEIN	CARBOHYDRATE		FAT	ALCOHOL
31%	66%		3%	0%
CALORIES	PRO-GM	CARB-GM	FAT-GM	SOD-MG
61.60	4.978	10.60	0.201	63.00
FOOD EXCHANGES					
MILK	VEG.	FRUIT	BREAD	MEAT	FAT
0.5	0.3	0.0	0.3	0.0	0.0

GAZPACHO

4   cups tomato juice, low
    sodium
½   cup cucumbers, chopped,
    unpeeled
¼   cup green pepper,
    chopped
¼   cup onion, finely
    chopped
¼   cup celery, finely
    chopped
1   tablespoon olive oil
2   tablespoons wine
    vinegar or herbal
    vinegar
½   teaspoon black pepper
1   teaspoon dried oregano
    or 2 teaspoons chopped
    fresh
1   teaspoon chopped fresh
    basil
1   clove garlic, minced

Combine all ingredients. Cover and chill overnight.

Servings: 6 (¾ cup serving)

NUTRIENT VALUES			
PROTEIN	CARBOHYDRATE	FAT	ALCOHOL
10%	55%	35%	0%
CALORIES	PRO-GM	CARB-GM	FAT-GM	SOD-MG
54.40	1.463	8.425	2.411	21.20
FOOD EXCHANGES					
MILK	VEG.	FRUIT	BREAD	MEAT	FAT
0.0	1.3	0.0	0.0	0.0	0.4

BLUEBERRY SOUP

2 cups blueberries
¾ cup apple juice
¼ cup orange juice
1 drop lemon extract
Dash of freshly grated
   nutmeg

Place the blueberries, juices, and lemon extract in a small saucepan. Bring to a boil over medium heat.

Reduce heat and simmer for 1 minute. Add nutmeg.

Pour the soup into a blender and process until smooth. Chill the soup.

Garnish with orange, kiwi, or apple slices.

Servings: 3 (½ cup serving)

NUTRIENT VALUES					
PROTEIN 3%	CARBOHYDRATE 93%		FAT 4%		ALCOHOL 0%
CALORIES 92.30	PRO-GM 0.806	CARB-GM 23.00	FAT-GM 0.467		SOD-MG 8.250
FOOD EXCHANGES					
MILK 0.0	VEG. 0.0	FRUIT 1.7	BREAD 0.0	MEAT 0.0	FAT 0.0

CHILLED MELON SOUP

2 cups cantalope, chopped
2 cups honeydew melon,
   chopped
½ cup fresh orange juice
2 tablespoons fresh lime
   juice
½ cup champagne

Puree melon in a blender with orange juice and lime juice. Chill for 30 minutes.

Add chilled champagne and serve.

Servings: 6 (¾ cup serving)

NUTRIENT VALUES					
PROTEIN 6%	CARBOHYDRATE 80%		FAT 3%		ALCOHOL 10%
CALORIES 56.00	PRO-GM 0.884	CARB-GM 12.40	FAT-GM 0.239		SOD-MG 10.90
FOOD EXCHANGES					
MILK 0.0	VEG. 0.0	FRUIT 0.8	BREAD 0.0	MEAT 0.0	FAT 0.0

STRAWBERRY-MELON SOUP

½ cantalope, cubed
1 cup apple juice
1 cup strawberries
¼ teaspoon ground cardamom

Puree the cantalope, apple juice, strawberries, and cardamom in a blender. Process until smooth. Chill. Garnish with extra strawberries.

Servings: 6 (½ cup serving)

Calories: 46

NUTRIENT VALUES			
PROTEIN	CARBOHYDRATE	FAT	ALCOHOL
5%	90%	5%	0%
CALORIES	PRO-GM	CARB-GM	FAT-GM	SOD-MG
45.80	0.643	11.10	0.285	6.167

FOOD EXCHANGES					
MILK	VEG.	FRUIT	BREAD	MEAT	FAT
0.0	0.0	1.2	0.0	0.0	0.0

Freshly Special . . .

SALADS & SALAD DRESSINGS

BLUE CHEESE DRESSING I

1   ounce blue cheese
2   tablespoons reduced-
    calorie mayonnaise
1   tablespoon lemon juice
2   tablespoons lowfat
    cottage cheese
¼   cup lowfat buttermilk
⅛   teaspoon dill weed
⅛   teaspoon garlic powder
¼   teaspoon white pepper
¼   cup nonfat yogurt

Combine all ingredients in a blender and process 30 seconds. Refrigerate.

Yields: 1 cup (1 tablespoon serving)

NUTRIENT VALUES					
PROTEIN	CARBOHYDRATE		FAT		ALCOHOL
22%	19%		58%		0%
CALORIES	PRO-GM	CARB-GM	FAT-GM		SOD-MG
16.40	0.923	0.796	1.060		39.10
FOOD EXCHANGES					
MILK	VEG.	FRUIT	BREAD	MEAT	FAT
0.1	0.0	0.0	0.0	0.1	0.2

BLUE CHEESE DRESSING II

⅔   cup 2% fat (or less)
    cottage cheese
2   ounces blue cheese,
    crumbled
1   teaspoon dry mustard
1   tablespoon white wine
    vinegar
1   teaspoon safflower oil
1   teaspoon onion, minced
½   teaspoon white pepper

Combine all ingredients in a blender container. Blend until smooth. Chill to blend flavors.

Yields: 1 cup (1 tablespoon serving)

NUTRIENT VALUES					
PROTEIN	CARBOHYDRATE		FAT		ALCOHOL
35%	9%		56%		0%
CALORIES	PRO-GM	CARB-GM	FAT-GM		SOD-MG
23.90	2.064	0.539	1.486		87.70
FOOD EXCHANGES					
MILK	VEG.	FRUIT	BREAD	MEAT	FAT
0.0	0.0	0.0	0.0	0.3	0.2

BUTTERMILK DRESSING I

1 cup lowfat buttermilk
¼ cup reduced-calorie
   mayonnaise
1 tablespoon minced fresh
   parsley
¾ teaspoon onion powder
½ teaspoon garlic powder
½ teaspoon white pepper

Combine all ingredients in a bowl, stirring until well blended. Cover and refrigerate.

Yields: 1¼ cups (1 tablespoon serving)

NUTRIENT VALUES					
PROTEIN 14%	CARBOHYDRATE 29%		FAT 58%		ALCOHOL 0%
CALORIES 14.20	PRO-GM 0.480	CARB-GM 1.019	FAT-GM 0.903		SOD-MG 15.10
FOOD EXCHANGES					
MILK 0.1	VEG. 0.0	FRUIT 0.0	BREAD 0.0	MEAT 0.0	FAT 0.2

BUTTERMILK DRESSING II

1 cup lowfat buttermilk
1 cup lowfat cottage
   cheese (2% fat or less)
1 tablespoon chopped
   onion
1 clove garlic, crushed
2 tablespoons lemon juice
1 teaspoon sugar
1 teaspoon chives

Place all ingredients in a blender and process until smooth. Chill.

Yields: 20 (1 tablespoon serving)

NUTRIENT VALUES					
PROTEIN 50%	CARBOHYDRATE 36%		FAT 13%		ALCOHOL 0%
CALORIES 15.10	PRO-GM 1.867	CARB-GM 1.353	FAT-GM 0.217		SOD-MG 61.00
FOOD EXCHANGES					
MILK 0.1	VEG. 0.0	FRUIT 0.0	BREAD 0.0	MEAT 0.2	FAT 0.0

CHEESY DRESSING

½ cup lowfat cottage
  cheese
¼ cup lowfat buttermilk
½ medium-sized tomato,
  peeled, seeded and
  chopped
¼ teaspoon celery seed
1 teaspoon white pepper
1 teaspoon fresh chopped
  basil
½ teaspoon fresh lemon
  thyme
1 clove garlic

In a blender or food processor combine the cottage cheese and buttermilk and process until smooth. Add the remaining ingredients and blend until creamy. Store in the refrigerator.

Yields: 1 cup (1 tablespoon serving)

NUTRIENT VALUES			
PROTEIN	CARBOHYDRATE	FAT	ALCOHOL
56%	31%	13%	0%
CALORIES	PRO-GM	CARB-GM	FAT-GM	SOD-MG
7.756	1.059	0.591	0.114	33.70
FOOD EXCHANGES					
MILK	VEG.	FRUIT	BREAD	MEAT	FAT
0.0	0.0	0.0	0.0	0.1	0.0

CITRUS HONEY DRESSING

1½ cups fresh orange juice
½ cup fresh lemon juice
1½ tablespoons honey
½ teaspoon paprika
1 garlic clove, minced

In a medium jar, add orange juice, lemon juice, honey, paprika and garlic. Cover and shake well. Refrigerate.

Yields: 1⅔ cups (1 tablespoon serving)

NUTRIENT VALUES			
PROTEIN	CARBOHYDRATE	FAT	ALCOHOL
4%	94%	2%	0%
CALORIES	PRO-GM	CARB-GM	FAT-GM	SOD-MG
11.20	0.115	2.861	0.027	0.500
FOOD EXCHANGES					
MILK	VEG.	FRUIT	BREAD	MEAT	FAT
0.0	0.0	0.1	0.1	0.0	0.0

CREAMY GARLIC DRESSING

¼ cup nonfat yogurt
¼ cup reduced-calorie
    mayonnaise
½ cup lowfat buttermilk
2 teaspoons fresh parsley,
    finely minced
3 cloves garlic, minced
½ teaspoon onion powder
¼ teaspoon black pepper

Combine all ingredients and refrigerate.

Yields: 1 cup

NUTRIENT VALUES					
PROTEIN	CARBOHYDRATE		FAT		ALCOHOL
12%	29%		59%		0%
CALORIES	PRO-GM	CARB-GM		FAT-GM	SOD-MG
16.30	0.503	1.177		1.068	12.20
FOOD EXCHANGES					
MILK	VEG.	FRUIT	BREAD	MEAT	FAT
0.1	0.0	0.0	0.0	0.0	0.3

CREAMY HERB DRESSING

3 sprigs watercress
4 springs cilantro
¼ cup minced green onion
2 tablespoons chopped
    parsley
½ teaspoon dill weed or 1
    teaspoon fresh minced
½ teaspoon oregano or 1
    teaspoon fresh minced
2 tablespoons white wine
    vinegar or herbal
½ cup lowfat buttermilk
¼ cup part-skim ricotta
    cheese
¼ cup nonfat yogurt cheese

Mix all ingredients in a blender and process until smooth.

Refrigerate.

Yields: 2 cups (1 tablespoon serving)

NUTRIENT VALUES					
PROTEIN	CARBOHYDRATE		FAT		ALCOHOL
33%	37%		30%		0%
CALORIES	PRO-GM	CARB-GM		FAT-GM	SOD-MG
5.616	0.465	0.527		0.188	8.593
FOOD EXCHANGES					
MILK	VEG.	FRUIT	BREAD	MEAT	FAT
0.0	0.0	0.0	0.0	0.0	0.0

CREAMY TOMATO DRESSING

½ cup lowfat cottage cheese
¼ cup lowfat buttermilk
2 canned whole tomatoes, drained
1 clove garlic, minced
1 tablespoon basil vinegar
½ teaspoon tarragon
¼ teaspoon pepper
½ teaspoon fresh minced oregano

Mix all ingredients in a blender and process until smooth. Chill.

Yields: 1¼ cups (1 tablespoon serving)

NUTRIENT VALUES			
PROTEIN	CARBOHYDRATE	FAT	ALCOHOL
52%	35%	13%	0%
CALORIES	PRO-GM	CARB-GM	FAT-GM	SOD-MG
6.541	0.859	0.573	0.093	33.20
FOOD EXCHANGES					
MILK	VEG.	FRUIT	BREAD	MEAT	FAT
0.0	0.0	0.0	0.0	0.1	0.0

CUCUMBER DRESSING

1 cup cucumber, peeled, seeded and chopped
½ cup nonfat yogurt cheese
2 tablespoons onion, chopped
1 clove garlic
1 tablespoon fresh dill weed, or 1½ teaspoons dried
1 teaspoon Dijon mustard
¼ teaspoon black pepper
2 teaspoons lemon juice

Combine all ingredients in a blender and process for 30 seconds. Chill and allow flavors to blend.

Yields: 1 cup (1 tablespoon serving)

NUTRIENT VALUES			
PROTEIN	CARBOHYDRATE	FAT	ALCOHOL
34%	65%	2%	0%
CALORIES	PRO-GM	CARB-GM	FAT-GM	SOD-MG
9.281	0.774	1.482	0.018	14.60
FOOD EXCHANGES					
MILK	VEG.	FRUIT	BREAD	MEAT	FAT
0.1	0.0	0.0	0.0	0.0	0.0

CUCUMBER-DILL DRESSING

1 medium cucumber, peeled and sliced
12 ounces lowfat cottage cheese
2 tablespoons prepared horseradish
3 tablespoons fresh dill or 2 tablespoons dried dill

Combine all ingredients in blender; process until smooth. Store in an airtight container in refrigerator.

Yields: 2¼ cups (1 tablespoon serving)

NUTRIENT VALUES					
PROTEIN 56%	CARBOHYDRATE 32%		FAT 12%	ALCOHOL 0%	
CALORIES 9.024	PRO-GM 1.277	CARB-GM 0.718	FAT-GM 0.118	SOD-MG 48.20	
FOOD EXCHANGES					
MILK 0.0	VEG. 0.0	FRUIT 0.0	BREAD 0.0	MEAT 0.2	FAT 0.0

GINGER YOGURT DRESSING

2 tablespoons fresh lemon juice
1 teaspoon safflower oil
1 tablespoon apple juice
1½ teaspoons grated fresh ginger
½ cup nonfat yogurt
1 teaspoon honey

Mix all ingredients together and chill.

Yields: ¾ cup (1 tablespoon serving)

NUTRIENT VALUES					
PROTEIN 16%	CARBOHYDRATE 54%		FAT 30%	ALCOHOL 0%	
CALORIES 11.10	PRO-GM 0.473	CARB-GM 1.547	FAT-GM 0.382	SOD-MG 6.783	
FOOD EXCHANGES					
MILK 0.0	VEG. 0.0	FRUIT 0.0	BREAD 0.0	MEAT 0.0	FAT 0.1

GREEN GODDESS DRESSING

½ cup reduced-calorie
    mayonnaise
½ cup nonfat yogurt
2 tablespoons minced
    green onions
2 tablespoons minced
    parsley
1 teaspoon tarragon
    vinegar
1 teaspoon lemon juice
½ garlic clove, minced

Place the ingredients in blender and process until well combined.

Store in the refrigerator in a tightly covered container.

Yields: 1¼ cups (1 tablespoon serving)

NUTRIENT VALUES				
PROTEIN	CARBOHYDRATE		FAT	ALCOHOL
6%	19%		75%	0%
CALORIES	PRO-GM	CARB-GM	FAT-GM	SOD-MG
19.10	0.294	0.901	1.602	4.199
FOOD EXCHANGES					
MILK	VEG.	FRUIT	BREAD	MEAT	FAT
0.0	0.0	0.0	0.0	0.0	0.4

LOW CAL ITALIAN I

2 tablespoons cider or
    wine vinegar
½ cup tomato juice, low
    sodium
2 teaspoons minced onion
½ teaspoon dried parsley
    or 1 teaspoons minced
    fresh
½ teaspoon dried oregano
    or 1 teaspoon minced
    fresh
¼ teaspoon dried basil or
    ½ teaspoon minced fresh
1 clove garlic, minced

Combine all ingredients in a jar and shake.

Store in refrigerator.

Yields: ½ cup (1 tablespoon serving)

NUTRIENT VALUES				
PROTEIN	CARBOHYDRATE		FAT	ALCOHOL
13%	83%		4%	0%
CALORIES	PRO-GM	CARB-GM	FAT-GM	SOD-MG
3.859	0.152	0.992	0.021	1.664
FOOD EXCHANGES					
MILK	VEG.	FRUIT	BREAD	MEAT	FAT
0.0	0.1	0.0	0.0	0.0	0.0

LOW CALORIE ITALIAN DRESSING II

1   teaspoon unflavored
    gelatin
1⅓ cups water, divided
½   cup white wine vinegar
6   cloves garlic, chopped
¼   cup chopped chives
⅓   cup green olives,
    chopped
¼   cup Parmesan cheese,
    freshly grated
4   teaspoons lemon juice
4   teaspoons anchovy paste
2   teaspoons sugar
1   teaspoon freshly ground
    black pepper
2   teaspoons dried Italian
    herb mix
3   tablespoons chopped
    fresh parsley

Add gelatin to ⅔ cup water in a small saucepan, let stand one minute. Cook over low heat, stirring constantly, until gelatin is dissolved. Remove from heat and stir in remaining ⅔ cup water.

Combine gelatin with remaining ingredients in a blender and mix for 30 seconds. Chill and allow flavors to blend.

Yields: 2 cups (1 tablespoon serving)

NUTRIENT VALUES			
PROTEIN	CARBOHYDRATE	FAT	ALCOHOL
22%	34%	43%	0%
CALORIES	PRO-GM	CARB-GM	FAT-GM	SOD-MG
8.363	0.513	0.792	0.444	40.30

FOOD EXCHANGES					
MILK	VEG.	FRUIT	BREAD	MEAT	FAT
0.0	0.0	0.0	0.0	0.0	0.1

POPPY SEED DRESSING I

½ cup nonfat yogurt
½ cup lowfat cottage
   cheese
2 teaspoons lowfat
   buttermilk
2 tablespoons chives,
   chopped
2 teaspoons poppy seeds
¼ teaspoon salt
2 teaspoons sugar
2 tablespoons strawberry
   vinegar

Place all ingredients in a blender and process until smooth. Chill.

Excellent on fruit or spinach salad.

Yields: 1¾ cups (1 tablespoon serving)

NUTRIENT VALUES					
PROTEIN	CARBOHYDRATE		FAT		ALCOHOL
40%	43%		16%		0%
CALORIES	PRO-GM	CARB-GM		FAT-GM	SOD-MG
7.400	0.751	0.809		0.135	37.20
FOOD EXCHANGES					
MILK	VEG.	FRUIT	BREAD	MEAT	FAT
0.0	0.0	0.0	0.0	0.1	0.0

POPPY SEED DRESSING II

1 cup nonfat yogurt
1 tablespoon honey
4 teaspoons lemon juice
1 teaspoon poppy seed

Combine all ingredients, mixing well. Chill.

Yields: 1 cup

NUTRIENT VALUES					
PROTEIN	CARBOHYDRATE		FAT		ALCOHOL
23%	71%		6%		0%
CALORIES	PRO-GM	CARB-GM		FAT-GM	SOD-MG
12.20	0.724	2.214		0.078	10.10
FOOD EXCHANGES					
MILK	VEG.	FRUIT	BREAD	MEAT	FAT
0.1	0.0	0.0	0.1	0.0	0.0

RUSSIAN DRESSING

6 tablespoons nonfat
   yogurt
2 tablespoons tomato paste
¼ cup reduced-calorie
   mayonnaise
3 tablespoons white
   vinegar
¼ teaspoon salt
¼ teaspoon paprika
¼ teaspoon mustard
   powder

Combine all ingredients in blender and process until smooth.

Yields: 1 cup (1 tablespoon serving)

NUTRIENT VALUES					
PROTEIN	CARBOHYDRATE		FAT		ALCOHOL
9%	31%		60%		0%
CALORIES	PRO-GM	CARB-GM		FAT-GM	SOD-MG
14.70	0.340	1.169		1.022	35.70
FOOD EXCHANGES					
MILK	VEG.	FRUIT	BREAD	MEAT	FAT
0.0	0.1	0.0	0.0	0.0	0.3

TAHINI DRESSING

1 cup nonfat yogurt
2 cloves garlic, minced
3 tablespoons tahini
   (sesame butter)
2 tablespoons green
   onions, chopped
2 teaspoons lemon juice
½ teaspoon black pepper

Put all ingredients in blender and process until smooth. Chill.

Yields: 2 cups (1 tablespoon serving)

NUTRIENT VALUES					
PROTEIN	CARBOHYDRATE		FAT		ALCOHOL
20%	30%		50%		0%
CALORIES	PRO-GM	CARB-GM		FAT-GM	SOD-MG
12.30	0.644	0.947		0.706	6.493
FOOD EXCHANGES					
MILK	VEG.	FRUIT	BREAD	MEAT	FAT
0.0	0.0	0.0	0.0	0.0	0.1

THOUSAND ISLAND DRESSING

2   tablespoons reduced-
     calorie mayonnaise
¼   cup nonfat yogurt
1   tablespoon catsup
3   tablespoons skim milk
3   tablespoons chopped
     onion
2   tablespoons chopped dill
     pickle
1   clove garlic, minced
¼   teaspoon dried oregano
     or ½ teaspoon minced
     fresh
½   teaspoon dried parsley
     or 1 teaspoon minced
     fresh

Combine all ingredients and chill before serving.

Yields: 1 cup (1 tablespoon serving)

NUTRIENT VALUES					
PROTEIN	CARBOHYDRATE		FAT		ALCOHOL
13%	40%		47%		0%
CALORIES	PRO-GM	CARB-GM		FAT-GM	SOD-MG
9.716	0.310	0.982		0.515	28.40
FOOD EXCHANGES					
MILK	VEG.	FRUIT	BREAD	MEAT	FAT
0.0	0.0	0.0	0.0	0.0	0.1

TOMATO-HERB DRESSING

½ cup unsalted tomato juice
½ cup red wine vinegar
1 teaspoon dried dill or 2 teaspoons minced fresh
¼ teaspoon dried chervil
¼ teaspoon dried basil or ½ teaspoon minced fresh
½ teaspoon dried oregano or 1 teaspoon minced fresh
½ clove garlic, minced
1 cup lowfat buttermilk

Combine all ingredients. Keep refrigerated.

Yields: 1½ cups (1 tablespoon serving)

NUTRIENT VALUES			
PROTEIN	CARBOHYDRATE	FAT	ALCOHOL
25%	63%	12%	0%
CALORIES	PRO-GM	CARB-GM	FAT-GM	SOD-MG
6.391	0.432	1.072	0.092	13.10

FOOD EXCHANGES					
MILK	VEG.	FRUIT	BREAD	MEAT	FAT
0.0	0.0	0.0	0.0	0.0	0.0

VINAIGRETTE I

1 tablespoon olive oil
⅓ cup lemon juice
2 teaspoons Dijon mustard
2 tablespoons minced shallots
1 tablespoon grated Parmesan cheese
1 tablespoon white wine or herbal vinegar

Combine all ingredients in a small jar with a lid. Shake well until thoroughly combined.

Store in the refrigerator in a tightly covered container. Return to room temperature before using.

Yields: ½ cup (1 tablespoon serving)

NUTRIENT VALUES			
PROTEIN	CARBOHYDRATE	FAT	ALCOHOL
6%	17%	76%	0%
CALORIES	PRO-GM	CARB-GM	FAT-GM	SOD-MG
22.40	0.363	0.993	1.922	30.90

FOOD EXCHANGES					
MILK	VEG.	FRUIT	BREAD	MEAT	FAT
0.0	0.0	0.1	0.0	0.1	0.3

GREEN CHILI VINAIGRETTE

½ cup green chile pesto
¼ cup lemon vinegar or
    wine vinegar
3   tablespoons fresh lemon
    juice
2   tablespoons water

Mix all ingredients well. Refrigerate.

Yields: 10 tablespoons (1 tablespoon serving)

Use as salad dressing, as marinade for cold vegetables, or with pasta.

NUTRIENT VALUES			
PROTEIN 15%	CARBOHYDRATE 20%	FAT 65%	ALCOHOL 0%
CALORIES 25.10	PRO-GM 1.041	CARB-GM 1.364	FAT-GM 1.960	SOD-MG 45.70
FOOD EXCHANGES					
MILK 0.0	VEG. 0.0	FRUIT 0.0	BREAD 0.0	MEAT 0.0	FAT 0.0

HERBED VINAIGRETTE

1   tablespoon olive oil
⅓ cup lemon juice
2   teaspoons Dijon mustard
2   tablespoons minced
    shallots
1   tablespoon grated
    Parmesan cheese
1   tablespoon minced fresh
    parsley or 1 teaspoon
    dried
1   tablespoon minced fresh
    thyme or ½ teaspoon
    dried
1   teaspoon minced fresh
    marjoram or ½ teaspoon
    dried

Combine the ingredients in a small jar with a lid. Shake well until thoroughly combined. Refrigerate.

Yields: 10 tablespoons (1 tablespoon per serving)

NUTRIENT VALUES			
PROTEIN 7%	CARBOHYDRATE 23%	FAT 70%	ALCOHOL 0%
CALORIES 19.60	PRO-GM 0.360	CARB-GM 1.146	FAT-GM 1.548	SOD-MG 25.10
FOOD EXCHANGES					
MILK 0.0	VEG. 0.0	FRUIT 0.1	BREAD 0.0	MEAT 0.1	FAT 0.3

SPICY VINAIGRETTE

2   cloves garlic, minced
3   tablespoons fresh orange juice
4   tablespoons red wine vinegar
¼   teaspoon dry mustard
½   teaspoon chili powder or paprika
1   teaspoon honey
1   tablespoon oil

Combine all ingredients. Mix well.

Yields: 9 tablespoons (1 tablespoon per serving)

NUTRIENT VALUES			
PROTEIN 1%	CARBOHYDRATE 33%	FAT 66%	ALCOHOL 0%
CALORIES 19.70	PRO-GM 0.073	CARB-GM 1.693	FAT-GM 1.526	SOD-MG 0.440
FOOD EXCHANGES					
MILK 0.0	VEG. 0.0	FRUIT 0.1	BREAD 0.1	MEAT 0.0	FAT 0.3

YOGURT DILL DRESSING

1   cup nonfat yogurt
2   teaspoons onion powder
1   teaspoon lemon juice
2   teaspoons chopped fresh dill
¼   teaspoon garlic powder
1   teaspoon white wine vinegar
¼   teaspoon dry mustard

Mix together all ingredients and chill.

Yields: 1 cup (1 tablespoon serving)

NUTRIENT VALUES			
PROTEIN 36%	CARBOHYDRATE 64%	FAT 0%	ALCOHOL 0%
CALORIES 8.007	PRO-GM 0.722	CARB-GM 1.286	FAT-GM 0.003	SOD-MG 10.10
FOOD EXCHANGES					
MILK 0.1	VEG. 0.0	FRUIT 0.0	BREAD 0.0	MEAT 0.0	FAT 0.0

APPLE WALDORF SALAD

1 Granny Smith apple
1 Red Delicious apple
½ cup celery, chopped
1 tablespoon pecan halves
1 tablespoon fresh lemon juice
¼ cup nonfat yogurt
Dash of cinnamon
Dash of grated nutmeg

Chop apples, do not peel; sprinkle with lemon juice. Add celery, yogurt, pecans and spices. Serve on purple cabbage leaf or lettuce leaf.

Servings: 4

NUTRIENT VALUES			
PROTEIN	CARBOHYDRATE	FAT	ALCOHOL
6%	75%	19%	0%
CALORIES	PRO-GM	CARB-GM	FAT-GM	SOD-MG
61.80	1.068	12.70	1.405	23.80
FOOD EXCHANGES					
MILK	VEG.	FRUIT	BREAD	MEAT	FAT
0.1	0.0	0.8	0.0	0.0	0.4

CONGEALED FRUIT SALAD

2 envelopes unflavored gelatin
⅓ cup cold water
1 cup pineapple juice, unsweetened
1 tablespoon honey
¼ cup orange juice, fresh or frozen
¼ cup lemon juice
1 cup grated carrots
1 cup orange segments, cut in small pieces
1½ cups unsweetened, crushed pineapple, drained
Green leaf lettuce
½ cup nonfat yogurt

Soften gelatin in cold water. Heat pineapple juice, remove from heat. Stir in softened gelatin and stir to dissolve. Add honey, orange juice and lemon juice.

Refrigerate to cool mixture. When mixture begins to thicken, fold in carrot, oranges and pineapple.

Transfer gelatin mixture to a 4-cup mold and chill. Unmold when thickened. Garnish with lettuce and yogurt.

Servings: 8 (½ cup serving)

NUTRIENT VALUES			
PROTEIN	CARBOHYDRATE	FAT	ALCOHOL
15%	84%	1%	0%
CALORIES	PRO-GM	CARB-GM	FAT-GM	SOD-MG
75.20	2.912	16.70	0.132	17.90
FOOD EXCHANGES					
MILK	VEG.	FRUIT	BREAD	MEAT	FAT
0.1	0.3	0.9	0.1	0.0	0.0

PINEAPPLE ORANGE SALAD

1   cup canned pineapple
    chunks, unsweetened,
    and drained
1   cup canned Mandarin
    orange slices,
    unsweetened, and
    drained
1   cup nonfat yogurt
¼   teaspoon coconut extract
2   teaspoons shredded
    coconut, unsweetened
1   teaspoon vanilla extract
2   teaspoons honey

Combine all ingredients and toss to mix well.
Chill to blend flavors.

Servings: 5 (½ cup serving)

NUTRIENT VALUES			
PROTEIN	CARBOHYDRATE	FAT	ALCOHOL
16%	80%	4%	0%
CALORIES	PRO-GM	CARB-GM	FAT-GM	SOD-MG
65.80	2.772	13.90	0.313	32.90

FOOD EXCHANGES					
MILK	VEG.	FRUIT	BREAD	MEAT	FAT
0.3	0.0	0.6	0.1	0.0	0.0

APPLE AND CABBAGE SLAW

4 cups finely shredded
   cabbage
1 cup carrots, grated
1 apple, diced
2 tablespoons raisins
¼ cup celery, sliced
2 tablespoons fresh parsley

DRESSING
¼ cup lemon juice
1 tablespoon honey
1 tablespoon grated onions
2 teaspoons prepared
   mustard
1 tablespoon sesame seeds
1 tablespoon cinnamon/
   clove vinegar

In a large salad bowl, combine cabbage, carrots, apples, raisins, celery, and parsley.

In a separate bowl, mix together lemon juice, honey, onion, mustard, sesame seeds and vinegar.

Pour the dressing over the salad mixture and toss to mix.

Servings: 7 (1 cup serving)

NUTRIENT VALUES			
PROTEIN	CARBOHYDRATE	FAT	ALCOHOL
8%	80%	12%	0%
CALORIES	PRO-GM	CARB-GM	FAT-GM	SOD-MG
58.70	1.302	12.90	0.837	38.50
FOOD EXCHANGES					
MILK	VEG.	FRUIT	BREAD	MEAT	FAT
0.0	0.8	0.4	0.1	0.0	0.2

FRUIT SLAW

2 **cups green cabbage, shredded**
¼ **cup green pepper, chopped**
½ **cup canned crushed pineapple, unsweetened and drained**
2 **tablespoons strawberry or raspberry vinegar**
2 **tablespoons reduced-calorie mayonnaise**
2 **tablespoons nonfat yogurt**
2 **teaspoons minced onion**
¼ **teaspoon curry powder**
¼ **teaspoon celery seed**

Combine cabbage, green pepper and pineapple in a large bowl.

Stir vinegar, mayonnaise, yogurt and seasonings in a separate bowl. Pour over cabbage mixture. Toss to blend well. Chill.

Servings: 4 (¾ cup serving)

NUTRIENT VALUES				
PROTEIN	CARBOHYDRATE		FAT	ALCOHOL
7%	60%		34%	0%
CALORIES	PRO-GM	CARB-GM	FAT-GM	SOD-MG
53.70	0.992	8.654	2.160	12.00
FOOD EXCHANGES					
MILK	VEG.	FRUIT	BREAD	MEAT	FAT
0.0	0.4	0.4	0.0	0.0	0.5

VEGETABLE SLAW

1 cup red cabbage, shredded
2 cups green cabbage, shredded
1 cup yellow squash or zucchini, julienned

DRESSING
¼ cup nonfat yogurt
2 teaspoons reduced-calorie mayonnaise
1½ teaspoons Dijon mustard
1 teaspoon minced green onion
1 teaspoon fresh lemon juice
1½ teaspoons herbal vinegar (basil or tarragon)

Combine vegetables in large bowl. Make dressing and pour over vegetables. Mix well. Refrigerate until ready to serve.

Servings: 4 (1 cup serving)

NUTRIENT VALUES			
PROTEIN	CARBOHYDRATE	FAT	ALCOHOL
19%	61%	20%	0%
CALORIES	PRO-GM	CARB-GM	FAT-GM	SOD-MG
36.30	1.860	5.820	0.838	45.00
FOOD EXCHANGES					
MILK	VEG.	FRUIT	BREAD	MEAT	FAT
0.1	0.9	0.0	0.0	0.0	0.1

ARTICHOKE AND GREEN BEAN SALAD

14 ounces canned artichoke hearts, drained
1 cup mushrooms, sliced
¼ cup fresh lime or lemon juice
1 red onion, cut in rings
1½ cups green beans, frozen or fresh
1 clove garlic, minced
½ cup herbal vinegar
1 tablespoon vegetable oil
Coarsely ground pepper to taste
2 tablespoons parsley, chopped
¼ cup green onions, chopped
1 teaspoon dried mustard
¼ teaspoon thyme or ½ teaspoon minced fresh lemon thyme

Squeeze fresh lime or lemon juice over artichoke hearts and mushrooms. Add onions and beans. Mix the remaining ingredients. Pour over vegetables and marinate 8 hours, tossing once. Serve on lettuce bed with a sprinkle of paprika.

Servings: 7 (¾ cup serving)

NUTRIENT VALUES			
PROTEIN	CARBOHYDRATE	FAT	ALCOHOL
11%	46%	42%	0%
CALORIES	PRO-GM	CARB-GM	FAT-GM	SOD-MG
81.60	2.650	10.70	4.355	2.536

FOOD EXCHANGES					
MILK	VEG.	FRUIT	BREAD	MEAT	FAT
0.0	1.6	0.1	0.0	0.0	0.8

BASIL AND BEAN SALAD

1 cup cooked pinto beans*
¼ cup chopped onion
1 cup cherry tomatoes, halved
½ cucumber, chopped

DRESSING
¼ cup chopped parsley
1 tablespoon chopped basil
1½ teaspoons olive oil
1 tablespoon white wine vinegar
1 tablespoon lemon juice
¼ teaspoon black pepper
1 teaspoon sugar

*May substitute kidney or black beans.

In a mixing bowl, combine the beans, onion, cherry tomatoes and cucumber.

Combine the parsley, basil, oil, vinegar, lemon juice, pepper and sugar in a blender. Blend until smooth. Mix with the bean and vegetable mixture. Serve on a lettuce leaf.

Servings: 4 (½ cup serving)

NUTRIENT VALUES					
PROTEIN	CARBOHYDRATE		FAT	ALCOHOL	
16%	65%		18%	0%	
CALORIES	PRO-GM	CARB-GM	FAT-GM	SOD-MG	
94.20	4.046	16.20	2.020	5.398	
FOOD EXCHANGES					
MILK	VEG.	FRUIT	BREAD	MEAT	FAT
0.0	1.0	0.0	0.6	0.0	0.4

BEAN AND PEA SALAD

1 cup cooked kidney beans
¾ cup cooked garbanzo
   beans (chick peas)
1 red bell pepper, chopped
½ cup thinly sliced celery
2 green onions, chopped
2 teaspoons olive oil
2 tablespoons vinegar
¼ teaspoon chili powder
½ teaspoon Dijon-style
   mustard
1 teaspoon low-sodium
   soy sauce
Minced fresh parsley

In a medium bowl, toss together the kidney beans, garbanzos, peppers, celery and onions. In a separate bowl, combine the oil, vinegar, mustard, chili powder and soy sauce.

Pour the dressing over the salad and toss well. Chill before serving. Garnish with parsley.

Servings: 6 (½ cup serving)

NUTRIENT VALUES					
PROTEIN 18%	CARBOHYDRATE 59%		FAT 23%	ALCOHOL 0%	
CALORIES 86.20	PRO-GM 4.108	CARB-GM 13.20	FAT-GM 2.264	SOD-MG 325.0	
FOOD EXCHANGES					
MILK 0.0	VEG. 1.5	FRUIT 0.0	BREAD 0.5	MEAT 0.0	FAT 0.5

BEET AND CARROT SALAD

2 cups grated red beets
   (fresh or canned)
1 cup grated carrots
¼ cup lemon juice
2 teaspoons sunflower oil
2 tablespoons apple juice
1 tablespoon grated fresh
   ginger
2 teaspoons honey
6 cups chopped spinach
   leaves
1 cup nonfat yogurt

Combine the lemon juice, oil, apple juice, ginger, honey and yogurt in a small bowl. Set aside.

In a large bowl, toss together the carrots, beets, and dressing. Chill before serving. Place beet-carrot mixture on spinach.

Servings: 6 (½ cup beet-carrot mixture on 1 cup spinach leaves.)

NUTRIENT VALUES					
PROTEIN 18%	CARBOHYDRATE 65%		FAT 17%	ALCOHOL 0%	
CALORIES 88.20	PRO-GM 4.362	CARB-GM 15.60	FAT-GM 1.817	SOD-MG 294.0	
FOOD EXCHANGES					
MILK 0.0	VEG. 2.0	FRUIT 0.0	BREAD 0.0	MEAT 0.0	FAT 0.5

BROCCOLI AND CAULIFLOWER SALAD

1   green onion, chopped
¼   cup nonfat yogurt
1   teaspoon honey
2   tablespoons reduced-calorie mayonnaise
1½ teaspoons herbal vinegar
½   teaspoon low-sodium soy sauce
1   tablespoon picante sauce
1   tablespoon Mrs. Dash
3   cups cauliflower florets
3   cups broccoli florets

Combine cauliflower and broccoli in a medium mixing bowl. In a separate bowl, combine remaining ingredients. Pour dressing over vegetables and chill several hours before serving.

Servings: 6 (1 cup serving)

NUTRIENT VALUES			
PROTEIN	CARBOHYDRATE	FAT	ALCOHOL
21%	52%	27%	0%
CALORIES	PRO-GM	CARB-GM	FAT-GM	SOD-MG
46.90	2.846	7.023	1.616	73.00

FOOD EXCHANGES					
MILK	VEG.	FRUIT	BREAD	MEAT	FAT
0.1	1.0	0.0	0.1	0.0	0.3

CAESAR SALAD

3   cups Romaine lettuce
2   teaspoons Parmesan cheese
4   egg whites
1   tablespoon lemon juice
3   tablespoons white wine vinegar
1   clove garlic, minced
1   teaspoon low-sodium soy sauce
1   teaspoon Worcestershire
1   slice whole wheat bread, toasted and cut into cubes for croutons

Mix egg whites, lemon juice, vinegar, garlic, soy sauce and Worcestershire. Place chilled Romaine in mixing bowl. Add dressing, stirring to coat. Serve on salad plate and sprinkle with Parmesan cheese and top with croutons.

Servings: 3

NUTRIENT VALUES			
PROTEIN	CARBOHYDRATE	FAT	ALCOHOL
42%	46%	12%	0%
CALORIES	PRO-GM	CARB-GM	FAT-GM	SOD-MG
63.10	7.037	7.672	0.907	281.0

FOOD EXCHANGES					
MILK	VEG.	FRUIT	BREAD	MEAT	FAT
0.0	0.3	0.0	0.3	0.5	0.0

CABBAGE PECAN SALAD

3   cups finely shredded
green cabbage
½   cup red seedless grapes,
halved
½   red apple, diced
2   tablespoons chopped
pecans
½   cup Poppy Seed
Dressing (see p. 167)

Place the cabbage in a large serving bowl. Add the grapes, apples and pecans. Add dressing and toss.

Servings: 6 (¾ cup serving)

NUTRIENT VALUES					
PROTEIN 14%	CARBOHYDRATE 53%		FAT 33%		ALCOHOL 0%
CALORIES 46.50	PRO-GM 1.784	CARB-GM 6.805		FAT-GM 1.844	SOD-MG 57.60
FOOD EXCHANGES					
MILK 0.0	VEG. 0.4	FRUIT 0.2	BREAD 0.0	MEAT 0.0	FAT 0.4

CARROT RAISIN SALAD

2   cups grated carrots
2   tablespoons seedless
raisins
1   tablespoon reduced-
calorie mayonnaise
3   tablespoons nonfat
yogurt
2   tablespoons fresh lemon
juice
2   teaspoons brown sugar

Mix carrots and raisins together. Set aside. In a small mixing bowl, mix mayonnaise, yogurt, lemon juice, and sugar. Pour over carrot mixture and mix thoroughly. Refrigerate.

Servings: 3 (⅔ cup serving)

NUTRIENT VALUES					
PROTEIN 7%	CARBOHYDRATE 78%		FAT 15%		ALCOHOL 0%
CALORIES 84.20	PRO-GM 1.667	CARB-GM 17.40		FAT-GM 1.495	SOD-MG 37.00
FOOD EXCHANGES					
MILK 0.2	VEG. 1.2	FRUIT 0.3	BREAD 0.2	MEAT 0.0	FAT 0.3

CAULIFLOWER AND CARROT SALAD

2 cups chopped cauliflower
1 cup sliced carrots
½ cup chopped bell pepper
½ cup lemon juice
¼ cup chopped parsley
2 cloves garlic, finely minced
1 shallot, chopped (2 tablespoons)

In a covered pot, steam the cauliflower, carrot and bell pepper until tender-crisp. Cool and drain. Combine the lemon juice, parsley, garlic and shallot in a small bowl. Mix the vegetables and dressing together in a large bowl. Chill and serve.

Servings: 4 (¾ cup serving)

NUTRIENT VALUES			
PROTEIN	CARBOHYDRATE	FAT	ALCOHOL
14%	82%	4%	0%
CALORIES	PRO-GM	CARB-GM	FAT-GM	SOD-MG
46.00	1.922	11.30	0.243	36.60
FOOD EXCHANGES					
MILK	VEG.	FRUIT	BREAD	MEAT	FAT
0.0	1.3	0.1	0.0	0.0	0.0

CURRIED SPINACH SALAD

1½ tablespoon skim milk
¾ teaspoon curry powder
½ cup nonfat yogurt
2 teaspoons lemon juice
1 teaspoon honey
¼ teaspoon cinnamon

To make dressing, mix first six ingredients together, mixing well, chill.

Servings: ⅔ cups

1 teaspoon lemon juice
4 cups torn fresh spinach leaves
½ banana, thinly sliced
½ unpeeled pear, cut into chunks
½ cup sunflower sprouts, or alfalfa sprouts
¼ cup Thompson seedless grapes, halved
¼ cup celery, sliced
1 tablespoon chopped walnuts

Toss banana and pear with lemon juice to prevent browning. Set aside. In a separate bowl, toss together spinach, banana, pear, sprouts, grapes, celery and walnuts. Place salad on plates and divide dressing over salad.

Servings: 7 (1 cup salad serving with 1½ tablespoons dressing)

NUTRIENT VALUES					
PROTEIN 19%	CARBOHYDRATE 65%		FAT 16%		ALCOHOL 0%
CALORIES 44.30	PRO-GM 2.398	CARB-GM 8.074		FAT-GM 0.900	SOD-MG 42.70
FOOD EXCHANGES					
MILK 0.1	VEG. 0.3	FRUIT 0.3	BREAD 0.1	MEAT 0.0	FAT 0.1

GREEN BEAN SALAD

2½ cups fresh green beans
2 cups fresh wax beans
1 shallot, minced
1 garlic clove, minced
2 teaspoons olive oil
2 tablespoons red wine vinegar or herbal vinegar
1 teaspoon Italian seasoning
2 tablespoons minced fresh Italian parsley leaves

Trim and wash the green and wax beans, and cut them into 1-inch lengths. Steam the beans until tender-crisp. Allow to cool and drain well. Place the beans in a bowl.

Combine shallot, garlic, the oil, vinegar, and Italian seasoning in a large bowl. Mix well. Add beans and toss. Sprinkle the salad with parsley and serve.

Servings: 6 (¾ cup serving)

NUTRIENT VALUES			
PROTEIN	CARBOHYDRATE	FAT	ALCOHOL
13%	59%	28%	0%
CALORIES	PRO-GM	CARB-GM	FAT-GM	SOD-MG
50.30	1.914	8.462	1.781	4.076
FOOD EXCHANGES					
MILK	VEG.	FRUIT	BREAD	MEAT	FAT
0.0	1.3	0.0	0.0	0.0	0.3

JICAMA AND ORANGE SALAD

SALAD

4 oranges
2 red sweet peppers
1 small jicama
(approximately ½ pound)

DRESSING

¼ cup white vinegar
1 tablespoon safflower oil
¼ teaspoon white pepper
¼ teaspoon chile powder or paprika
1 clove garlic, peeled and halved
Lime wedges for garnish

Peel oranges, remove the membrane and separate the fruit into sections. Place in a bowl and squeeze any juices from the peel over the sections.

Seed the peppers and slice into strips and set aside.

Use a sharp knife to remove outer peel from jicama, then remove inner fibrous peel as well. Peeled jicama will resemble a peeled potato. Cube peeled jicama.

Combine all dressing ingredients and mix well. All of the ingredients can be prepared a few hours ahead of serving, but the salad should be assembled just before serving.

Toss oranges, jicama and peppers with dressing. Arrange salad on lettuce-lined plates and garnish with lime wedges.

Servings: 7

NUTRIENT VALUES					
PROTEIN	CARBOHYDRATE		FAT		ALCOHOL
4%	75%		21%		0%
CALORIES	PRO-GM	CARB-GM		FAT-GM	SOD-MG
89.30	0.930	17.90		2.218	0.826
FOOD EXCHANGES					
MILK	VEG.	FRUIT	BREAD	MEAT	FAT
0.0	0.2	0.6	0.4	0.0	0.4

MARINATED ARTICHOKE HEARTS

1 cup canned artichoke
   hearts, drained
1 clove garlic, minced
1 teaspoon safflower oil
2 tablespoons basil vinegar
¼ teaspoon dried oregano
   or ½ teaspoon fresh
¼ teaspoon dried basil or
   ½ teaspoon fresh
1 teaspoon sugar
¼ teaspoon white pepper

Combine all ingredients in a glass bowl. Cover and refrigerate overnight. Serve on a lettuce leaf.

Servings: 2

NUTRIENT VALUES			
PROTEIN	CARBOHYDRATE	FAT	ALCOHOL
12%	65%	24%	0%
CALORIES	PRO-GM	CARB-GM	FAT-GM	SOD-MG
82.60	2.744	15.20	2.495	75.00
FOOD EXCHANGES					
MILK	VEG.	FRUIT	BREAD	MEAT	FAT
0.0	2.0	0.0	0.0	0.0	0.5

MINTED CUCUMBER SALAD

2 fresh cucumbers, sliced
   thickly (peel if waxed)
Mint vinegar (½ cup–¾ cup)
Ice cubes
½ onion, sliced thinly
¼ cup fresh mint, chopped

Layer cucumbers, onion, mint, then ice in a bowl. Pour a little mint vinegar over each layer. (Ice makes cucumbers crispy without salt.) Leave in refrigerator for 1–2 hours to marinate. Serve chilled.

Servings: 4

Trisha Shirey

NUTRIENT VALUES			
PROTEIN	CARBOHYDRATE	FAT	ALCOHOL
11%	83%	6%	0%
CALORIES	PRO-GM	CARB-GM	FAT-GM	SOD-MG
32.20	1.066	8.180	0.250	3.800
FOOD EXCHANGES					
MILK	VEG.	FRUIT	BREAD	MEAT	FAT
0.0	0.5	0.0	0.3	0.0	0.0

MUSHROOM SALAD

2 cups sliced mushrooms
1 cup thinly sliced
   zucchini
½ cup chopped tomato
¼ cup sliced green onions
2 tablespoons grated
   Parmesan cheese
4 tablespoons low calorie
   Italian dressing (see page
   166)
2 tablespoons basil vinegar
   or balsamic vinegar
1 teaspoon dried whole
   marjoram
½ teaspoon freshly ground
   pepper

Combine mushrooms, zucchini, tomato and onion in a medium bowl. Mix remaining ingredients in a small bowl. Pour over vegetables and mix. Allow to marinate in refrigerator 4 hours. Serve chilled or at room temperature.

Servings: 5 (⅔ cup serving)

NUTRIENT VALUES					
PROTEIN	CARBOHYDRATE		FAT		ALCOHOL
19%	36%		45%		0%
CALORIES	PRO-GM	CARB-GM		FAT-GM	SOD-MG
39.80	2.118	3.919		2.152	144.0
FOOD EXCHANGES					
MILK	VEG.	FRUIT	BREAD	MEAT	FAT
0.0	0.6	0.0	0.0	0.1	0.4

MUSHROOM-TOMATO SALAD

2   cups small mushrooms,
    cleaned and halved
1   cup cherry tomatoes,
    halved—10 items
2   tablespoons parsley
    sprigs
2   tablespoons chopped
    green onions
1   teaspoon olive oil
2   teaspoons lemon juice
½   teaspoon black pepper
2   teaspoons water

Steam mushrooms for 5 minutes. Chill. Place chilled mushrooms in a medium mixing bowl and combine with remaining ingredients.

Servings: 4

NUTRIENT VALUES			
PROTEIN	CARBOHYDRATE	FAT	ALCOHOL
12%	44%	45%	0%
CALORIES	PRO-GM	CARB-GM	FAT-GM	SOD-MG
23.10	0.758	2.843	1.287	4.171

FOOD EXCHANGES					
MILK	VEG.	FRUIT	BREAD	MEAT	FAT
0.0	0.4	0.0	0.0	0.0	0.3

OLD FASHIONED POTATO SALAD

4   medium-sized potatoes (approximately 1 pound)
½   cup finely chopped celery
½   cup finely chopped green peppers
¼   cup chopped onion
¼   cup chopped dill pickle
¼   cup chopped parsley
2   tablespoons chopped fresh dill
2   tablespoons chopped fresh savory
1   tablespoon chopped pimento

Peel potatoes and cut into ¼″ thick slices; cook in boiling water until tender, about 5–7 minutes. Drain and cool to room temperature. Place potatoes in large salad bowl. Gently toss with next eight ingredients.

¾   cup nonfat yogurt
1   tablespoon Dijon mustard
1   tablespoon lemon juice
1   teaspoon lemon rind, grated
¼   teaspoon black pepper

In glass measuring cup, beat together yogurt, mustard, lemon juice, lemon rind, and black pepper. Pour over salad, toss gently to combine. Chill until serving time.

Servings: 8 (½ cup serving)

NUTRIENT VALUES			
PROTEIN	CARBOHYDRATE	FAT	ALCOHOL
12%	86%	1%	0%
CALORIES	PRO-GM	CARB-GM	FAT-GM	SOD-MG
90.80	2.791	19.80	0.142	109.0
FOOD EXCHANGES					
MILK	VEG.	FRUIT	BREAD	MEAT	FAT
0.1	0.1	0.0	1.0	0.0	0.0

ENSALADA DE NARANJAS (ORANGE AND ONION SALAD)

1   cup salad greens
2–3 orange slices
2   red onion slices
1   tablespoon Spicy
    Vinaigrette (see page
    172)

Arrange salad greens (approximately 1 cup) on plate. Place orange slices (2–3 per plate) and red onion rings (1–2 rings) on top of greens. For a milder onion taste, soak rings in ice cubes and small amount of water with a dash of vinegar; this also makes them crisp. Before serving, dress with Spicy Vinaigrette, using one tablespoon per serving.

Servings: 1

NUTRIENT VALUES					
PROTEIN 9%	CARBOHYDRATE 61%		FAT 29%	ALCOHOL 0%	
CALORIES 49.20	PRO-GM 1.226	CARB-GM 8.286	FAT-GM 1.764	SOD-MG 5.611	
FOOD EXCHANGES					
MILK 0.0	VEG. 0.5	FRUIT 0.5	BREAD 0.0	MEAT 0.0	FAT 0.5

ORIENTAL TOMATO SALAD

3   tablespoons rice wine
    vinegar
2   teaspoons sesame oil
2   teaspoons soy sauce
1   teaspoon fresh grated
    ginger
½   teaspoon sesame seeds
2   cups fresh snow peas
1   cup cherry tomatoes, cut
    in half
Lettuce leaves

Mix all ingredients together except lettuce leaves. Toss together. Serve on lettuce leaves.

Servings: 4 (¾ cup serving)

NUTRIENT VALUES					
PROTEIN 16%	CARBOHYDRATE 48%		FAT 36%	ALCOHOL 0%	
CALORIES 62.70	PRO-GM 2.688	CARB-GM 7.884	FAT-GM 2.671	SOD-MG 178.0	
FOOD EXCHANGES					
MILK 0.0	VEG. 1.4	FRUIT 0.0	BREAD 0.0	MEAT 0.0	FAT 0.5

ORIENTAL VEGETABLE SALAD

1 **cup snow peas, strings removed**
½ **cup sliced water chestnuts**
2 **cups bok choy, thinly sliced**
½ **cup bean sprouts**
¼ **cup finely chopped celery**
¼ **cup chopped green onions**

Mix vegetables in a large bowl. Pour dressing over vegetables and mix to coat vegetables.

DRESSING
2 **tablespoons Dijon mustard**
¼ **cup water**
1½ **teaspoons sesame oil**
1 **teaspoon white vinegar**

In a small mixing bowl, mix mustard and water until smooth. Add oil and vinegar and mix well.

Servings: 5 (1 cup serving)

NUTRIENT VALUES					
PROTEIN	CARBOHYDRATE		FAT		ALCOHOL
16%	52%		32%		0%
CALORIES	PRO-GM	CARB-GM		FAT-GM	SOD-MG
45.50	1.746	5.547		1.512	104.0
FOOD EXCHANGES					
MILK	VEG.	FRUIT	BREAD	MEAT	FAT
0.0	1.0	0.0	0.0	0.0	0.3

POTATO SALAD

2   cups potatoes, diced,
    cooked
1   tablespoon pimento,
    chopped
½   cup diced celery
2   tablespoons chopped
    onion
4   teaspoons minced
    parsley
1½ teaspoons vinegar
1   teaspoon dry mustard
2   tablespoons reduced-
    calorie mayonnaise
2   tablespoons nonfat
    yogurt
2   tablespoons minced
    fresh dill
1   tablespoon dill or salad
    burnet vinegar

Combine all ingredients. Toss lightly and chill.

Servings: 5 (½ cup serving)

NUTRIENT VALUES			
PROTEIN	CARBOHYDRATE	FAT	ALCOHOL
8%	78%	14%	0%
CALORIES	PRO-GM	CARB-GM	FAT-GM	SOD-MG
109.0	2.258	21.70	1.751	19.80

FOOD EXCHANGES					
MILK	VEG.	FRUIT	BREAD	MEAT	FAT
0.0	0.1	0.0	1.2	0.0	0.4

SAUERKRAUT SALAD

2   cups sauerkraut, rinsed
    and drained
¼   cup finely chopped
    celery
3   tablespoons finely
    chopped green pepper
3   tablespoons finely
    chopped onion
1   tablespoon sugar
2   tablespoons herbal
    vinegar or wine vinegar
1½ teaspoons safflower oil
2   tablespoons water

In a large bowl, mix sauerkraut, celery, green pepper and onion. Set aside. In a separate bowl, mix sugar, vinegar, oil and water. Whisk until well mixed. Pour over sauerkraut mixture and mix well. Cover. Refrigerate overnight to allow flavors to blend. Serve chilled.

Servings: 4 (¾ cup serving)

NUTRIENT VALUES					
PROTEIN	CARBOHYDRATE		FAT		ALCOHOL
8%	63%		28%		0%
CALORIES	PRO-GM	CARB-GM		FAT-GM	SOD-MG
55.60	1.310	9.843		1.945	788.0
FOOD EXCHANGES					
MILK	VEG.	FRUIT	BREAD	MEAT	FAT
0.0	1.1	0.0	0.1	0.0	0.4

SPANISH TOMATO SALAD

4   fresh tomatoes, cut into
    sixths
¼   cup fresh cilantro,
    chopped
4   green onions, chopped
1   red bell pepper, finely
    chopped
3   tablespoons fresh lemon
    juice
1   tablespoon soy sauce

Mix ingredients together. Allow flavors to blend.

Servings: 4 (1 cup serving)

NUTRIENT VALUES					
PROTEIN	CARBOHYDRATE		FAT		ALCOHOL
17%	76%		8%		0%
CALORIES	PRO-GM	CARB-GM		FAT-GM	SOD-MG
38.00	1.878	8.485		0.374	269.0
FOOD EXCHANGES					
MILK	VEG.	FRUIT	BREAD	MEAT	FAT
0.0	1.1	0.1	0.0	0.0	0.0

SPINACH-STRAWBERRY SALAD

10 ounces spinach, cleaned
1 cup hulled and halved strawberries
½ cup thinly sliced mushrooms
½ cup Poppy Seed Dressing (see page 167)

Divide spinach evenly on 4 serving plates. Place the strawberries and mushrooms on spinach. Top each salad with 2 tablespoons dressing.

Servings: 4

NUTRIENT VALUES						
PROTEIN 31%		CARBOHYDRATE 56%		FAT 12%		ALCOHOL 0%
CALORIES 43.80		PRO-GM 3.972	CARB-GM 7.178	FAT-GM 0.703		SOD-MG 132.0
FOOD EXCHANGES						
MILK 0.0	VEG. 0.9	FRUIT 0.3	BREAD 0.0		MEAT 0.0	FAT 0.0

THREE BEAN SALAD

2 cups canned green beans or fresh steamed
2 cups canned wax beans or fresh steamed
2 cups red kidney beans
½ cup chopped green pepper
½ cup chopped onion
1 tablespoon safflower oil
⅓ cup wine vinegar or herbal vinegar
½ teaspoon black pepper

Drain beans and put into a glass bowl. Add other ingredients. Refrigerate overnight to marinate flavors.

Servings: 10 (½ cup serving)

NUTRIENT VALUES						
PROTEIN 19%		CARBOHYDRATE 63%		FAT 18%		ALCOHOL 0%
CALORIES 80.60		PRO-GM 4.088	CARB-GM 13.60	FAT-GM 1.749		SOD-MG 169.0
FOOD EXCHANGES						
MILK 0.0	VEG. 2.5	FRUIT 0.0	BREAD 0.0		MEAT 0.0	FAT 0.3

WILTED ORIENTAL SALAD

DRESSING
1   tablespoon sesame oil
2   tablespoons rice wine
    vinegar
1   tablespoon low-sodium
    soy sauce
1   teaspoon honey
4   ounce can Mandarin
    oranges, drained with 2
    tablespoons reserved
    liquid
½   bag of crunched up "top
    ramen" noodles

4   cups Boston Bibb lettuce,
    torn

Heat the first six ingredients, including noodles, thoroughly and pour over lettuce. Top with small slices of green pepper and sesame seeds.

Servings: 4 (1¼ cup serving)

Ellen McCullough

NUTRIENT VALUES			
PROTEIN	CARBOHYDRATE	FAT	ALCOHOL
9%	50%	41%	0%
CALORIES	PRO-GM	CARB-GM	FAT-GM	SOD-MG
116.0	2.888	15.60	5.755	470.0
FOOD EXCHANGES					
MILK	VEG.	FRUIT	BREAD	MEAT	FAT
0.0	0.4	0.3	0.6	0.0	1.0

BULGUR SALAD

1½ cups bulgur, raw
3   cups boiling water
½   cup finely chopped
    onion
2   tablespoons parsley,
    chopped
1   tablespoon grated
    horseradish

Place the bulgur in a large heatproof mixing bowl. Stir in the boiling water. Soak 2 hours. Stir occasionally. Chill in the refrigerator.

Add onion, parsley and horseradish to bulgur.

DRESSING

2   teaspoons sesame oil
2   tablespoons rice wine
    vinegar or herbal
    vinegar
2   tablespoons lemon juice
½   teaspoon pepper
¼   teaspoon dry mustard

In a small cup, whisk together the oil, vinegar, lemon juice, pepper and mustard. Fold the dressing into the bulgur salad. Serve chilled or room temperature.

Excellent served as an accompaniment to grilled or baked chicken or double serving size for lunch entree!

Servings: 7 (1½ cup serving)

NUTRIENT VALUES					
PROTEIN	CARBOHYDRATE		FAT	ALCOHOL	
9%	80%		11%	0%	
CALORIES	PRO-GM	CARB-GM	FAT-GM	SOD-MG	
153.0	3.487	31.60	1.871	24.40	
FOOD EXCHANGES					
MILK	VEG.	FRUIT	BREAD	MEAT	FAT
0.0	0.1	0.0	1.9	0.0	0.3

BROWN RICE SALAD

2½ cups cooked brown rice
3   stalks celery, chopped
¼   cup chopped green onion
3   tablespoons dill pickle
    relish
¼   cup fresh chopped
    parsley
2   teaspoons finely
    chopped fresh dill
¼   cup sliced radishes
2   tablespoons Dijon
    mustard
1   teaspoon sesame oil
2   teaspoons Mrs. Dash

Combine all ingredients and chill to allow flavors to blend. Serve on lettuce leaf and garnish with radishes and carrot slices.

Servings: 6 (½ cup serving)

NUTRIENT VALUES					
PROTEIN	CARBOHYDRATE		FAT		ALCOHOL
7%	81%		12%		0%
CALORIES	PRO-GM	CARB-GM	FAT-GM		SOD-MG
96.50	1.667	18.50	1.176		130.0
FOOD EXCHANGES					
MILK	VEG.	FRUIT	BREAD	MEAT	FAT
0.0	0.0	0.0	1.2	0.0	0.2

LENTIL SALAD

2 cups cooked lentils, drained
3 tablespoons herbal or white wine vinegar
2 teaspoons olive oil
1 teaspoon savory
1 teaspoon sugar
½ medium onion, finely chopped
1 stalk celery, finely chopped
½ cup cooked garbanzo beans (chick peas)
½ teaspoon fresh ground black pepper

Combine all ingredients and chill thoroughly. Serve over a bed of chopped lettuce.

Servings: 7 (½ cup serving)

NUTRIENT VALUES					
PROTEIN	CARBOHYDRATE		FAT		ALCOHOL
23%	67%		9%		0%
CALORIES	PRO-GM	CARB-GM		FAT-GM	SOD-MG
90.40	5.517	15.90		0.979	71.10
FOOD EXCHANGES					
MILK	VEG.	FRUIT	BREAD	MEAT	FAT
0.0	0.1	0.0	1.0	0.1	0.1

LENTIL-RICE SALAD

⅔ cup lentils (uncooked)
2 teaspoons olive oil
2½ tablespoons lemon juice
¼ cup chopped green onions
1 cup cooked brown rice
½ teaspoon dried oregano or 1 teaspoon fresh
⅓ cup nonfat yogurt
½ teaspoon black pepper

Place lentils in saucepan with 2 cups water, bring to boil, then reduce heat and simmer just until tender (about 40 minutes). Drain. Toss immediately with oil, lemon juice, onions, rice, and oregano. Chill.

Just before serving, stir in yogurt and pepper.

Servings: 5 (½ cup serving)

NUTRIENT VALUES					
PROTEIN	CARBOHYDRATE		FAT		ALCOHOL
21%	64%		15%		0%
CALORIES	PRO-GM	CARB-GM		FAT-GM	SOD-MG
144.0	7.419	23.20		2.405	14.80
FOOD EXCHANGES					
MILK	VEG.	FRUIT	BREAD	MEAT	FAT
0.1	0.0	0.0	1.6	0.0	0.4

TABBOULEH

1 cup bulgur wheat
2 cups boiling water
1 cup chopped tomato
½ cup minced fresh parsley
¼ cup chopped green
    onions
1 tablespoon minced fresh
    mint leaves
¼ cup lemon juice
1 tablespoon olive oil
¼ teaspoon salt
¼ teaspoon pepper

Pour boiling water over bulgur and let stand for 2 hours. Drain bulgur. Add tomato, parsley, onion, and mint. In a separate bowl, combine remaining ingredients. Pour over bulgur and stir to combine. Chill before serving.

Servings: 7 (½ cup serving)

NUTRIENT VALUES			
PROTEIN	CARBOHYDRATE	FAT	ALCOHOL
8%	74%	18%	0%
CALORIES	PRO-GM	CARB-GM	FAT-GM	SOD-MG
115.0	2.522	21.90	2.346	73.60
FOOD EXCHANGES					
MILK	VEG.	FRUIT	BREAD	MEAT	FAT
0.0	0.1	0.1	1.2	0.0	0.4

Specialties from the Garden . . .

VEGETABLES

ASPARAGUS WITH STRAWBERRY VINAIGRETTE

1   **pound fresh asparagus**

DRESSING
¼   **cup strawberry vinegar**
2   **teaspoons walnut oil**
¼   **cup water**
1   **teaspoon honey**

Trim the asparagus and steam it until it is tender crisp. Plunge it into ice water. Drain and cut each stalk into thirds. Combine the dressing ingredients and toss the asparagus with the dressing. Chill well before serving. Serve on a lettuce bed.

Servings: 3 (¾ cup serving)

NUTRIENT VALUES					
PROTEIN	CARBOHYDRATE		FAT		ALCOHOL
18%	45%		37%		0%
CALORIES	PRO-GM	CARB-GM		FAT-GM	SOD-MG
73.10	3.914	9.542		3.470	7.001
FOOD EXCHANGES					
MILK	VEG.	FRUIT	BREAD	MEAT	FAT
0.0	1.5	0.0	0.2	0.0	0.7

LEMON GREEN BEANS

4   **cups fresh green beans, strings removed and cut in 2″ pieces**
½   **cup sliced red pepper**
½   **teaspoon dried whole basil**
2   **tablespoons lemon juice**
2   **teaspoons sesame seeds, toasted**

Steam beans and red pepper until tender crisp. Drain and transfer to a large bowl. Add lemon juice, sesame seeds, and basil, mixing well.

Servings: 6 (½ cup serving)

NUTRIENT VALUES					
PROTEIN	CARBOHYDRATE		FAT		ALCOHOL
17%	67%		16%		0%
CALORIES	PRO-GM	CARB-GM		FAT-GM	SOD-MG
37.80	1.898	7.495		0.766	3.208
FOOD EXCHANGES					
MILK	VEG.	FRUIT	BREAD	MEAT	FAT
0.0	1.3	0.0	0.0	0.0	0.2

BEETS IN CITRUS SAUCE

1   16-ounce can beets,
    sliced or whole, drained
    (reserve liquid)
½   cup and 3 tablespoons
    beet juice
1   tablespoon cornstarch
2   tablespoons orange juice
    concentrate
⅛   teaspoon cloves
1   teaspoon honey
1   teaspoon reduced-calorie
    margarine

Place ½ cup beet juice in small saucepan and cook over medium heat. Dissolve cornstarch in 3 tablespoons beet juice and add to saucepan, stirring constantly. Add orange juice concentrate and honey. When thickened and clear, add cloves and beets and cook 1–2 minutes more until beets are heated through. Remove from heat and stir in orange peel and margarine. Serve hot.

Servings: 4 (½ cup serving)

Trisha Shirey

NUTRIENT VALUES					
PROTEIN	CARBOHYDRATE		FAT		ALCOHOL
7%	81%		12%		0%
CALORIES	PRO-GM	CARB-GM		FAT-GM	SOD-MG
68.70	1.295	14.50		0.975	342.0
FOOD EXCHANGES					
MILK	VEG.	FRUIT	BREAD	MEAT	FAT
0.0	1.4	0.3	0.3	0.0	0.2

SAVORY CABBAGE

4   cups green cabbage,
     shredded
1½   cups water
2   teaspoons reduced-
     calorie margine, melted
2   teaspoons prepared
     horseradish
2   tablespoons fresh lemon
     juice
1   teaspoon honey
1   teaspoon white wine
     vinegar

In a 3-quart saucepan, bring water to a boil. Add cabbage. Return to boil then reduce heat. Cover, and simmer for 10 minutes. Remove from heat and drain. Mix cabbage with margarine, horseradish, lemon juice, honey, and vinegar. Serve warm.

Servings: 3 (¾ cup serving)

NUTRIENT VALUES					
PROTEIN	CARBOHYDRATE		FAT		ALCOHOL
11%	66%		23%		0%
CALORIES	PRO-GM	CARB-GM		FAT-GM	SOD-MG
51.20	1.536	9.603		1.483	87.40
FOOD EXCHANGES					
MILK	VEG.	FRUIT	BREAD	MEAT	FAT
0.0	1.2	0.0	0.2	0.0	0.3

RED CABBAGE WITH APPLES

3 cups red cabbage, shredded
½ cup chicken broth, defatted
1 medium cooking apple, peeled, cored, and sliced thin
½ cup chopped onion
1 cup water
2 tablespoons red wine vinegar or herbal vinegar
2 teaspoons honey
½ teaspoon black pepper
1 bay leaf

Place apples, onion, and stock in a large saucepan. Saute 10 minutes over medium heat. Add cabbage, water, vinegar, honey, pepper, and bay leaf. Mix well and bring to a boil. Reduce heat. Cover and simmer 10 to 15 minutes, stirring occasionally. Remove bay leaf and serve.

Servings: 3 (1 cup serving)

NUTRIENT VALUES					
PROTEIN 8%	CARBOHYDRATE 86%		FAT 5%		ALCOHOL 0%
CALORIES 71.10	PRO-GM 1.698	CARB-GM 17.30		FAT-GM 0.449	SOD-MG 8.039
FOOD EXCHANGES					
MILK 0.0	VEG. 1.2	FRUIT 0.5	BREAD 0.2	MEAT 0.0	FAT 0.0

GINGER CARROTS

2 cups julienned carrots
1 teaspoon reduced-calorie margarine
1 teaspoon brown sugar
⅛ teaspoon ground ginger

Steam carrots until tender crisp. Meanwhile, melt margarine in a medium saucepan, stir in sugar and ginger. Cook until sugar dissolves, over medium heat. Stir often. Add carrots, continue cooking, stirring gently for 2 minutes.

Servings: 2 (1 cup serving)

NUTRIENT VALUES					
PROTEIN 7%	CARBOHYDRATE 80%		FAT 13%		ALCOHOL 0%
CALORIES 87.30	PRO-GM 1.710	CARB-GM 18.60		FAT-GM 1.297	SOD-MG 126.0
FOOD EXCHANGES					
MILK 0.0	VEG. 2.5	FRUIT 0.0	BREAD 0.0	MEAT 0.0	FAT 0.3

HERBED CARROTS AND ZUCCHINI

2   teaspoons olive oil
¼   cup minced shallots
1   pound carrots, peeled
    and julienned
¼   cup water
½   teaspoon sugar
2   cups, julienned zucchini
2   tablespoons fresh sage,
    finely chopped
2   tablespoons fresh mint,
    finely chopped
2   tablespoons fresh
    parsley, finely chopped
Freshly ground black pepper

Heat the oil in a large nonstick skillet over medium heat. Add the shallots and cook until soft but not brown, about 5 minutes. Add the carrots, water, and sugar, cover and cook stirring occasionally, until they begin to soften, about 10 minutes. Add the zucchini and cook, uncovered, until the zucchini just begins to soften, about 3 minutes. Remove from heat, add herbs and pepper, and lightly toss. Serve warm.

Servings: 6 (⅔ cup per serving)

NUTRIENT VALUES					
PROTEIN 8%	CARBOHYDRATE 66%		FAT 25%		ALCOHOL 0%
CALORIES 56.10	PRO-GM 1.282	CARB-GM 10.00		FAT-GM 1.696	SOD-MG 29.00
FOOD EXCHANGES					
MILK 0.0	VEG. 1.4	FRUIT 0.0	BREAD 0.1	MEAT 0.0	FAT 0.3

HONEYED CARROTS

1   pound carrots, sliced
    thinly
¼   cup water
1   teaspoon reduced-calorie
    margarine
½   teaspoon nutmeg
1   teaspoon honey
1   tablespoon apple juice
    concentrate
2   tablespoons fresh
    chopped parsley

Steam carrots in water until easily pierced with fork. Drain. Combine remaining ingredients except parsley in a medium saucepan. Simmer till bubbling. Remove from heat. Pour over carrots, add parsley and toss till well mixed. Serve warm.

Servings: 6 (½ cup serving)

NUTRIENT VALUES					
PROTEIN 7%	CARBOHYDRATE 83%		FAT 10%		ALCOHOL 0%
CALORIES 45.30	PRO-GM 0.817	CARB-GM 10.00		FAT-GM 0.534	SOD-MG 34.90
FOOD EXCHANGES					
MILK 0.0	VEG. 1.3	FRUIT 0.1	BREAD 0.1	MEAT 0.0	FAT 0.1

CARROTS MARSALA

2 cups sliced carrots
¼ cup marsala wine
½ cup water
1 tablespoon reduced-calorie margaine
⅛ teaspoon pepper
1½ tablespoons chopped fresh parsley

Combine all ingredients except parsley in a medium saucepan. Bring to a boil; cover. Reduce heat and simmer 10 minutes. Stir occasionally as carrots cook. Remove from heat, place in serving dish and sprinkle with parsley.

Servings: 4 (½ cup serving)

NUTRIENT VALUES					
PROTEIN 7%	CARBOHYDRATE 65%		FAT 28%		ALCOHOL 0%
CALORIES 49.60	PRO-GM 0.919	CARB-GM 8.546		FAT-GM 1.602	SOD-MG 86.00
FOOD EXCHANGES					
MILK 0.0	VEG. 1.3	FRUIT 0.0	BREAD 0.0	MEAT 0.0	FAT 0.3

MEXICAN CARROT TOSS

2½ cups zucchini, grated
5 large carrots, grated
2 tablespoons chopped green olives
2 tablespoons chopped green onion
⅓ cup nonfat yogurt
1½ tablespoons red wine vinegar, or herbal vinegar
¼ teaspoon garlic powder
1 teaspoon Dijon mustard
¼ teaspoon ground cumin

Combine all ingredients in a medium bowl. Toss to mix. Serve on lettuce leaves.

Servings: 6 (⅔ cup serving)

NUTRIENT VALUES					
PROTEIN 16%	CARBOHYDRATE 77%		FAT 7%		ALCOHOL 0%
CALORIES 43.10	PRO-GM 1.948	CARB-GM 9.074		FAT-GM 0.366	SOD-MG 58.10
FOOD EXCHANGES					
MILK 0.1	VEG. 1.4	FRUIT 0.0	BREAD 0.0	MEAT 0.0	FAT 0.0

MINTED CARROTS

2   cups sliced carrots
¼   cup water
½   teaspoon reduced-calorie
     margarine
2   teaspoons finely
     chopped fresh mint

Steam carrots until tender. Drain. Add margarine, mint. Toss gently and serve immediately.

Yields: 4 (½ cup serving)

Trisha Shirey

NUTRIENT VALUES					
PROTEIN 9%	CARBOHYDRATE 82%		FAT 9%		ALCOHOL 0%
CALORIES 37.10	PRO-GM 0.850	CARB-GM 8.150	FAT-GM 0.407		SOD-MG 57.40
FOOD EXCHANGES					
MILK 0.0	VEG. 1.3	FRUIT 0.0	BREAD 0.0	MEAT 0.0	FAT 0.0

SWEET AND SOUR CARROTS

1   tablespoon reduced-
      calorie margarine
1½ teaspoons cornstarch
½   cup skim milk
½   teaspoon dry mustard
¾   teaspoon brown sugar
1   teaspoon white vinegar
      or herbal vinegar
2   cups steamed carrots
1   teaspoon minced
      pineapple sage

In a medium saucepan melt, margarine over medium heat. Mix cornstarch with 1 tablespoon milk until smooth. Add cornstarch mixture to saucepan, stirring until bubbly. Add remaining ingredients and cook, stirring constantly until smooth and creamy. Pour over steamed carrots. Sauce may also be used over greens or green beans.

Yields: 4 (½ cup serving)

NUTRIENT VALUES					
PROTEIN 11%	CARBOHYDRATE 67%		FAT 22%		ALCOHOL 0%
CALORIES 65.70	PRO-GM 1.947	CARB-GM 11.50	FAT-GM 1.671		SOD-MG 101.0
FOOD EXCHANGES					
MILK 0.1	VEG. 1.3	FRUIT 0.0	BREAD 0.0	MEAT 0.0	FAT 0.3

TROPICAL CARROTS

2 cups julienned carrots
¼ cup unsweetened
  pineapple tidbits,
  undrained
2 teaspoons cornstarch
¼ teaspoon ground ginger
1 teaspoon fresh lemon
  juice

Steam carrots until they are tender crisp. Combine lemon juice, pineapple, cornstarch, ginger and cooked carrots in a small saucepan. Cook over low heat, stirring constantly until thickened.

Servings: 4 (½ cup serving)

NUTRIENT VALUES			
PROTEIN	CARBOHYDRATE	FAT	ALCOHOL
8%	89%	3%	0%
CALORIES	PRO-GM	CARB-GM	FAT-GM	SOD-MG
59.00	1.246	14.00	0.242	39.60
FOOD EXCHANGES					
MILK	VEG.	FRUIT	BREAD	MEAT	FAT
0.0	1.9	0.1	0.1	0.0	0.0

CAULIFLOWER TOSS

4 cups chopped
  cauliflower
1 teaspoon toasted sesame
  seeds
1 teaspoon soy sauce
2 tablespoons lemon juice
1 tablespoon pineapple
  juice concentrate
¼ teaspoon sesame oil

Steam the cauliflower. Toss with remaining ingredients and serve warm or chill.

Servings: 4 (1 cup serving)

Barbara Stetzelberger

NUTRIENT VALUES			
PROTEIN	CARBOHYDRATE	FAT	ALCOHOL
20%	64%	16%	0%
CALORIES	PRO-GM	CARB-GM	FAT-GM	SOD-MG
40.80	2.326	7.592	0.833	102.0
FOOD EXCHANGES					
MILK	VEG.	FRUIT	BREAD	MEAT	FAT
0.0	1.0	0.1	0.0	0.0	0.1

STEWED CORN, OKRA AND TOMATOES

1 tablespoon reduced-calorie margarine
1 onion, chopped
1 pound okra, sliced in 1-inch pieces
4 medium tomatoes, peeled and chopped
½ cup defatted chicken broth
¼ teaspoon Tabasco sauce
¼ teaspoon paprika
2 cups corn (fresh or frozen)
2 tablespoons minced fresh parsley
1 tablespoon minced fresh basil or rosemary
Vegetable coating spray

Spray a large heavy stew pot with coating spray. Melt margarine and cook onion until clear, 5–7 minutes. Add okra and cook 5 minutes, stirring frequently. Add stock, tabasco and paprika and cover. Simmer for 15 minutes or until okra is tender. Add corn and cook for an additional 5–7 minutes until corn is done. Remove from heat, stir in herbs and serve.

Servings: 6 (1 cup serving)

Trisha Shirey

NUTRIENT VALUES					
PROTEIN 14%	CARBOHYDRATE 74%		FAT 11%		ALCOHOL 0%
CALORIES 107.0	PRO-GM 4.382	CARB-GM 22.80		FAT-GM 1.546	SOD-MG 37.40
FOOD EXCHANGES					
MILK 0.0	VEG. 2.0	FRUIT 0.0	BREAD 0.8	MEAT 0.0	FAT 0.2

CUCUMBER WITH DILL

1   cucumber (peel if waxed) sliced
¼   cup cider vinegar or herbal vinegar
1   tablespoon fresh minced dill weed
1   teaspoon honey
Dash salt and pepper

Combine all ingredients and refrigerate several hours before serving.

Servings: 2 (½ cup serving)

NUTRIENT VALUES					
PROTEIN 9%	CARBOHYDRATE 86%		FAT 5%	ALCOHOL 0%	
CALORIES 35.50	PRO-GM 0.915	CARB-GM 8.983	FAT-GM 0.217	SOD-MG 4.417	
FOOD EXCHANGES					
MILK 0.0	VEG. 0.3	FRUIT 0.0	BREAD 0.5	MEAT 0.0	FAT 0.0

√ OVEN FRIED EGGPLANT

1   medium eggplant, sliced in ½-inch slices (approx. 1 lb.)
3   slices whole wheat bread, made into crumbs
⅛   teaspoon freshly ground black pepper
1   teaspoon fresh minced oregano
1   clove garlic, minced
3   tablespoons lowfat buttermilk
Vegetable coating spray

Bake bread slices in 250° oven until very dry. Cool and crush to crumbs with a rolling pin or in blender or food processor. Combine crumbs and seasonings in a shallow pan. Combine egg whites and buttermilk. Dip eggplant slices in egg mixture then bread crumbs, coating well. Place on cookie sheet that has been sprayed with vegetable coating spray. Bake at 450° for 15–20 minutes until golden brown, turning once.

Servings: 6

NUTRIENT VALUES					
PROTEIN 22%	CARBOHYDRATE 66%		FAT 12%	ALCOHOL 0%	
CALORIES 59.40	PRO-GM 3.515	CARB-GM 10.60	FAT-GM 0.880	SOD-MG 106.0	
FOOD EXCHANGES					
MILK 0.0	VEG. 0.8	FRUIT 0.0	BREAD 0.4	MEAT 0.2	FAT 0.1

CREAMED ONIONS AND SAGE

12 ounces pearl onions, trimmed and left whole
1 tablespoon reduced-calorie margarine
1 tablespoon unbleached white flour
⅔ cup defatted chicken broth
¼ teaspoon white pepper, coarsely cracked
3 fresh sage leaves or ¼ teaspoon dried sage
2 tablespoons nonfat yogurt
1 tablespoon minced fresh parsley

Melt margarine in a saucepan and brown onions, stirring often. Add flour and stir constantly until browned about 2 minutes. Add broth gradually, stirring. Add sage, then allow to cook covered 10–12 minutes until onions are clear and done. Remove from heat, remove sage leaves if using fresh sage and add remaining ingredients. Mix well and serve.

Yields: 4 (½ cup serving)

Trisha Shirey

NUTRIENT VALUES					
PROTEIN 13%	CARBOHYDRATE 60%		FAT 27%		ALCOHOL 0%
CALORIES 54.80	PRO-GM 1.886	CARB-GM 8.470		FAT-GM 1.724	SOD-MG 39.70
FOOD EXCHANGES					
MILK 0.0	VEG. 1.0	FRUIT 0.0	BREAD 0.1	MEAT 0.0	FAT 0.3

HERB POTATOES

1 pound new potatoes, scrubbed (peel if desired)
1 tablespoon reduced-calorie margarine
1 tablespoon chopped mint or basil, no stems
Freshly ground pepper to taste

Cut up potatoes if large. Steam 3–5 minutes or until done. Should be easily pierced with a fork.

Add herb of choice and margarine and toss lightly until mixed. Add pepper. Serve hot.

Servings: 4 (4 ounce serving)

Trisha Shirey

NUTRIENT VALUES					
PROTEIN 9%	CARBOHYDRATE 74%		FAT 17%		ALCOHOL 0%
CALORIES 77.50	PRO-GM 1.795	CARB-GM 14.60		FAT-GM 1.503	SOD-MG 35.40
FOOD EXCHANGES					
MILK 0.0	VEG. 0.0	FRUIT 0.0	BREAD 0.9	MEAT 0.0	FAT 0.3

HERBED LAYERED POTATOES

3–4 medium-size baking
    potatoes (about 1 pound),
    thinly sliced
Vegetable coating spray
¼ cup minced chives
3   tablespoons minced
    fresh parsley
½ teaspoon black pepper
½ teaspoon paprika
1   teaspoon fresh minced
    rosemary

Layer ⅓ of potatoes in a 8 × 8 baking pan coated with vegetable coating spray. Sprinkle with ⅓ chives, parsley, pepper, paprika, and rosemary. Repeat layers until all ingredients are used. Cover with foil. Bake at 350° for 45 minutes or until done.

Servings: 6

NUTRIENT VALUES					
PROTEIN	CARBOHYDRATE		FAT		ALCOHOL
11%	85%		4%		0%
CALORIES	PRO-GM	CARB-GM	FAT-GM		SOD-MG
46.30	1.325	10.10	0.218		2.632
FOOD EXCHANGES					
MILK	VEG.	FRUIT	BREAD	MEAT	FAT
0.0	0.0	0.0	0.6	0.0	0.0

OVEN FRENCH FRIES

16 ounces potatoes, cleaned
2   teaspoons safflower oil
1   teaspoon paprika
Dash salt (optional)
1   teaspoon crushed dried
    rosemary (optional)

Cut potatoes into julienned strips. Place in bowl and toss with oil and seasonings. Spread on nonstick baking sheet and bake at 450° for 20–25 minutes or until brown.

Servings: 4

NUTRIENT VALUES					
PROTEIN	CARBOHYDRATE		FAT		ALCOHOL
8%	67%		25%		0%
CALORIES	PRO-GM	CARB-GM	FAT-GM		SOD-MG
86.30	1.851	14.80	2.413		63.80
FOOD EXCHANGES					
MILK	VEG.	FRUIT	BREAD	MEAT	FAT
0.0	0.0	0.0	0.9	0.0	0.5

SWEET POTATO CASSEROLE

4 cups cooked sliced sweet potatoes (4–5 medium potatoes)
3 navel oranges
1 tablespoon cornstarch
2 teaspoons grated orange peel
¾ cup orange juice
3 tablespoons honey
¼ teaspoon cloves
¼ teaspoon cinnamon
1 tablespoon slivered almonds, toasted
1 tablespoon unsweetened coconut, toasted
Vegetable coating spray

Cut potatoes into thirds and steam until tender and can be pierced easily with a fork. Drain and cool. Peel and cut into ¼-inch thick slices.

Grate orange peel and set aside. Peel oranges and cut into ¼-inch slices. Spray 8 × 8 glass baking dish with vegetable spray. Line dish with sweet potatoes, then oranges, and finish with a layer of sweet potatoes.

In a one-quart saucepan, dissolve cornstarch in a small amount of orange juice. Add remaining juice, spices, honey and cook, stirring until thickened. Pour juice mixture over sweet potatoes and top with coconut and almonds. Bake at 375° for 20–25 minutes until bubbling.

Servings: 12 (½ cup each)

Trisha Shirey

NUTRIENT VALUES			
PROTEIN	CARBOHYDRATE	FAT	ALCOHOL
5%	88%	6%	0%
CALORIES	PRO-GM	CARB-GM	FAT-GM	SOD-MG
79.30	1.191	19.10	0.626	4.524
FOOD EXCHANGES					
MILK	VEG.	FRUIT	BREAD	MEAT	FAT
0.0	0.0	0.4	0.8	0.0	0.1

SPINACH SOUFFLE

1 **package (10 ounces) frozen chopped spinach, cooked, drained**
3 **tablespoons chopped onion**
½ **cup lowfat cottage cheese**
1 **teaspoon lemon juice**
¼ **teaspoon nutmeg**
¼ **teaspoon black pepper**
1 **egg white**

Preheat oven to 350°. Combine all ingredients except egg white and puree in blender. Beat egg white to stiff peaks. Gently fold in spinach mixture. Place mixture in an ungreased souffle dish, small casserole dish or lined muffin tin. Bake at 350° for 25 minutes. Serve immediately.

Yields: 3 servings

NUTRIENT VALUES			
PROTEIN	CARBOHYDRATE	FAT	ALCOHOL
51%	41%	8%	0%
CALORIES	PRO-GM	CARB-GM	FAT-GM	SOD-MG
63.60	8.903	7.221	0.615	251.0
FOOD EXCHANGES					
MILK	VEG.	FRUIT	BREAD	MEAT	FAT
0.0	1.3	0.0	0.0	0.8	0.0

HERBED YELLOW SQUASH

4 **cups sliced yellow squash**
½ **cup diced onion**
¼ **cup water or vegetable stock**
½ **cup nonfat yogurt**
1 **teaspoon dill, mint, thyme or marjoram**

Steam squash and onion in water until tender, 5–7 minutes. Drain and stir gently over low heat to dry excess water. Stir in yogurt and herbs and serve while warm.

Servings: 4 (½ cup serving)

Trisha Shirey

NUTRIENT VALUES			
PROTEIN	CARBOHYDRATE	FAT	ALCOHOL
28%	67%	5%	0%
CALORIES	PRO-GM	CARB-GM	FAT-GM	SOD-MG
40.70	3.158	7.486	0.235	23.40
FOOD EXCHANGES					
MILK	VEG.	FRUIT	BREAD	MEAT	FAT
01.	1.0	0.0	0.0	0.0	0.0

MARINATED SQUASH

2 cups sliced yellow
   squash
½ green pepper, cut into
   thin strips
¼ cup chopped green
   onions
⅓ cup unsweetened apple
   juice
2 tablespoons white wine
   vinegar or basil vinegar
¼ teaspoon black pepper
¼ teaspoon dry mustard
¼ teaspoon dried whole
   basil or 2 teaspoons
   fresh minced basil

Saute yellow squash, peppers and onion in water in a nonstick skillet over low heat until squash is tender crisp. Remove from heat and place vegetables in a serving bowl. Set aside. Combine apple juice, vinegar, and seasonings in a small saucepan and bring mixture to a boil. Remove from heat. Pour juice over squash. Let cool. Cover and refrigerate a minimum of 4 hours before serving.

Servings: 2 (1¼ cup serving)

NUTRIENT VALUES				
PROTEIN	CARBOHYDRATE		FAT	ALCOHOL
15%	80%		5%	0%
CALORIES	PRO-GM	CARB-GM	FAT-GM	SOD-MG
52.20	2.204	12.00	0.357	6.039
FOOD EXCHANGES					
MILK	VEG.	FRUIT	BREAD	MEAT	FAT
0.0	1.3	0.3	0.0	0.0	0.0

OVEN FRIED YELLOW SQUASH

½ cup cornmeal
¼ teaspoon salt
¼ teaspoon pepper
½ teaspoon garlic powder
2 egg whites
1 tablespoon water
3 medium-size yellow squash, cut into ¼ inch slices
Vegetable coating spray

Combine cornmeal, salt, pepper, and garlic powder. Set aside. Combine egg whites and water; beat well. Dip squash in egg mixture, dredge in cornmeal mixture. Spray a baking pan with coating spray. Place squash slices in a single layer in pan. Bake at 450° for 35 minutes or until golden brown, turning once. Alternate suggestions—*Mexican fried squash*—increase garlic to 1 teaspoon, add ½ teaspoon ground cumin; ½ teaspoon chili powder. *Italian fried squash*—increase garlic to 1 teaspoon; add 1 teaspoon dried oregano or 2 teaspoon fresh; and 1 teaspoon dried basil or 2 teaspoon fresh.

Servings: 6

NUTRIENT VALUES			
PROTEIN	CARBOHYDRATE	FAT	ALCOHOL
19%	75%	6%	0%
CALORIES	PRO-GM	CARB-GM	FAT-GM	SOD-MG
60.90	3.043	11.70	0.410	100.0
FOOD EXCHANGES					
MILK	VEG.	FRUIT	BREAD	MEAT	FAT
0.0	0.5	0.0	0.6	0.2	0.0

ZUCCHINI BOATS

2   zucchini (approx. 1 pound)
½   cup chopped tomato
2   tablespoons chopped green pepper
2   tablespoons green onion
½   teaspoon dried basil or 1 teaspoon fresh (or use oregano, or dill)
1   clove garlic, minced
½   teaspoon marjoram
¼   cup grated part-skim mozzarella

Wash squash, cut in half lengthwise, scoop out middle, reserving pulp. Steam zucchini shells 5 minutes. Chop one half of the reserved pulp and combine with other vegetables and spices. Stuff squash. Place in baking dish; bake at 400° for 15 minutes. Sprinkle with cheese. Return to oven for 5 minutes to brown. Serve warm.

Servings: 4

NUTRIENT VALUES					
PROTEIN	CARBOHYDRATE		FAT		ALCOHOL
29%	44%		27%		0%
CALORIES	PRO-GM	CARB-GM	FAT-GM		SOD-MG
42.40	3.426	5.181	1.381		37.90
FOOD EXCHANGES					
MILK	VEG.	FRUIT	BREAD	MEAT	FAT
0.0	1.0	0.0	0.0	0.3	0.1

ZUCCHINI WITH DILL

2   cups sliced zucchini
¼   cup vegetable stock
2   tablespoons herbal vinegar
1   tablespoon chopped fresh dill
2   tablespoons evaporated skim milk

Steam zucchini in stock until tender crisp. Drain and toss gently over low heat to evaporate excess water. Remove from heat, adding vinegar, dill, and milk. Stir well to mix. Serve warm.

Servings: 3 (½ cup serving)

NUTRIENT VALUES					
PROTEIN	CARBOHYDRATE		FAT		ALCOHOL
26%	69%		5%		0%
CALORIES	PRO-GM	CARB-GM	FAT-GM		SOD-MG
23.20	1.417	3.812	0.120		8.333
FOOD EXCHANGES					
MILK	VEG.	FRUIT	BREAD	MEAT	FAT
0.0	0.5	0.0	0.0	0.0	0.0

BROILED MINTED TOMATOES

3 medium ripe, firm tomatoes
2 tablespoons reduced-calorie margarine
2 tablespoons roughly chopped spearmint leaves (no stems)
5 tablespoons whole wheat breadcrumbs
3 tablespoons freshly grated Parmesan cheese
2 tablespoons finely chopped spearmint leaves

Slice tomatoes into ½ inch slices. Place tomatoes in a glass baking dish or baking sheet. Melt margarine and add roughly chopped spearmint. Saute over low heat. Combine butter and mint with the breadcrumbs, cheese and finely chopped mint. Top tomatoes with bread crumb mix. Broil until golden brown and serve warm.

Servings: 4

Trisha Shirey

NUTRIENT VALUES					
PROTEIN	CARBOHYDRATE		FAT		ALCOHOL
16%	31%		52%		0%
CALORIES	PRO-GM	CARB-GM		FAT-GM	SOD-MG
75.30	3.239	6.259		4.618	182.0
FOOD EXCHANGES					
MILK	VEG.	FRUIT	BREAD	MEAT	FAT
0.0	0.8	0.0	0.1	0.3	0.6

OVEN FRIED GREEN TOMATOES

½ cup cornmeal
¼ teaspoon pepper, freshly ground
2 egg whites
1 tablespoon water
3 medium-size green tomatoes, cut into ¼-inch slices
Vegetable coating spray

Spray a nonstick baking pan with vegetable coating spray; set aside. Combine cornmeal and pepper; set aside. Combine egg whites and water; beat well. Dip tomatoes in egg mixture; dredge in cornmeal mixture. Place tomatoes in a single layer on baking pan. Bake at 400° for 35 minutes or until browned, turning once.

Yields: 6 (3–4 slices per serving)

NUTRIENT VALUES					
PROTEIN	CARBOHYDRATE		FAT		ALCOHOL
17%	77%		6%		0%
CALORIES	PRO-GM	CARB-GM		FAT-GM	SOD-MG
61.60	2.643	12.10		0.432	22.20
FOOD EXCHANGES					
MILK	VEG.	FRUIT	BREAD	MEAT	FAT
0.0	0.5	0.0	0.6	0.2	0.0

SPINACH STUFFED TOMATOES

2   tomatoes, halved
2   tablespoons vegetable stock
½   small onion, chopped
1   garlic clove, minced
4   teaspoons whole wheat breadcrumbs
1½   teaspoons fresh parsley, minced
¼   teaspoon dried thyme or 1 teaspoon fresh
¼   teaspoon dried oregano or 1 teaspoon fresh
¼   teaspoon dried marjoram
¼   teaspoon dried basil or 2 teaspoons chopped fresh
5   teaspoons Parmesan cheese
½   cup cooked and well-drained spinach

Remove pulp from tomatoes and chop; invert "shells" to drain. Saute onions and garlic until translucent in stock or broth. Add tomato pulp and herbs. Mix crumbs and cheese. Add sauteed mixture. Spray baking pan with vegetable coating spray. Spoon spinach into the tomato halves. Top each with the crumb mixture and sprinkle with Parmesan. Or mix crumbs and spinach together and stuff. Bake at 350° for 20 minutes until tender.

Servings: 4

NUTRIENT VALUES			
PROTEIN	CARBOHYDRATE	FAT	ALCOHOL
24%	56%	20%	0%
CALORIES	PRO-GM	CARB-GM	FAT-GM	SOD-MG
44.10	2.882	6.814	1.105	84.80
FOOD EXCHANGES					
MILK	VEG.	FRUIT	BREAD	MEAT	FAT
0.0	1.0	0.0	0.0	0.1	0.0

TOMATOES PROVENCALE

2   medium-size ripe
    tomatoes
1   tablespoon fresh minced
    parsley
1   teaspoon olive oil
1   garlic clove, minced
1   teaspoon minced fresh
    oregano or ½ teaspoon
    dried
¼   cup whole wheat
    breadcrumbs
1   tablespoon Parmesan
    cheese

Prepare fire to grill. Cut each tomato in half crosswise. Squeeze halves slightly to remove some of the seeds. Mix remaining ingredients together. With small spoon, spread ¼ of the mixture evenly over each tomato pressing mixture down into tomato. When fire is medium-hot, grill tomatoes 12 minutes or until done.

Servings: 4 (½ tomato each)

NUTRIENT VALUES					
PROTEIN	CARBOHYDRATE		FAT		ALCOHOL
15%	45%		40%		0%
CALORIES	PRO-GM	CARB-GM		FAT-GM	SOD-MG
39.40	1.621	4.717		1.880	55.00
FOOD EXCHANGES					
MILK	VEG.	FRUIT	BREAD	MEAT	FAT
0.0	0.5	0.0	0.1	0.1	0.3

TOMATOES STUFFED WITH BASIL

4   large tomatoes
1   tablespoon grated
    Parmesan cheese
2   teaspoons low-calorie
    margarine
4   tablespoons minced
    fresh basil
¼   cup whole wheat
    breadcrumbs (½ slice)

Remove core and stem from tomatoes. Leave tomato intact removing only core and not pulp. Mix remaining ingredients and stuff the tomato cavities. Bake at 350° for 30 minutes or until tomatoes are done.

Servings: 4

NUTRIENT VALUES					
PROTEIN	CARBOHYDRATE		FAT		ALCOHOL
16%	54%		30%		0%
CALORIES	PRO-GM	CARB-GM		FAT-GM	SOD-MG
50.80	2.201	7.543		1.854	81.40
FOOD EXCHANGES					
MILK	VEG.	FRUIT	BREAD	MEAT	FAT
0.0	1.0	0.0	0.1	0.1	0.3

TURNIPS WITH PARSLEY

4 cups turnips, scrubbed
  and quartered
½ teaspoon freshly ground
  black pepper
½ cup nonfat yogurt
2 tablespoons fresh
  minced parsley
2 teaspoons minced lemon
  thyme

Steam turnips in a small amount of water until easily pierced with a fork. Drain and stir over low heat until excess water is evaporated. Add remaining ingredients, toss gently and serve immediately.

Servings: 4 (½ cup serving)

NUTRIENT VALUES			
PROTEIN	CARBOHYDRATE	FAT	ALCOHOL
20%	78%	2%	0%
CALORIES	PRO-GM	CARB-GM	FAT-GM	SOD-MG
43.10	2.558	9.948	0.140	98.90
FOOD EXCHANGES					
MILK	VEG.	FRUIT	BREAD	MEAT	FAT
01.	1.3	0.0	0.0	0.0	0.0

STIR-FRIED VEGETABLES

1 ounce dried Chinese
  mushrooms
4 cups sliced zucchini
1 cup sliced onion
1 small red pepper, sliced
  in strips
4 ounces sliced water
  chestnuts, drained
2 teaspoons safflower oil
2 large garlic cloves,
  minced
¼ cup oyster sauce

Cover mushrooms with hot water and soak until soft, about 20 minutes. Drain. Cut large mushrooms in half. Cut away any tough stems.

Heat oil in wok or in large nonstick skillet and cook garlic until light brown. And zucchini and onion. Cook over high heat, stirring often for 4 minutes. Add red pepper, water chestnuts, and mushrooms and cook until tender crisp. Add oyster sauce and heat thoroughly, about 1 minute more. Serve immediately.

Servings: 6 (1 cup serving)

NUTRIENT VALUES			
PROTEIN	CARBOHYDRATE	FAT	ALCOHOL
14%	58%	28%	0%
CALORIES	PRO-GM	CARB-GM	FAT-GM	SOD-MG
54.30	2.063	8.796	1.862	5.279
FOOD EXCHANGES					
MILK	VEG.	FRUIT	BREAD	MEAT	FAT
0.0	1.4	0.0	0.0	0.0	0.3

VEGETABLE KABOBS

½ **pound eggplant, cut into cubes**
1 **cup cherry tomatoes**
2 **cups fresh mushrooms**
1 **bell pepper, cut into 1-inch squares**
1 **onion, cut into chunks**

MARINADE:
1½ **teaspoons vegetable oil**
10 **tablespoons white wine vinegar**
1 **tablespoon red wine**
1 **clove garlic, minced**
¼ **teaspoon basil**
¼ **teaspoon oregano**
½ **teaspoon black pepper**
¼ **cup water**

Steam eggplant until it begins to soften. Do not overcook. Should still be firm, not mushy. Clean remaining vegetables.

Combine all marinade ingredients in a large bowl. Add vegetables and marinate at least four hours.

Place vegetables on skewer and grill over hot coals until done.

Wonderful served on a bed of rice and sprinkled with Parmesan or serve with grilled chicken.

Servings: 4

NUTRIENT VALUES			
PROTEIN	CARBOHYDRATE	FAT	ALCOHOL
12%	62%	23%	3%
CALORIES	PRO-GM	CARB-GM	FAT-GM	SOD-MG
76.60	2.627	13.70	2.293	7.310

FOOD EXCHANGES					
MILK	VEG.	FRUIT	BREAD	MEAT	FAT
0.0	1.4	0.0	0.3	0.0	0.4

Meatless Specialties...

VEGETARIAN ENTREES

PIZZA

TOMATO SAUCE

4–5 ripe tomatoes (or canned)
1   clove garlic
2   tablespoons minced
**   onion**
1   tablespoon fresh basil or
**   1½ teaspoon dried**
1   tablespoon fresh oregano
**   or 1½ teaspoon dried**
1   tablespoon olive oil
½   cup water

Skin and finely dice tomatoes. Then mince onion and garlic. Chop basil and oregano. Heat olive oil in nonstick skillet; add onion and garlic. Saute until onion is clear, then add tomatoes, basil, oregano and ½ cup water. Simmer 5 minutes.

PIZZA TOPPINGS
1   large red onion cut into
**   rings or chopped if you**
**   prefer**
2   cups tomato sauce
**   (recipe above)**
1   cup sliced mushrooms
1   large red & green bell
**   pepper, sliced thin**
15 black olives, sliced
8   whole wheat tortillas
6   ounces farmers cheese

Preheat oven to 350°. On baking sheet, place tortillas and heat until crisp (approximately 8–10 minutes). Remove from oven and spread tortillas with ¼ cup tomato sauce. Distribute vegetables evenly among each tortilla. Top each tortilla with ¾ ounce cheese and return to oven until cheese has melted. Serve immediately.

Servings: 8

Marlo Neale

NUTRIENT VALUES					
PROTEIN	CARBOHYDRATE		FAT		ALCOHOL
16%	45%		39%		0%
CALORIES	PRO-GM	CARB-GM		FAT-GM	SOD-MG
273.0	10.50	28.70		11.20	136.0
FOOD EXCHANGES					
MILK	VEG.	FRUIT	BREAD	MEAT	FAT
0.5	1.1	0.0	1.4	0.0	1.3

LASAGNA

SAUCE INGREDIENTS:
1 onion, chopped
2 cloves garlic
3 cups sliced mushrooms
2 bay leaves
1½ teaspoons oregano
1½ teaspoons basil
½ teaspoon thyme
¼ cup chopped parsley
6 cups tomatoes, diced
(fresh or canned)
5 cups water

OTHER INGREDIENTS:
2 10-ounce packags frozen
spinach
1 cup part skim ricotta,
thinned with ½ cup
skim milk
8 ounces whole wheat
lasagna noodles
½ pound part skim
mozzarella, sliced thin
¼ cup grated parmesan
cheese
vegetable coating spray

To prepare sauce, saute garlic and onion in water in a large saucepan until onions are clear. Add remaining sauce ingredients. Simmer for 30 minutes. Remove bay leaf.

Cook lasagna noodles in boiling water until tender and drain. Rinse in cold water to prevent sticking.

Spray a 9 × 13 baking dish with vegetable coating spray.

Cook frozen spinach. Squeeze all excess water from spinach. Spread thin layer of sauce on the bottom of pan. Layer noodles on top of sauce. Spread more sauce on top of noodles. Place ½ of spinach evenly over sauce. Distribute ½ ricotta evenly. Sprinkle ½ mozzarella as next layer. Layer more noodles and repeat the process, ending with a layer of noodles, tomato sauce and remaining mozzarella. Bake uncovered for 30 minutes at 375°. Uncover and bake until brown. Let stand for 15 minutes before serving. Sprinkle with parmesan cheese.

Servings: 8

NUTRIENT VALUES				
PROTEIN	CARBOHYDRATE		FAT	ALCOHOL
26%	48%		26%	0%
CALORIES	PRO-GM	CARB-GM	FAT-GM	SOD-MG
307.0	20.40	37.60	9.223	315.0
FOOD EXCHANGES					
MILK	VEG.	FRUIT	BREAD	MEAT	FAT
0.1	2.2	0.0	1.6	1.8	0.8

RATATOUILLE

2 small eggplants (about 2 pounds in all) cut into 1½ inch cubes (8 cups cubed)
2 cups chopped onion
4 medium zucchini, washed, trimmed, quartered lengthwise and cut into 2 inch strips
1 medium sweet red pepper, stemmed, seeded, and cut in ½ inch strips
1 tablespoon garlic, minced
24 ounces Italian peeled plum tomatoes, drained
3 tablespoons tomato paste
2 tablespoons chopped fresh parsley
2 tablespoons chopped fresh dill
1 tablespoon dried basil or 2 tablespoons fresh
1 teaspoon dried oregano or 1 tablespoon fresh
Freshly ground black pepper, to taste

Steam eggplant until it begins to soften. Do not overcook. Set aside.

In a large skillet, saute onion, squash, peppers and garlic over medium heat until wilted, approximately 15 minutes. Add tomatoes, tomato paste, parsley, dill, basil, oregano, and black pepper. Simmer 10 minutes stirring occasionally. Add cubed eggplant to tomato mixture and simmer for another 10 minutes. Serve hot or at room temperature.

Servings: 7 (1 cup serving)

Serve over brown rice, whole grains, pasta or as a potato topper.

NUTRIENT VALUES					
PROTEIN	CARBOHYDRATE			FAT	ALCOHOL
17%	75%			8%	0%
CALORIES	PRO-GM	CARB-GM		FAT-GM	SOD-MG
96.30	4.861	21.10		0.944	167.0
FOOD EXCHANGES					
MILK	VEG.	FRUIT	BREAD	MEAT	FAT
0.0	3.6	0.0	0.0	0.0	0.1

EGGPLANT PARMESAN

½ cup whole wheat flour
4 egg whites, slightly beaten
2½ cups whole wheat bread crumbs
½ teaspoon basil
½ teaspoon garlic powder
½ teaspoon black pepper
1 medium size eggplant (1–1¼ lb.)
2 cups tomato sauce or lowfat spaghetti sauce
1 cup grated part-skim mozzarella
6 tablespoons grated parmesan cheese

Prepare three bowls for dipping eggplant slices.

1. whole wheat flour

2. egg whites

3. bread crumbs, basil, garlic and pepper

Preheat oven to 350°.

Cut eggplant into ⅛ inch slices. Dip into flour mixture, egg mixture, then cracker mixture.

Lay one half of the eggplant slices in a layer in a 9″ × 13″ baking dish. Sprinkle with ½ tomato sauce and parmesan. Repeat layers. Cover and bake for 30 minutes. Remove from oven; top with mozzarella and bake uncovered 15 additional minutes.

Servings: 8

NUTRIENT VALUES				
PROTEIN 26%	CARBOHYDRATE 50%		FAT 24%	ALCOHOL 0%
CALORIES 170.0	PRO-GM 11.30	CARB-GM 21.50	FAT-GM 4.569	SOD-MG 299.0
FOOD EXCHANGES					
MILK 01.	VEG. 0.0	FRUIT 0.0	BREAD 1.5	MEAT 0.9	FAT 0.4

EGGPLANT AND BASIL CHEESE CASSEROLE

1 large or 2 small
  eggplants, sliced ½ inch
  thick
2 large tomatoes, peeled,
  seeded, chopped, and
  drained
½ cup part skim ricotta
  cheese
2 egg whites
2 cloves garlic, minced
⅛ teaspoon cayenne pepper
½ cup freshly grated
  Parmesan cheese
½ cup nonfat yogurt
12–15 large basil leaves
¼ cup whole wheat bread
  crumbs
Vegetable coating spray

Spray a cookie sheet with vegetable coating spray. Place eggplant slices in a single layer on the sheet and spray top of eggplant with vegetable coating spray. Broil until golden brown, turn slices and broil other side. Set aside.

Combine ricotta, egg whites, garlic, cayenne, ¼ cup parmesan cheese, and yogurt.

Spray an 8 × 8 inch glass dish with vegetable coating spray. Place a single layer of eggplant in bottom. Cover eggplant with basil leaves. Spoon half the chopped tomatoes over the basil leaves. Then top with half the cheese mixture. Make a second layer of eggplant, then basil and finish with the cheese mixture. Top with remaining Parmesan cheese. Bake at 350° for 40 minutes until browned and bubbling. Serve hot.

Servings: 6

Trisha Shirey

NUTRIENT VALUES			
PROTEIN 30%	CARBOHYDRATE 38%	FAT 32%	ALCOHOL 0%
CALORIES 124.4	PRO-GM 9.802	CARB-GM 12.36	FAT-GM 4.660	SOD-MG 228.0

FOOD EXCHANGES					
MILK 0.1	VEG. 1.4	FRUIT 0.0	BREAD 0.2	MEAT 1.0	FAT 0.3

EGGPLANT SANDWICH MELTS

4 slices whole wheat bread
1 cup Italian sauce (See p. 82)
4 ounces part skim mozzarella or part skim Swiss, thinly sliced
1 recipe oven fried eggplant (See p. 213)
Vegetable coating spray

Spray a cookie sheet with vegetable coating spray. Place bread slices on sprayed cookie sheet. Top with eggplant slices. Top each sandwich with ¼ cup Italian sauce, then 1 ounce cheese. Broil until cheese is melted and bubbly.

Servings: 4

Trisha Shirey

NUTRIENT VALUES				
PROTEIN 23%	CARBOHYDRATE 46%		FAT 31%	ALCOHOL 0%
CALORIES 246.0	PRO-GM 15.10	CARB-GM 30.00	FAT-GM 8.950	SOD-MG 500.0
FOOD EXCHANGES					
MILK 0.0	VEG. 0.9	FRUIT 0.0	BREAD 1.8	MEAT 1.0	FAT 1.0

CORN & TOMATO CASSEROLE

6 ears fresh corn or 3 cups frozen corn
1 medium onion, chopped
1 medium green pepper, chopped
2 tablespoons defatted chicken stock
5 medium tomatoes, sliced ½ inch thick
½ teaspoon freshly ground black pepper
½ cup whole wheat bread crumbs
1 tablespoon reduced calorie margarine, melted
Vegetable coating spray

Cut corn from cob or thaw corn if frozen. Saute corn, onion, green peppers and black pepper in chicken stock for 5 minutes. Spoon half the corn mixture in a 2 quart casserole dish sprayed with coating spray. Top with half the tomato slices. Repeat the layers. Combine bread crumbs and margarine. Top casserole with bread crumbs and bake at 375° for 30 minutes.

Servings: 6 (1 cup serving)

Trisha Shirey

NUTRIENT VALUES				
PROTEIN 13%	CARBOHYDRATE 76%		FAT 11%	ALCOHOL 0%
CALORIES 122.10	PRO-GM 4.367	CARB-GM 26.50	FAT-GM 1.689	SOD-MG 62.20
FOOD EXCHANGES					
MILK 0.0	VEG. 1.3	FRUIT 0.0	BREAD 1.3	MEAT 0.0	FAT 0.2

VEGETARIAN CHILI

1	cup dried kidney beans
1	cup dried pinto beans
½	cup dried black beans
5	celery stalks and leaves, chopped
1	carrot, shredded
14	ounce can stewed tomatoes
1	green pepper, chopped
1	medium onion, chopped
2	cloves garlic, minced
1	bay leaf
6	tablespoons fresh parsley, minced
½	teaspoon whole dillweed
¾	teaspoon whole basil
¾	teaspoon oregano
½	teaspoon ground cumin
½	teaspoon ground allspice

Dash of ground pepper

Sort and wash beans; place in a large pot. Cover with water 2 inches above beans; bring to a boil. Let stand with no heat for 1 hour. Drain and rinse beans. Add fresh water to cover beans. Return to simmer for 1 hour. Add remaining ingredients, simmer 30 minutes to 1 hour or until beans are tender and chili is thickened (add more water if necessary). Remove and discard bay leaf. Garnish with red onion ring and parsley sprig. Freezes well for 2–3 months.

Servings: 9 (1 cup serving)

NUTRIENT VALUES			
PROTEIN	CARBOHYDRATE	FAT	ALCOHOL
23%	70%	7%	0%
CALORIES	PRO-GM	CARB-GM	FAT-GM	SOD-MG
264.0	15.90	48.60	2.067	201.0

FOOD EXCHANGES					
MILK	VEG.	FRUIT	BREAD	MEAT	FAT
0.0	0.9	0.0	2.1	0.0	0.5

TAMALE PIE

2 cups cooked pinto or kidney beans
¼ cup water
½ cup chopped onion
1 clove garlic minced
1 teaspoon cumin
1 teaspoon chili powder
2 tablespoons tomato paste
½ cup fresh corn or frozen
½ cup chopped green pepper
1 tablespoon chopped cilantro
2½ cups cold water
1½ cups cornmeal
¼ cup grated part skim mozzarella cheese

Mash beans with a potato masher. In a skillet, saute onion in water until soft. Add beans, and next seven ingredients. Cook over low heat until heated through.

Combine the cornmeal and water in a heavy pan, and cook over medium heat until cornmeal thickens. You have to stir this constantly or the cornmeal will stick.

Spray an 8" × 8"nonstick pan with vegetable coating spray and spread two thirds of the cornmeal mixture over the bottom and sides; then pour the bean mixture into the cornmeal crust and spread the remaining one third of the cornmeal on the top. Sprinkle with grated cheese. Bake at 350° for 45–50 minutes.

Servings: 6

NUTRIENT VALUES				
PROTEIN 16%	CARBOHYDRATE 78%		FAT 6%	ALCOHOL 0%
CALORIES 285.0	PRO-GM 11.90	CARB-GM 56.30	FAT-GM 1.897	SOD-MG 32.30
FOOD EXCHANGES					
MILK 0.0	VEG. 1.7	FRUIT 0.0	BREAD 3.1	MEAT 0.2	FAT 0.1

SOFT BEAN TACO

2   whole wheat tortillas
6   tablespoons cooked long
    grain brown rice
2   tablespoons cooked pinto
    beans, mashed
2   tablespoons chopped
    green onion
¼   cup chopped tomato
4   teaspoons grated lowfat
    cheese
¼   cup chopped lettuce

Mix rice and beans. Heat rice and bean mixture. Divide and place in warm tortilla. Divide remaining ingredients in half and place in order listed inside tortilla. Fold in half and serve.

Servings: 2

NUTRIENT VALUES			
PROTEIN	CARBOHYDRATE	FAT	ALCOHOL
14%	69%	17%	0%
CALORIES	PRO-GM	CARB-GM	FAT-GM	SOD-MG
169.0	6.001	29.40	3.200	186.0
FOOD EXCHANGES					
MILK	VEG.	FRUIT	BREAD	MEAT	FAT
0.0	0.5	0.0	1.8	0.3	0.5

ENCHILADA BAKE

1 green pepper, chopped
1 onion, chopped
1 clove garlic, minced
5-6 mushrooms, sliced (⅓ cup)
1½ cups beans (kidney or pinto), cooked or canned
1½ cups diced tomatoes
1 tablespoon chili powder
1 teaspoon cumin seed, ground
6 corn tortillas
2 ounces Monterey Jack or farmer's cheese, grated
½ cup ricotta cheese, part skim
¼ cup nonfat yogurt

Saute onion, garlic, mushrooms, and pepper over medium heat until onion is translucent. Add beans, tomato, chili powder and cumin. Simmer gently for about 30 minutes. Meanwhile mix ricotta and yogurt together in a small bowl and set aside. Soften tortillas by steaming in the oven or microwave. (or dip in hot stock to soften) On each tortilla place 3 teaspoons grated cheese and 2 tablespoons yogurt mixture. Roll tortilla around cheese mixture and place in baking dish seam side down. Repeat procedure with remaining tortillas. Top tortillas with bean mixture. Bake at 350° for 15–20 minutes or until cheese melts. Serve hot.

Servings: 6

(Freezes well—freeze before baking).

NUTRIENT VALUES			
PROTEIN	CARBOHYDRATE	FAT	ALCOHOL
21%	57%	22%	0%
CALORIES	PRO-GM	CARB-GM	FAT-GM	SOD-MG
252.0	13.10	35.80	6.240	139.0

FOOD EXCHANGES					
MILK	VEG.	FRUIT	BREAD	MEAT	FAT
0.3	2.2	0.0	2.2	0.4	0.8

EGGPLANT ENCHILADAS

Vegetable coating spray
1 cup chopped onion
2 cloves garlic, minced
¼ cup defatted chicken broth
1 teaspoon Worcestershire sauce
6 cups peeled, cubed eggplant (2 small)
1 cup chopped green pepper
1 cup sliced fresh mushrooms
2 tablespoons chopped, toasted almonds
1 teaspoon freshly ground black pepper
1 cup grated Monterey Jack cheese
1 tablespoon minced fresh parsley
12 whole wheat flour tortillas
Stock for softening tortillas

Saute onion and garlic in stock in a large skillet. Cook 5 minutes then stir in eggplant, green pepper, mushrooms and Worcestershire sauce. Cook 10–12 minutes or until eggplant is soft. Remove from heat; add almonds, parsley, pepper and ¾ cup cheese. Simmer small amount of stock in a small frying pan. Dip tortillas in individually on each side to soften. Put a portion of eggplant mix in each tortilla and roll tightly. Place in a glass baking dish sprayed with vegetable coating spray. Top with remaining cheese and bake 20 minutes at 350°.

Servings: 12 (1 enchilada each)

Trisha Shirey

NUTRIENT VALUES					
PROTEIN	CARBOHYDRATE		FAT	ALCOHOL	
16%	54%		30%	0%	
CALORIES	PRO-GM	CARB-GM	FAT-GM	SOD-MG	
158.0	6.575	22.30	5.408	218.0	
FOOD EXCHANGES					
MILK	VEG.	FRUIT	BREAD	MEAT	FAT
0.0	1.3	0.0	0.9	0.3	0.8

CHEESE ENCHILADAS

8   corn tortillas
½   cup vegetable stock
¾   cup chopped onion
¼   cup chopped bell pepper
½   pound tofu, mashed
½   cup chopped parsley
1   cup grated zucchini
1   cup grated carrots
⅓   cup cheddar cheese
Vegetable coating spray

ENCHILADA SAUCE
3   tablespoons chopped
    onion
16 ounces tomato sauce, low
    sodium
1   tablespoon vinegar
3   tablespoon chili powder
1   tablespoon cumin
2   cloves garlic, minced
8   ounces water

Combine all ingredients for enchilada sauce in a large saucepan. Bring to a boil, reduce heat and simmer for 30 minutes.

Saute onion and bell pepper in stock until soft. Add tofu, zucchini, and parsley. Cook and stir until tofu is fairly dry. Mix cheese and carrots and set aside. Soften tortillas in oven or in warm chicken stock. Fill softened tortillas with 2 tablespoons of tofu mixture and 1 tablespoon of cheese and carrot mixture and roll up. Arrange side by side in a small baking dish sprayed with vegetable coating spray.

Pour enchilada sauce over the top of rolled enchiladas and sprinkle with remaining cheese and carrot mixture. Cover and bake at 350° for 30 minutes.

Servings: 8

NUTRIENT VALUES			
PROTEIN	CARBOHYDRATE	FAT	ALCOHOL
18%	57%	25%	0%
CALORIES	PRO-GM	CARB-GM	FAT-GM	SOD-MG
161.0	7.825	24.30	4.762	139.0

FOOD EXCHANGES					
MILK	VEG.	FRUIT	BREAD	MEAT	FAT
0.0	0.9	0.0	1.3	0.2	1.0

CHEESE CHALUPA

1 corn tortilla
¼ cup cooked pinto beans
2 tablespoons chopped onion
¼ cup chopped tomato
½ cup chopped lettuce
½ ounce grated part skim mozzarella cheese

Bake tortilla in 300° oven 10–15 minutes or until crisp. Cook beans according to Basic Bean Recipe (See pg. 114). Mash ¼ cup cooked beans.

Layer on tortilla shell: beans, onion, lettuce, chopped tomatoes, and top with grated cheese. Serve with pico de gallo. (See pg. 65)

Servings: 1

NUTRIENT VALUES				
PROTEIN	CARBOHYDRATE		FAT	ALCOHOL
21%	63%		16%	0%
CALORIES	PRO-GM	CARB-GM	FAT-GM	SOD-MG
215.0	11.80	34.70	3.902	126.0
FOOD EXCHANGES					

MILK	VEG.	FRUIT	BREAD	MEAT	FAT
0.0	2.0	0.0	2.0	0.5	0.0

STUFFED BELL PEPPERS

¾ cup long-grain brown
    rice, raw
2 cups water
4 green bell peppers,
    halved lengthwise and
    seeded
1 tablespoon chicken
    stock, defatted
⅔ cup chopped onion
1 clove garlic, minced
½ cup mushrooms, sliced
1 tablespoon chopped
    fresh parsley
1 teaspoon dried oregano
    or 2 teaspoon fresh
½ teaspoon dried basil or 1
    teaspoon fresh
1 teaspoon low sodium soy
    sauce
½ cup lowfat cottage
    cheese
2 egg whites
½ carrot, chopped
1 tomato, sliced
4 tablespoons grated
    lowfat cheese

Bring water to a boil, add rice. Return to boil, reduce heat, cover and simmer 45 minutes. Drain. Steam the pepper halves over boiling water for 5 minutes.

Heat the stock in a large skillet and saute the onions and garlic until tender. Add the mushrooms and cook for 2 minutes longer.

Stir in the parsley, oregano, basil and soy sauce.

Add the cooked rice, egg whites, carrot and cottage cheese. Cook, stirring gently, for a minute or two. Fill the pepper halves with the rice mixture.

Set in a baking pan and place 1 tablespoon grated cheese on top of each pepper. Bake at 350° covered for 30 minutes. Remove cover and bake 15 additional minutes or until cheese is brown.

Servings: 4 (2 pepper halves each)

NUTRIENT VALUES			
PROTEIN	CARBOHYDRATE	FAT	ALCOHOL
20%	69%	11%	0%
CALORIES	PRO-GM	CARB-GM	FAT-GM	SOD-MG
221.0	11.50	38.70	2.698	281.0
FOOD EXCHANGES					
MILK	VEG.	FRUIT	BREAD	MEAT	FAT
0.0	1.9	0.0	1.6	1.0	0.5

CORN STUFFED PEPPERS

4 small green bell peppers (well-shaped) or red bell peppers

3 cups fresh or frozen corn (about 3 ears)

¼ cup water

3 green onions and tops, chopped

1 medium tomato, peeled, seeded, diced

2 teaspoons minced fresh basil

¼ teaspoon freshly ground white pepper

Vegetable coating spray

Carefully remove tops from peppers, remove seeds and membranes. Cook peppers, covered in boiling water for 5 minutes. Drain and set aside. Combine corn and ¼ cup water and bring to a boil. Cover and reduce heat. Simmer 7–8 minutes. Drain and add onion, tomato, basil and pepper. Spoon corn mix into peppers and place in an 8 × 8 glass baking dish, sprayed with coating spray. Cover with foil and bake 350° for 15 minutes.

Servings: 4

Trish Shirey

NUTRIENT VALUES					
PROTEIN	CARBOHYDRATE		FAT	ALCOHOL	
13%	83%		4%	0%	
CALORIES	PRO-GM	CARB-GM	FAT-GM	SOD-MG	
128.0	4.700	30.90	0.676	10.90	
FOOD EXCHANGES					
MILK	VEG.	FRUIT	BREAD	MEAT	FAT
0.0	1.0	0.0	1.6	0.0	0.0

STUFFED CHARD LEAVES

8–12 large Swiss chard
leaves
1¼ cups cooked brown rice,
cold
½ cup chopped onion
2 tablespoons water
¾ cup lowfat cottage
cheese
2 egg whites
2 tablespoons raisins
½ teaspoon dried dill weed
or 1½ teaspoons fresh
2 tablespoons chopped
parsley

Preheat oven to 350°

Saute onion in water until tender. Mix all ingredients except chard. Quickly steam chard leaves to soften. Place 2 tablespoons of filling on the underside of a leaf. Fold over the sides of the leaf and roll up into a square packet. Place seam-side down in a nonstick dish. Cover and bake for 30 minutes. Serve hot.

Servings: (2–3 each)

NUTRIENT VALUES			
PROTEIN	CARBOHYDRATE	FAT	ALCOHOL
30%	64%	6%	0%
CALORIES	PRO-GM	CARB-GM	FAT-GM	SOD-MG
119.0	8.996	19.30	0.860	256.0
FOOD EXCHANGES					
MILK	VEG.	FRUIT	BREAD	MEAT	FAT
0.0	0.5	0.3	0.8	0.9	0.0

MUSHROOM BARLEY CASSEROLE

¼ cup water
1 cup chopped onion
½ pound fresh mushrooms,
cleaned and sliced
1 cup barley
2½ cups vegetable stock
½ teaspoon salt
¼ teaspoon pepper
½ teaspoon marjoram

Saute onion and mushrooms in water until tender; stir in barley and saute until slightly brown. Add stock and seasonings, mix well. Cover tightly and cook over low heat for about 1 hour, until barley is tender and liquid absorbed.

Servings: 4

NUTRIENT VALUES			
PROTEIN	CARBOHYDRATE	FAT	ALCOHOL
11%	86%	4%	0%
CALORIES	PRO-GM	CARB-GM	FAT-GM	SOD-MG
212.0	6.012	46.90	0.858	248.0
FOOD EXCHANGES					
MILK	VEG.	FRUIT	BREAD	MEAT	FAT
0.0	1.1	0.0	2.5	0.0	0.0

RICE AND BEAN CASSEROLE

2 cups brown rice, cooked (See pg. 115)
2 cups cooked black beans
2 tablespoons defatted chicken stock
3 cloves garlic, minced
1 large onion, chopped
1 tablespoon chili powder
1-4 ounce can chopped green chiles
1½ cups grated part skim mozzarella
1 cup part skim ricotta cheese
¼ cup skim milk
Vegetable coating spray

Saute onion and garlic in stock for 5–7 minutes until onions are clear. Combine onion, garlic, rice, beans, chiles and chili powder. Combine ricotta and milk and blend until smooth, add 1 cup mozzarella cheese. Spray 1½ quart casserole with coating spray. Layer beans and rice with cheese mixture, ending with rice mix. Bake covered at 350° for 30 minutes. Uncover, top with remaining ½ cup mozzarella, and bake uncovered 5 minutes until cheese is melted. Serve hot.

Servings: 6 (1 cup serving)

Trisha Shirey

NUTRIENT VALUES			
PROTEIN	CARBOHYDRATE	FAT	ALCOHOL
26%	46%	28%	0%
CALORIES	PRO-GM	CARB-GM	FAT-GM	SOD-MG
289.0	19.10	33.80	8.983	209.0

FOOD EXCHANGES					
MILK	VEG.	FRUIT	BREAD	MEAT	FAT
0.1	0.4	0.0	0.8	1.8	0.8

RICE-CARROT LOAF

1   cup carrots, grated
1   small onion, chopped
1   cup vegetable stock or
    chicken stock, defatted
2   egg whites
1½ cups cooked brown rice,
    cold
⅔   cup part-skim
    mozzarella, grated
¼   teaspoon oregano
¼   white pepper
2   tablespoons dried bread
    crumbs
Vegetable coating spray

Saute onions and carrots in stock until tender. Add egg whites, rice, cheese and spices and stir well. Place in baking dish sprayed with vegetable coating spray. Top with bread crumbs and bake in 350° oven for 30 minutes.

Servings: 4

NUTRIENT VALUES					
PROTEIN	CARBOHYDRATE		FAT		ALCOHOL
22%	57%		21%		0%
CALORIES	PRO-GM	CARB-GM		FAT-GM	SOD-MG
153.2	8.376	21.8		3.576	126.0
FOOD EXCHANGES					
MILK	VEG.	FRUIT	BREAD	MEAT	FAT
0.0	1.0	0.0	0.9	0.9	0.3

SPINACH RICE CASSEROLE

2 cups cooked long-grain brown rice, cold
1 pound fresh spinach, chopped
½ cup chopped onion
1 clove minced garlic
2 tablespoons chicken stock, defatted
2 egg whites, beaten
½ cup skim milk
2 ounces part-skim mozzarella cheese, grated (½ cup grated)
¼ cup chopped parsley
1½ teaspoons low-sodium soy sauce
¼ teaspoon nutmeg
Paprika

Saute onions and garlic in stock until onions are clear. Combine with all remaining ingredients except paprika in a large mixing bowl.

Place mixture in a 8″ square baking dish that has been sprayed with vegetable coating spray. Sprinkle with paprika. Bake for 1 hour at 350° or until done.

Servings: 4

NUTRIENT VALUES			
PROTEIN	CARBOHYDRATE	FAT	ALCOHOL
26%	58%	16%	0%
CALORIES	PRO-GM	CARB-GM	FAT-GM	SOD-MG
178.0	12.00	26.90	3.325	329.0
FOOD EXCHANGES					
MILK	VEG.	FRUIT	BREAD	MEAT	FAT
0.1	1.4	0.0	1.1	0.8	0.3

LENTIL AND BULGUR CASSEROLE

¾ cup dry green lentils, washed

2½ cups defatted chicken broth

1 tablespoon olive oil

1 medium onion, chopped

8 ounces fresh mushrooms, sliced

¾ cup dry bulgur

½ teaspoon freshly ground black pepper

2 tablespoons minced fresh parsley

1 cup nonfat yogurt

1 tablespoon minced fresh chives

Vegetable coating spray

Combine lentils and stock in saucepan and cook over medium heat for 20 minutes. Lentils should be tender but firm. Saute onion and mushrooms in olive oil for 2–3 minutes. Add bulgur and cook 5 minutes more, stirring constantly. Add the pepper, parsley and lentils to bulgur and mix well. Pour into a 1½ quart glass baking dish that has been sprayed with coating spray. Bake 25–30 minutes at 350°until lentils are done. Mix the yogurt and chives and top the casserole before serving.

Servings: 6 (1 cup serving)

NUTRIENT VALUES				
PROTEIN	CARBOHYDRATE		FAT	ALCOHOL
20%	67%		14%	0%
CALORIES	PRO-GM	CARB-GM	FAT-GM	SOD-MG
214.0	10.60	36.00	3.319	31.90
FOOD EXCHANGES					
MILK	VEG.	FRUIT	BREAD	MEAT	FAT
0.3	0.4	0.0	2.2	0.0	0.4

LENTIL BURGERS

1 **cup cooked lentils**
½ **cup whole wheat bread crumbs (1 slice)**
¼ **cup wheat bran**
¼ **cup finely chopped onion**
2 **egg whites, lightly beaten**
2 **tablespoons picante sauce**
Vegetable coating spray

In a medium bowl, mash the lentils. Add the next five ingredients and shape into patties. Spray a nonstick skillet or griddle with vegetable coating spray. Over medium heat cook the burgers until brown. Use ¼ cup lentil mixture per burger.

Serve in whole wheat pita or on whole wheat hamburger buns with chopped tomatoes and shredded lettuce.

Servings: 7

NUTRIENT VALUES			
PROTEIN	CARBOHYDRATE	FAT	ALCOHOL
27%	66%	7%	0%
CALORIES	PRO-GM	CARB-GM	FAT-GM	SOD-MG
56.40	4.416	10.60	0.489	68.80

FOOD EXCHANGES					
MILK	VEG.	FRUIT	BREAD	MEAT	FAT
0.0	0.1	0.0	0.8	0.1	0.1

ORIENTAL PEPPERS AND TOFU

¼ cup defatted chicken broth
2 cloves garlic, minced
1 teaspoon grated fresh ginger
2 carrots, sliced
1 red pepper, sliced in thin strips
1 green pepper, sliced in thin strips
5 green onions, sliced in 1 inch pieces
1 tablespoon low sodium soy sauce
1 tablespoon vinegar (Ginger-Garlic is good)
½ pound tofu, cubed

Heat stock in a large skillet. Add garlic, ginger and carrots and stir fry three minutes. Add peppers and stir fry three more minutes. Add green onions and cook one minute. Add soy sauce, vinegar and tofu and stir gently. Cover and simmer for 5–6 minutes.

Servings: 3 (1 cup serving)

Trisha Shirey

NUTRIENT VALUES					
PROTEIN 28%	CARBOHYDRATE 42%		FAT 30%		ALCOHOL 0%
CALORIES 93.70	PRO-GM 7.264	CARB-GM 10.80	FAT-GM 3.518		SOD-MG 24.20
FOOD EXCHANGES					
MILK 0.0	VEG. 2.2	FRUIT 0.0	BREAD 0.0	MEAT 0.0	FAT 1.2

CHEESY BAKED TOFU

¾ cup whole wheat bread crumbs

1 teaspoon dried oregano or 2 teaspoons fresh

1 teaspoon dried basil or 2 teaspoons fresh

2 egg whites

1 teaspoon low sodium soy sauce

1 clove garlic, minced

1 pound tofu, drained

¼ cup whole wheat flour

½ cup tomato sauce (low sodium)

¼ cup thinly sliced fresh mushrooms

10 pitted black olives, sliced

Vegetable coating spray

Slice tofu into five slices then halve to make 10 slices. Blot with paper towels. Combine bread crumbs and herbs in a small bowl. Mix egg whites, garlic and soy sauce in a separate bowl. Dip tofu slices in flour, then egg mixture, then in bread crumbs. Place in a shallow baking dish sprayed with coating spray. Bake for 25 minutes at 375° until golden crisp. Remove from oven and place in an 8 × 8 glass baking dish sprayed with coating spray. Pour tomato sauce over tofu, distributing evenly. Place shredded mozzerella over sauce, then add mushrooms and olives. Bake at 375° until cheese melts, about 15 minutes.

Servings: 5 (2 slices tofu each)

Trisha Shirey

NUTRIENT VALUES			
PROTEIN	CARBOHYDRATE	FAT	ALCOHOL
29%	36%	35%	0%
CALORIES	PRO-GM	CARB-GM	FAT-GM	SOD-MG
137.0	10.70	13.00	5.696	325.0
FOOD EXCHANGES					
MILK	VEG.	FRUIT	BREAD	MEAT	FAT
0.0	0.9	0.0	0.6	0.2	1.8

CHOW MEIN

2½ cups water
1 cup long grain brown rice, raw
½ cup chopped onion
1 clove garlic, minced
1 cup chopped celery
2 teaspoons sesame oil
½ cup sliced mushrooms
1 cup bean sprouts
½ cup sliced water chestnuts
1 cup sliced carrots
1 cup snow peas
½ cup vegetable stock
1 tablespoon cornstarch
2 tablespoons low sodium soy sauce
4 green onion tops, chopped

Place rice into 2½ cups boiling water. Reduce heat, cover and simmer for 45 minutes. Do not remove lid during cooking.

Saute onions, garlic and celery in the oil. Add the mushrooms and stir until they are just heated. Add the bean sprouts, water chestnuts, carrots and snow peas. Cook for 6–8 minutes, or until carrots are tender crisp.

In a bowl, combine the vegetable stock, cornstarch and soy sauce. Add the mixture to the vegetables and simmer until it thickens. Serve over hot rice. Garnish with chopped green onions or chives.

Servings: 4 (1 cup chow mein over ½ cup brown rice)

NUTRIENT VALUES				
PROTEIN	CARBOHYDRATE		FAT	ALCOHOL
13%	70%		17%	0%
CALORIES	PRO-GM	CARB-GM	FAT-GM	SOD-MG
153.0	5.126	27.80	2.999	573.0
FOOD EXCHANGES					
MILK	VEG.	FRUIT	BREAD	MEAT	FAT
0.0	2.3	0.0	1.0	0.0	0.6

BASIL TOMATO QUICHE

2 large tomatoes, peeled, seeded, chopped
6–8 basil leaves, torn into small pieces
4 egg whites
1 clove garlic, whole
1 cup evaporated skim milk
2 tablespoons grated Parmesan cheese
1½ cups grated part skim mozzarella cheese
Vegetable coating spray

Blot excess water from tomatoes with paper towel. Spray an 8 × 8 inch glass baking dish with vegetable coating spray. Spear the garlic clove with a fork and beat the eggs until frothy. Discard garlic. Add remaining ingredients and mix well. Pour into prepared pan. Bake at 350° for 30 minutes until browned. Serve warm.

Servings: 9

Trisha Shirey

NUTRIENT VALUES					
PROTEIN 40%	CARBOHYDRATE 24%		FAT 36%		ALCOHOL 0%
CALORIES 90.70	PRO-GM 8.941	CARB-GM 5.277		FAT-GM 3.569	SOD-MG 172.0
FOOD EXCHANGES					
MILK 0.3	VEG. 0.2	FRUIT 0.0	BREAD 0.0	MEAT 0.9	FAT 0.3

CRUSTLESS MEXICAN QUICHE

½ onion, chopped
1 small red bell pepper,
   chopped
1 small green bell pepper,
   chopped
3-4 tablespoons broth or
   water
10 ounces shredded
   Monterey Jack cheese
2 eggs or egg substitute
5 egg whites
1¼ cups skim milk
Dash of pepper
1 teaspoon dried whole
   basil
Paprika
Vegetable coating spray

Coat shallow baking dish or 8-inch pie pan with vegetable coating spray. Saute onion and bell peppers in broth or water until tender; drain and place in quiche pan. Sprinkle with cheese. Combine next four ingredients; pour over cheese. Sprinkle with paprika. Bake at 350 degrees for 30–40 minutes or until firm in center.

Servings: 8

NUTRIENT VALUES				
PROTEIN 30%	CARBOHYDRATE 10%		FAT 60%	ALCOHOL 0%
CALORIES 188.0	PRO-GM 14.10	CARB-GM 4.532	FAT-GM 12.60	SOD-MG 261.0
FOOD EXCHANGES					
MILK 0.2	VEG. 0.3	FRUIT 0.0	BREAD 0.0	MEAT 1.8	FAT 1.4

GREEN CHILE QUICHE

2   medium zucchini, shredded (squeeze excess water)
2   finely chopped green onions
¼   cup chopped green chiles, canned
4   beaten egg whites
2   eggs or egg substitute
1   cup grated part skim mozzarella
1   cup grated cheddar cheese
1½ cups evaporated skim milk
Vegetable coating spray

Saute squash and onion in a nonstick skillet over low heat, until tender. Add water if squash begins to stick. Mix all ingredients and pour into 9 inch pan sprayed with vegetable coating spary. Bake at 350° until firm and lightly browned.

Servings: 8

Trisha Shirey

NUTRIENT VALUES					
PROTEIN	CARBOHYDRATE		FAT		ALCOHOL
34%	18%		47%		0%
CALORIES	PRO-GM	CARB-GM		FAT-GM	SOD-MG
166.0	14.00	7.455		8.507	254.0
FOOD EXCHANGES					
MILK	VEG.	FRUIT	BREAD	MEAT	FAT
0.4	0.3	0.0	0.0	1.4	0.9

PIZZA QUICHE

Vegetable coating spray
1 teaspoon olive oil
½ cup sliced mushrooms
1 cup chopped onions
½ cup chopped green pepper
1 clove garlic, minced
4 medium tomatoes, peeled, seeded, chopped, drained
½ teaspoon dried basil or 1 teaspoon fresh
½ teaspoon dried oregano or 1 teaspoon fresh
2 tablespoons tomato paste
2 tablespoons minced fresh parsley
⅛ teaspoon freshly ground black pepper
4 egg whites, beaten until frothy
8 sliced pitted black olives
⅓ cup grated Parmesan cheese
1 cup part skim grated Swiss cheese

Preheat oven to 350°. Spray a heavy or non-stick skillet with coating spray. Add olive oil, saute onion, green peppers, mushrooms and garlic 5–7 minutes, until limp. Add tomatoes and stir briefly over low heat to dry tomatoes. Combine eggs, tomato paste, cheese and herbs. Stir in sauteed vegetables except olives and mix well. Pour into 9″ pan sprayed with nonstick spray. Top with olives. Bake at 350° for 30 minutes until browned.

Servings: 7

Trisha Shirey

NUTRIENT VALUES					
PROTEIN 27%	CARBOHYDRATE 32%		FAT 41%	ALCOHOL 0%	
CALORIES 130.0	PRO-GM 9.138	CARB-GM 11.00	FAT-GM 6.115	SOD-MG 148.0	
FOOD EXCHANGES					
MILK 0.4	VEG. 1.0	FRUIT 0.0	BREAD 0.1	MEAT 0.4	FAT 3.4

ZUCCHINI-TOMATO QUICHE

¼ cup vegetable stock
2 ripe tomatoes
1 onion, chopped in large pieces or thick rings
2 zucchini, sliced ¼″ thick
4 egg whites
2 eggs or egg substitute
1¼ cups skim milk
2 cups grated part skim mozzarella
Vegetable coating spray

Dip tomatoes briefly in boiling water to loosen skin then plunge into cold water. Skin, deseed, chop and set aside. Saute onions in broth until clear. Add zucchini and cook 4–5 minutes. Remove from heat. Beat eggs and egg whites until foamy. Add tomato, onions, zucchini and milk. Mix thoroughly. Mix in cheese and stir thoroughly. Spray 9-inch round or square baking dish with vegetable coating spray. Pour into prepared dish and bake at 350° until firm in center and lightly browned.

Servings: 8

Trisha Shirey

NUTRIENT VALUES					
PROTEIN 37%	CARBOHYDRATE 21%		FAT 42%		ALCOHOL 0%
CALORIES 135.0	PRO-GM 12.50	CARB-GM 7.105		FAT-GM 6.318	SOD-MG 200.0
FOOD EXCHANGES					
MILK 0.2	VEG. 0.7	FRUIT 0.0	BREAD 0.0	MEAT 1.4	FAT 0.6

BREAKFAST TACO

2 egg whites
1 tablespoon skim milk
2 tablespoons chopped onion
2 tablespoons red or chopped green pepper
½ teaspoon cumin
1 whole wheat flour torilla
Bottled picante sauce or pico de gallo (1–2 tablespoons) See pg. 65

Saute onion, pepper and cumin in nonstick pan coated with vegetable coating spray. Beat egg whites and milk in blender for one minute. Add to skillet, stirring to mix with vegetables. Cook until eggs are set. Place in warm whole wheat tortilla and roll up. Add picante or pico de gallo to taste.

Servings: 1

NUTRIENT VALUES					
PROTEIN 28%	CARBOHYDRATE 55%		FAT 17%		ALCOHOL 0%
CALORIES 141.5	PRO-GM 10.19	CARB-GM 19.93		FAT-GM 2.743	SOD-MG 488.7
FOOD EXCHANGES					
MILK 0.0	VEG. 0.5	FRUIT 0.0	BREAD 1.0	MEAT 1.0	FAT 0.5

HUEVAS CON PAPAS

1 tablespoon safflower oil
½ onion, sliced
1 pound potatoes, unpeeled and finely sliced
½ cup water
1 egg
6 egg whites
Black pepper to taste
½ teaspoon minced, fresh thyme or ¼ teaspoon dried
1 teaspoon minced fresh basil or ½ teaspoon dried

Heat the oil in a cast iron or nonstick skillet. Saute the onion and potatoes for about 5 minutes until lightly browned, stirring occasionally. Stir in water, cover, and cook on low heat for 10 minutes or until potatoes are tender. Sprinkle with pepper, thyme and basil. Beat eggs together in a blender for one minute. Pour eggs over potatoes, pat down firmly, cover and cook until set (5–10 minutes). Brown under the broiler and cut into 4 pieces and serve. Serve with picante or fresh pico de gallo.

Servings: 4

NUTRIENT VALUES			
PROTEIN	CARBOHYDRATE	FAT	ALCOHOL
23%	46%	30%	0%
CALORIES	PRO-GM	CARB-GM	FAT-GM	SOD-MG
146.0	8.567	16.90	4.931	95.20

FOOD EXCHANGES					
MILK	VEG.	FRUIT	BREAD	MEAT	FAT
0.0	0.3	0.0	0.9	0.9	0.8

MIGAS

¼ cup chopped green onions
2 corn tortillas, cut into 1-inch squares
½ cup vegetable stock
1 tomato, chopped
2 ounces chopped green chiles
2 whole eggs or egg substitute
4 egg whites
¼ teaspoon black pepper

Saute onions and tortillas in stock until onions are tender. Add tomato and heat. Beat eggs and egg whites slightly. Add eggs, pepper, and chiles to skillet. Continue to cook, stirring until mixture is evenly cooked. Add pepper.

Servings: 2

NUTRIENT VALUES			
PROTEIN	CARBOHYDRATE	FAT	ALCOHOL
31%	39%	30%	0%
CALORIES	PRO-GM	CARB-GM	FAT-GM	SOD-MG
204.0	16.00	20.00	6.907	228.0
FOOD EXCHANGES					
MILK	VEG.	FRUIT	BREAD	MEAT	FAT
0.0	0.8	0.0	0.8	1.8	0.8

SPANISH SCRAMBLED EGGS

Vegetable coating spray
1/4 cup chopped green pepper
1/4 cup chopped green onions
3 large eggs or egg substitute equivalent
4 egg whites
1/4 cup skim milk
1/8 teaspoon black pepper
1 tablespoon picante sauce
1/2 cup chopped tomato
1/4 cup grated cheddar cheese
Fresh parsley for garnish

Coat a heavy or nonstick skillet with vegetable coating spray. Place over medium heat, add green pepper and onion, cooking until tender and translucent. Set aside.

Combine eggs, milk, pepper and picante sauce, beat well and pour into skillet. Cook over low heat, stirring gently. Cook until eggs are set but still moist. Stir in green pepper, onion and tomato and heat. Sprinkle eggs with cheese and garnish with parsley.

Servings: 5

NUTRIENT VALUES			
PROTEIN 35%	CARBOHYDRATE 12%	FAT 52%	ALCOHOL 0%
CALORIES 96.00	PRO-GM 8.447	CARB-GM 2.968	FAT-GM 5.515	SOD-MG 146.0
FOOD EXCHANGES					
MILK 0.1	VEG. 0.2	FRUIT 0.0	BREAD 0.0	MEAT 1.1	FAT 0.6

EGGS WITH RICE

2 eggs
6 egg whites
1 cup cooked brown rice or wild rice, cold
1/4 cup skim milk
1 teaspoon Worcestershire
1 tablespoon Parmesan cheese
1/4 teaspoon oregano
Vegetable coating spray

Combine all ingredients except vegetable coating spray in a bowl; beat ingredients until well blended.

Coat a nonstick skillet with vegetable coating spray; place over medium heat. Pour in egg mixture. Cook until eggs are set but still moist.

Servings: 3

NUTRIENT VALUES			
PROTEIN 34%	CARBOHYDRATE 38%	FAT 28%	ALCOHOL 0%
CALORIES 163.0	PRO-GM 13.60	CARB-GM 15.00	FAT-GM 4.948	SOD-MG 212.0
FOOD EXCHANGES					
MILK 0.2	VEG. 0.0	FRUIT 0.0	BREAD 0.8	MEAT 1.7	FAT 0.3

VEGETABLE OMELET

1   cup chopped zucchini
½   cup chopped green
    onions
½   cup chopped tomatoes
¼   teaspoon black pepper
2   egg whites
2   whole eggs or egg
    substitute
2   tablespoons water
¼   teaspoon basil
¼   teaspoon celery salt
⅛   teaspoon black pepper
¼   cup shredded part-skim
    Swiss cheese
Vegetable coating spray

Coat a 6″ nonstick skillet with vegetable coating spray. Place over medium heat and add zucchini, onion and tomato. Saute until vegetables are tender. Stir in pepper. Remove vegetables from skillet and set aside. Wipe skillet dry with a paper towel.

Beat egg whites (room temperature) into stiff peaks. Set aside. Combine yolks, water, basil, celery salt and pepper. Beat until thick and lemon colored. Gently fold egg whites into yolk mixture.

Spread half of egg mixture into skillet. Cover, reduce heat and cook 4–5 minutes or until omelet is puffed and brown. Flip omelet and brown second side. Spoon half of the vegetable mixture over omelet. Fold in half. Sprinkle half of cheese over top of omelet. Repeat procedure for second serving. Serve immediately

Servings: 2

NUTRIENT VALUES			
PROTEIN	CARBOHYDRATE	FAT	ALCOHOL
33%	21%	45%	0%
CALORIES	PRO-GM	CARB-GM	FAT-GM	SOD-MG
169.0	14.20	9.197	8.631	124.0
FOOD EXCHANGES					
MILK	VEG.	FRUIT	BREAD	MEAT	FAT
0.5	0.8	0.0	0.0	1.5	1.0

SPINACH OMELET

1 **pound fresh spinach, cleaned and chopped**
¼ **cup chicken stock, defatted**
1 **clove garlic, minced**
¼ **cup grated Parmesan cheese**
2 **eggs or egg substitute**
4 **egg whites**
2 **tablespoons skim milk**
1 **tablespoon reduced-calorie margarine**
Vegetable coating spray

Combine spinach, stock and garlic in a small saucepan; cover and simmer for 10 minutes. Stir in Parmesan cheese; cook until cheese is melted, stirring constantly. Set aside.

Beat eggs and milk together. Spray a small nonstick skillet with vegetable coating spray. Place skillet over medium heat and melt 1 teaspoon margarine. Pour one-third of egg mixture into skillet. As mixture starts to cook, gently lift edges of omelet with a spatula and tilt pan so uncooked portion flows underneath.

When mixture is set, spread one-third of spinach mixture over half of omelet. Loosen omelet with a spatula; fold in half and slide onto a warm serving platter. Repeat procedure with remaining ingredients. Serve immediately.

Servings: 3

NUTRIENT VALUES				
PROTEIN	CARBOHYDRATE		FAT	ALCOHOL
38%	17%		45%	0%
CALORIES	PRO-GM	CARB-GM	FAT-GM	SOD-MG
170.0	17.00	7.531	8.967	438.0
FOOD EXCHANGES					
MILK	VEG.	FRUIT	BREAD	MEAT	FAT
0.0	1.5	0.0	0.2	1.7	0.8

EGG FOO YUNG

2   whole large eggs or egg
    substitute equivalent
6   egg whites
½   cup water
¼   cup chopped onions
½   cup fresh bean sprouts
½   cup fresh mushrooms,
    sliced
½   teaspoon black pepper
1   teaspoon low-sodium
    soy sauce
Vegetable coating spray

Beat eggs and water with an electric beater for about 4 minutes. Add onions, bean sprouts, mushrooms, pepper and soy sauce.

Spray nonstick skillet with vegetable coating spray and preheat pan. Pour in the egg mixture and turn the heat down. Cook about 3 minutes, turn and cook the other side about 3 minutes.

Servings: 4

NUTRIENT VALUES			
PROTEIN	CARBOHYDRATE	FAT	ALCOHOL
47%	15%	37%	0%
CALORIES	PRO-GM	CARB-GM	FAT-GM	SOD-MG
74.40	8.724	2.778	3.056	196.0
FOOD EXCHANGES					
MILK	VEG.	FRUIT	BREAD	MEAT	FAT
0.0	0.4	0.0	0.0	1.4	0.3

BROCCOLI FRITTATA

½ cup chopped onion
¼ cup vegetable stock
1 cup skim milk
2 tablespoons chopped fresh basil
1 teaspoon low-sodium soy sauce
4 egg whites, beaten
2 large eggs, beaten or equivalent egg substitute
¼ cup grated Parmesan cheese, divided
3 cups chopped fresh broccoli, steamed
Vegetable coating spray

Saute onion in stock until tender. Add milk, basil and soy sauce and heat. Add a small amount of hot mixture to beaten eggs in bowl, stirring constantly. Add remaining hot milk mixture, cooked broccoli and half of the Parmesan cheese. Mix well. Spray an 8" round baking dish with vegetable coating spray. Pour in egg mixture and sprinkle with remaining cheese. Bake at 350° for 30 minutes or until set.

Servings: 4

NUTRIENT VALUES					
PROTEIN 39%	CARBOHYDRATE 27%		FAT 34%		ALCOHOL 0%
CALORIES 136.0	PRO-GM 13.60	CARB-GM 9.453	FAT-GM 5.284		SOD-MG 338.0
FOOD EXCHANGES					
MILK 0.3	VEG. 1.0	FRUIT 0.0	BREAD 0.1	MEAT 1.3	FAT 0.4

BREAKFAST SUNDAE

6 tablespoons raisins
6 tablespoons water
½ teaspoon almond extract
3 bananas
3 oranges
3 cups lowfat cottage cheese

Combine raisins, water and extract. Cover and let stand overnight. In the morning, bring mixture to a boil. Reduce heat, cover and let simmer 10 minutes. For each serving, place ½ cup cottage cheese on serving plate. Divide sliced fruit evenly among servings: ½ orange and ½ banana per serving. Spoon hot raisin mixture over each.

Servings: 6

NUTRIENT VALUES					
PROTEIN 30%	CARBOHYDRATE 63%		FAT 7%		ALCOHOL 0%
CALORIES 195.0	PRO-GM 15.50	CARB-GM 31.90	FAT-GM 1.557		SOD-MG 461.0
FOOD EXCHANGES					
MILK 0.0	VEG. 0.0	FRUIT 2.1	BREAD 0.0	MEAT 1.8	FAT 0.0

SPINACH LINGUINE

12 ounces linguine, cooked according to package directions
½ cup vegetable stock
4 garlic cloves, minced
1 10-ounce package frozen chopped spinach, cooked
⅓ cup Parmesan cheese, grated
1½ teaspoons dried basil or 1 tablespoon fresh
½ teaspoon black pepper

Saute garlic in stock in large saucepan over medium heat for 2 minutes. Add cooked spinach, basil, and pepper. Cook for several minutes over low heat until heated through. Remove from heat. Mix cooked linguine, spinach mixture and Parmesan until well mixed. Serve warm.

Servings: 6 (1 cup serving)

NUTRIENT VALUES					
PROTEIN	CARBOHYDRATE			FAT	ALCOHOL
17%	74%			9%	0%
CALORIES	PRO-GM	CARB-GM		FAT-GM	SOD-MG
281.0	11.90	51.40		2.912	144.0
FOOD EXCHANGES					
MILK	VEG.	FRUIT	BREAD	MEAT	FAT
0.0	0.6	0.0	3.3	0.3	0.1

FETTUCCINI

5 ounces whole wheat fettuccini or linguini
1½ tablespoons reduced-calorie margarine
½ cup skim evaporated milk
¼ cup grated Parmesan cheese
¼ teaspoon black pepper
⅛ teaspoon nutmeg

Cook fettuccini according to package directions, drain. Melt butter in small saucepan. Add evaporated milk and heat just until hot. (Do not boil.) Place cooked fettuccini in serving bowl. Add milk and half of Parmesan cheese; toss until pasta is coated. Continue tossing pasta, gradually adding the pepper, nutmeg and remaining cheese. Serve immediately.

Servings: 3 (¾ cup each)

NUTRIENT VALUES					
PROTEIN	CARBOHYDRATE			FAT	ALCOHOL
18%	62%			20%	0%
CALORIES	PRO-GM	CARB-GM		FAT-GM	SOD-MG
295.0	13.10	43.80		6.301	280.0
FOOD EXCHANGES					
MILK	VEG.	FRUIT	BREAD	MEAT	FAT
0.3	0.0	0.0	2.7	0.5	0.7

FETTUCCINI WITH CHEESE SAUCE

4   ounces fettucini noodles
½   cup part-skim ricotta
2   tablespoons lowfat
    buttermilk
1   tablespoon grated
    Parmesan cheese
1   tablespoon chopped
    fresh basil leaves

Heat 2 quarts cold water in a large saucepan. Bring to a boil over high heat. Add the fettuccini and cook until the pasta is *al dente*. Drain the pasta in a colander. Mix the ricotta, milk, Parmesan cheese and basil in a saucepan and stir for 5 minutes over low heat. When warm and smooth, remove from heat and toss with the fettuccini noodles. Serve immediately.

Servings: 2 (1 cup serving)

NUTRIENT VALUES			
PROTEIN	CARBOHYDRATE	FAT	ALCOHOL
18%	67%	14%	0%
CALORIES	PRO-GM	CARB-GM	FAT-GM	SOD-MG
302.0	13.30	49.00	4.634	127.0
FOOD EXCHANGES					
MILK	VEG.	FRUIT	BREAD	MEAT	FAT
0.0	0.0	0.0	3.0	1.0	0.3

PASTA CANNELLONI

8   ounces shell pasta,
    eggless
½   cup vegetable stock
1   clove garlic, minced
½   cup chopped green
    pepper
1   cup chopped celery
1   cup chopped onion
½   cup chopped red pepper
1   teaspoon black pepper
2   tablespoons chopped
    fresh parsley
8   ounces tomato sauce, low
    sodium
1½ cups cannelloni beans or
    other white beans,
    cooked
1   cup water

Cook pasta according to package directions. Saute garlic, green and red pepper, onion and celery in stock until soft or tender. Add tomato sauce, water and seasonings. Cook on low for 15 minutes. Add beans and stir. Drain pasta, mix pasta and bean mixture. Toss well.

Servings: 6 (generous 1 cup serving)

NUTRIENT VALUES					
PROTEIN	CARBOHYDRATE		FAT	ALCOHOL	
18%	78%		4%	0%	
CALORIES	PRO-GM	CARB-GM	FAT-GM	SOD-MG	
231.0	11.00	48.00	1.152	31.80	
FOOD EXCHANGES					
MILK	VEG.	FRUIT	BREAD	MEAT	FAT
0.0	0.5	0.0	3.1	0.0	0.0

PASTA MARCO POLO

¼ cup chopped black olives
2 cloves garlic, chopped
3 tablespoons grated Parmesan cheese
½ cup evaporated skim milk
3 tablespoons fresh chopped parsley
1 teaspoon dried basil or 2 teaspoons fresh
1 teaspoon dried oregano or 2 teaspoons fresh
¼ teaspoon dried thyme or ½ teaspoon fresh
¼ teaspoon dried rosemary or ½ teaspoon fresh
¼ teaspoon black pepper
2 teaspoons olive oil
8 ounces fettuccini, cooked

Mix all ingredients except the pasta in a large bowl and set aside. Cook fettuccini according to package directions. Drain pasta. Toss pasta with cheese mixture. Serve hot.

Servings: 4 (1 cup serving)

NUTRIENT VALUES					
PROTEIN	CARBOHYDRATE		FAT		ALCOHOL
15%	63%		22%		0%
CALORIES	PRO-GM	CARB-GM		FAT-GM	SOD-MG
334.0	12.40	51.60		8.046	229.0
FOOD EXCHANGES					
MILK	VEG.	FRUIT	BREAD	MEAT	FAT
0.3	0.0	0.0	3.1	0.3	1.1

PASTA WITH TOMATOES AND BASIL

8	Roma tomatoes, quartered
4	cloves garlic, minced
1	green pepper, seeded and sliced into thin strips
20	leaves fresh basil, torn into large pieces
1	tablespoon vegetable oil or olive oil
1	tablespoon basil/red wine vinegar
¼	teaspoon freshly ground black pepper

Combine the first seven ingredients and let marinate at room temperature for at least 1 hour.

1	pound whole wheat pasta
¾	cup grated part-skim mozzarella
2	tablespoons grated Parmesan cheese

Cook pasta until done; drain and toss with mozzarella. Add tomato mixture and mix well. Place on serving plates and top with Parmesan cheese.

Servings: 8 (1 cup serving)

Trisha Shirey

NUTRIENT VALUES			
PROTEIN	CARBOHYDRATE	FAT	ALCOHOL
16%	68%	16%	0%
CALORIES	PRO-GM	CARB-GM	FAT-GM	SOD-MG
307.0	12.10	51.20	5.210	98.40

FOOD EXCHANGES					
MILK	VEG.	FRUIT	BREAD	MEAT	FAT
0.0	0.6	0.0	3.1	0.4	0.4

PASTA PRIMAVERA

8 ounces whole wheat
   fettuccini, cooked
   according to package
   directions
½ cup chopped onion
½ cup chopped green
   pepper
½ cup chopped red pepper
1 cup sliced fresh
   mushrooms
2 cloves garlic, minced
¼ cup evaporated skim
   milk
¼ cup grated Parmesan
   cheese
1½ teaspoons reduced-
   calorie margarine
1 egg white, beaten lightly
1 teaspoon olive oil
1 teaspoon crushed red
   pepper
1 teaspoon minced fresh
   oregano or ½ teaspoon
   dried

Saute onion, peppers, mushrooms, and garlic in ½ cup water over low heat until soft (about 10 minutes). Put sauteed vegetables in a large bowl, mix with olive oil. Add cooked pasta, margarine, milk, cheese, egg white, red pepper, and oregano.

Servings: 5 (generous 1 cup serving)

NUTRIENT VALUES			
PROTEIN	CARBOHYDRATE	FAT	ALCOHOL
17%	68%	15%	0%
CALORIES	PRO-GM	CARB-GM	FAT-GM	SOD-MG
255.0	10.70	42.10	4.117	142.0

FOOD EXCHANGES					
MILK	VEG.	FRUIT	BREAD	MEAT	FAT
0.1	0.5	0.0	2.6	0.4	0.4

GREEN PASTA SALAD

9 ounces dried spinach spaghetti
8 cups water
4 tablespoons reduced-calorie mayonnaise
4 tablespoons nonfat yogurt
2 garlic cloves, minced
3 tablespoons white wine vinegar
½ teaspoon saffron
10 asparagus spears (1 cup)
2 medium-size zucchini, sliced thin (2 cups)
¼ pound snow peas
¼ pound mushrooms, sliced
1 cup cherry tomatoes, halved
¼ cup parsley, minced (or 2 teaspoons dried)
¼ cup basil, minced (or 2 teaspoons dried)

Break the spaghetti in half. Cook the spaghetti in 8 cups of boiling water until tender (about 10 minutes). Drain and set aside.

Whisk together the mayonnaise, yogurt, garlic, vinegar and saffron. Add to the cooked spaghetti and mix.

Clean the asparagus and cut each spear into 1-inch pieces. Steam these pieces until tender crisp. Add to spaghetti.

Stir in zucchini, snow peas, mushrooms, cherry tomatoes, parsley and basil and toss.

Serve at room temperature.

Servings: 6

NUTRIENT VALUES			
PROTEIN	CARBOHYDRATE	FAT	ALCOHOL
15%	68%	18%	0%
CALORIES	PRO-GM	CARB-GM	FAT-GM	SOD-MG
254.0	9.195	42.90	5.028	109.0
FOOD EXCHANGES					
MILK	VEG.	FRUIT	BREAD	MEAT	FAT
0.1	1.3	0.0	2.3	0.0	0.8

PEKING PASTA SALAD

8 ounces pasta twirls
3 cups diced broccoli
 flowerets
1 cup diced sweet red
 pepper
1 cup diced asparagus tips
8 ounces snow peas
½ cup water
½ teaspoon hot red pepper
 flakes
2 tablespoons low-sodium
 soy sauce
1 teaspoon grated fresh
 ginger
2 cloves garlic, minced

Cook linguini "al dente" according to package directions. Drain and set aside. Saute the next 4 ingredients in water until tender crisp. Toss the cooked pasta, sautéed vegetables, and remaining ingredients.

Servings: 6 (1⅓ cup serving)

NUTRIENT VALUES			
PROTEIN	CARBOHYDRATE	FAT	ALCOHOL
19%	76%	5%	0%
CALORIES	PRO-GM	CARB-GM	FAT-GM	SOD-MG
195.0	9.895	39.10	1.146	359.0
FOOD EXCHANGES					
MILK	VEG.	FRUIT	BREAD	MEAT	FAT
0.0	1.5	0.0	2.2	0.0	0.0

PASTA PIGNOLIA SALAD

12 ounces mixed pasta
   twists
4 large, firm, ripe tomatoes
2 garlic cloves, minced
12 fresh basil leaves,
   chopped or 4 teaspoons
   dried basil
1 small red onion, finely
   chopped
1 red bell pepper,
   julienned
¼ cup pine nuts (pignolias)
1 tablespoon olive oil
6 tablespoons Parmesan
   cheese
¼ cup basil/garlic vinegar
   or white wine vinegar

Cook the pasta al dente in a large pot of boiling water. (8-10 minutes)

Meanwhile, cut tomatoes in small wedges. Mix the garlic, basil, onion, pepper, pine nuts, oil and vinegar in a medium bowl.

Toss cooked pasta with vegetables. Chill before serving. Sprinkle each serving with 1 tablespoon Parmesan.

Servings: 8 (1½ cups serving)

NUTRIENT VALUES			
PROTEIN	CARBOHYDRATE	FAT	ALCOHOL
16%	62%	22%	0%
CALORIES	PRO-GM	CARB-GM	FAT-GM	SOD-MG
254.0	10.70	41.00	6.395	95.20
FOOD EXCHANGES					
MILK	VEG.	FRUIT	BREAD	MEAT	FAT
0.0	0.8	0.0	2.4	0.4	0.9

PEA AND PASTA SALAD

1   pound vegetable or
    whole wheat fettuccini,
    cooked al dente
¾   cup skim milk
¼   teaspoon nutmeg
¾   cup lowfat cottage
    cheese
1   cup grated skim-milk
    Swiss Cheese
1   cup cooked green peas
¼   pound snow peas,
    steamed until tender
3   tablespoons grated
    Parmesan cheese
2   tablespoons chopped
    fresh parsley

Heat the milk until scalded. Add nutmeg, cottage cheese and Swiss Cheese and stir over low heat until cheese is melted. Drain pasta and add peas, cheese sauce, parsley and Parmesan. Toss gently and serve.

Servings: 8 (1 cup serving)

Trisha Shirey

NUTRIENT VALUES			
PROTEIN	CARBOHYDRATE	FAT	ALCOHOL
21%	67%	13%	0%
CALORIES	PRO-GM	CARB-GM	FAT-GM	SOD-MG
347.0	17.40	56.40	4.753	172.0
FOOD EXCHANGES					
MILK	VEG.	FRUIT	BREAD	MEAT	FAT
0.5	0.2	0.0	3.3	0.4	0.5

SESAME PASTA SALAD

8 ounces dry eggless pasta shells
½ cup broccoli flowerets
¼ cup green pepper, julienned
½ red pepper, julienned
2 tablespoons chopped green onion
¼ cup sliced water chestnuts

DRESSING:
4 teaspoons tahini
1 teaspoon sesame oil
¼ cup chicken stock, defatted
2 tablespons white wine vinegar
1 tablespoon low-sodium soy sauce
1½ teaspoons toasted sesame seeds

Cook the pasta in boiling water until al dente. Drain, rinse, and set aside. Steam the broccoli until tender crisp.

Combine all ingredients for the dressing except the sesame seeds in a blender. Process until smooth. Toss the dressing with the pasta, vegetables, and sesame seeds. Chill.

Servings: 4 (1 cup serving)

NUTRIENT VALUES			
PROTEIN	CARBOHYDRATE	FAT	ALCOHOL
15%	68%	17%	0%
CALORIES	PRO-GM	CARB-GM	FAT-GM	SOD-MG
293.0	11.50	51.30	5.749	267.0
FOOD EXCHANGES					
MILK	VEG.	FRUIT	BREAD	MEAT	FAT
0.0	0.5	0.0	3.3	0.1	1.0

Specialties from the Sea . . .

FISH

CHEESY FLOUNDER FILLETS

1½ pounds flounder fillets
⅓ cup yogurt cheese
2 teaspoons cornstarch
2 tablespoons grated Parmesan cheese
2 tablespoons fresh parsley, chopped
¼ cup minced onion
1 tablespoon fresh lemon juice
1 tablespoon fresh dill or 1 teaspoon dried (or use tarragon or marjoram)
Vegetable coating spray

Arrange fillets in a 13 × 9 baking pan sprayed with vegetable coating spray. Combine remaining ingredients, spread mixture evenly over fillets. Bake at 350° for 15 minutes or until fish flakes easily. If desired, place under broiler for 1–2 minutes until cheese mixture begins to brown.

Servings: 4

NUTRIENT VALUES				
PROTEIN 72%	CARBOHYDRATE 14%		FAT 14%	ALCOHOL 0%
CALORIES 158.0	PRO-GM 27.20	CARB-GM 5.306	FAT-GM 2.296	SOD-MG 256.0
FOOD EXCHANGES					
MILK 0.3	VEG. 0.1	FRUIT 0.0	BREAD 0.1	MEAT 2.6	FAT 0.0

DILL-ALMOND BAKED FISH

2 egg whites, beaten until foamy
2 tablespoons skim milk
1½ pounds flounder or white fish
¼ cup wheat germ
2 tablespoons ground almonds
¼ cup freshly grated Parmesan cheese
⅓ cup wheat bran
1 teaspoon fresh chopped dill or ½ teaspoon dried
Vegetable coating spray

Combine egg whites and milk in a shallow bowl. Mix bran, almonds, wheat germ, Parmesan and dill in a shallow pan. Dip fish in egg and milk and then in dry mix. Place the fish on shallow baking pan that has been sprayed with vegetable coating spray. Bake at 350° for 8–10 minutes or until fish flakes easily. Broil for 1 minute to brown. Garnish with dill, lemon and parsley.

Servings: 6

NUTRIENT VALUES				
PROTEIN 56%	CARBOHYDRATE 19%		FAT 25%	ALCOHOL 0%
CALORIES 150.0	PRO-GM 21.90	CARB-GM 7.445	FAT-GM 4.281	SOD-MG 211.0
FOOD EXCHANGES					
MILK 0.0	VEG. 0.0	FRUIT 0.0	BREAD 0.5	MEAT 2.3	FAT 0.6

"FRIED SNAPPER"

¼ cup evaporated skim milk
3 garlic cloves, mashed
1 teaspoon oregano
1 teaspoon lemon juice
2 (4–5 ounce) snapper fillets
¼ cup whole wheat breadcrumbs
1½ tablespoons grated Parmesan cheese

Combine milk, garlic, oregano and lemon and marinate fish in mixture 10–20 minutes per side. Combine crumbs and cheese and press fish fillets in mixture until well coated on each side. Place fish in non-stick baking dish and pour remaining milk mixture over top.

Bake at 450° 12–15 minutes or until fish flakes easily.

Servings: 2

Ellen McCullough

NUTRIENT VALUES					
PROTEIN 68%	CARBOHYDRATE 17%		FAT 14%		ALCOHOL 0%
CALORIES 202.0	PRO-GM 33.20	CARB-GM 8.470		FAT-GM 3.060	SOD-MG 261.0
FOOD EXCHANGES					
MILK 0.3	VEG. 0.0	FRUIT 0.0	BREAD 0.3	MEAT 3.3	FAT 0.0

SOUTHERN BAKED CATFISH

⅓ cup stoneground yellow cornmeal
¼ teaspoon freshly ground black pepper
2 tablespoons evaporated skim milk
2 tablespoons Dijon mustard
4 (5–6 ounce) catfish fillets
2 teaspoons olive oil

Heat oven to 425°. Coat a nonstick baking sheet with oil. Mix cornmeal and pepper in a shallow pan. Mix milk and mustard in a shallow bowl. Dip catfish in milk mixture then cornmeal and bake 10 minutes turning once or until fish flakes easily. Place under broiler 1–2 minutes to brown. Serve with Cocktail Sauce, pg. 70

Servings: 4

NUTRIENT VALUES					
PROTEIN 57%	CARBOHYDRATE 16%		FAT 27%		ALCOHOL 0%
CALORIES 253.0	PRO-GM 35.10	CARB-GM 9.870		FAT-GM 7.266	SOD-MG 107.0
FOOD EXCHANGES					
MILK 0.1	VEG. 0.0	FRUIT 0.0	BREAD 0.5	MEAT 3.9	FAT 0.5

MEXICAN BAKED FISH

1 **pound haddock fillet or other white fish**
1 **firm ripe tomato, chopped**
8 **black olives, sliced**
½ **onion, chopped**
2 **tablespoons fresh lime juice**
1 **tablespoon fresh cilantro, minced**
½ **to 1 teaspoon chopped jalapeno (canned or fresh)**
Vegetable coating spray

Preheat oven to 425°. Place fillets in shallow baking dish that has been sprayed with vegetable coating spray. Mix remaining ingredients and top each fillet. Bake 15–20 minutes or until fish flakes easily with a fork.

Servings: 4

NUTRIENT VALUES			
PROTEIN	CARBOHYDRATE	FAT	ALCOHOL
75%	12%	13%	0%
CALORIES	PRO-GM	CARB-GM	FAT-GM	SOD-MG
119.0	23.10	3.709	1.764	41.60

FOOD EXCHANGES					
MILK	VEG.	FRUIT	BREAD	MEAT	FAT
0.0	0.5	0.0	0.0	2.3	0.3

PESCADO MEXICANO

4 (6-ounce) fillets of sole or flounder
⅓ cup lime juice, fresh
2 green onions with tops, chopped finely
1 8-ounce can whole peeled green chiles, drained
Vegetable coating spray
½ cup chopped onions
2 cloves garlic, minced
¼ teaspoon dried oregano or ½ teaspoon fresh
⅛ teaspoon crushed whole allspice
2 bay leaves
¼ teaspoon ground coriander
⅛ teaspoon cinnamon
¼ cup orange juice
¼ cup nonfat yogurt
⅓ cup Parmesan cheese
½ teaspoon paprika
½ teaspoon black pepper
1 cup tomato sauce

Place fish fillets in shallow baking dish that has been sprayed with vegetable coating spray. Sprinkle fish fillets on both sides with fresh lime juice. Sprinkle fillets with the green onions. Cut the green chiles into long green strips (2"). Place the strips lengthwise on each fillet. Set aside. Spray nonstick skillet with coating spray and saute onions and garlic until translucent over low heat. Add oregano, allspice, bay leaves, coriander, cinnamon, tomato sauce and orange juice; simmer 10 minutes. Spread approximately 1 tablespoon yogurt on each fillet. Top with warm tomato sauce mixture. Sprinkle with Parmesan, paprika and pepper. Bake in 375° oven for 15–20 minutes or until fish flakes easily. Do not overcook. Garnish with lettuce leaf, orange slice and sprinkle with paprika.

Servings: 4

NUTRIENT VALUES			
PROTEIN 58%	CARBOHYDRATE 25%	FAT 17%	ALCOHOL 0%
CALORIES 212.0	PRO-GM 30.00	CARB-GM 13.10	FAT-GM 3.886	SOD-MG 355.0

FOOD EXCHANGES					
MILK 0.1	VEG. 0.6	FRUIT 0.1	BREAD 0.5	MEAT 2.9	FAT 0.1

RED SNAPPER VERACRUZANO

4 (5 ounce) snapper fillets
1 tablespoon lime juice
2 shallots, minced
1 garlic clove, minced
¼ cup dry white wine
4 canned tomatoes, drained and chopped
3 tablespoons fresh chopped cilantro
1 tablespoon fresh chopped oregano or 1½ teaspoon dried
1 tablespoon fresh chopped thyme or 1½ teaspoon dried
1 teaspoon Tabasco sauce

Spray a baking dish with vegetable coating spray and place fillets in dish. Sprinkle with lime juice. Saute minced shallots and garlic in white wine. Add tomatoes and Tabasco and cook five minutes. Add herbs. Pour tomato mixture over fish and cover. Place in a preheated 350° oven and bake 20–25 minutes. Use lime slices and fresh cilantro for garnish.

Servings: 4

NUTRIENT VALUES					
PROTEIN 78%	CARBOHYDRATE 13%		FAT 9%		ALCOHOL 0%
CALORIES 153.0	PRO-GM 29.00	CARB-GM 4.842	FAT-GM 1.531		SOD-MG 200.0
FOOD EXCHANGES					
MILK 0.0	VEG. 0.5	FRUIT 0.0	BREAD 0.0	MEAT 2.9	FAT 0.0

DILLED SALMON STEAKS

4 (6 ounce) salmon steaks
1 teaspoon safflower oil
2 tablespoons fresh lemon juice
2 tablespoons minced fresh dill or 1 tablespoon dried dill

Preheat oven to broil. Mix oil, lemon and dill and let stand 15 minutes. Dip salmon in oil and lemon mix and place on broiler rack and cook about 10 minutes. Turn and brush with more lemon and oil mixture. Cook another 10 minutes or until fish flakes and is browned. Garnish with additional dill if desired.

Servings: 4

NUTRIENT VALUES					
PROTEIN 57%	CARBOHYDRATE 5%		FAT 38%		ALCOHOL 0%
CALORIES 326.0	PRO-GM 46.40	CARB-GM 3.881	FAT-GM 13.80		SOD-MG 200.0
FOOD EXCHANGES					
MILK 0.0	VEG. 0.0	FRUIT 0.0	BREAD 0.0	MEAT 6.1	FAT 0.3

STUFFED FLOUNDER

¼ cup chicken stock, defatted

½ pound fresh mushrooms, thinly sliced

1 cup celery, finely chopped

2 slices whole wheat bread, toasted

¼ cup chicken stock, defatted

2 tablespoons fresh parsley, minced

2 tablespoons minced onion

1 teaspoon poultry seasoning

1 teaspoon chopped fresh lemon thyme

¼ teaspoon pepper

4 flounder or sole fillets (about 1½ pounds)

2 teaspoons lemon juice

Vegetable coating spray

Saute mushrooms, celery and ¼ cup chicken stock in nonstick skillet 10 minutes or until vegetables are tender and liquid is evaporated.

Crumble bread in a medium bowl; add sauteed vegetables, remaining stock, parsley, onion, seasonings and pepper. Arrange 2 fillets in an 8 × 10 baking dish coated with vegetable coating spray. Top with stuffing mixture; cover with remaining 2 fillets.

Sprinkle lemon juice evenly over fillets; bake, uncovered at 350° for 25–30 minutes or until fillets flake easily with a fork.

Servings: 4

NUTRIENT VALUES				
PROTEIN	CARBOHYDRATE		FAT	ALCOHOL
63%	25%		12%	0%
CALORIES	PRO-GM	CARB-GM	FAT-GM	SOD-MG
171.0	26.80	10.50	2.226	279.0
FOOD EXCHANGES					
MILK	VEG.	FRUIT	BREAD	MEAT	FAT
0.0	0.8	0.0	0.5	2.5	0.1

MOM'S FISH CASSEROLE

1½ pounds white fish fillets
  (bass, flounder, haddock)
1   small onion, diced
½   cup diced green pepper
8   ounces mushrooms,
    sliced
1   10-ounce can low-
    sodium mushroom soup
2   tablespoons dry white
    wine
1   teaspoon tarragon or
    Mexican marigold mint
Vegetable coating spray

Saute onion, pepper and mushrooms in wine over low heat until limp. Stir in undiluted soup and tarragon. Pour over fish fillets in an 8 × 8 glass baking dish that has been sprayed with vegetable coating spray. Bake uncovered at 400° for 30 minutes until golden brown and bubbling.

Servings: 6

Trisha Shirey

NUTRIENT VALUES			
PROTEIN	CARBOHYDRATE	FAT	ALCOHOL
58%	20%	22%	0%
CALORIES	PRO-GM	CARB-GM	FAT-GM	SOD-MG
186.0	26.30	9.250	4.350	473.0

FOOD EXCHANGES					
MILK	VEG.	FRUIT	BREAD	MEAT	FAT
0.0	1.3	0.0	0.1	2.5	0.5

SALMON-DILL LOAF

1 7½-ounce can salmon, drained, boned, and flaked
2 cups soft, whole wheat bread crumbs (3 slices)
3 egg whites and 1 yolk, beaten
⅓ cup skim milk
½ cup chopped onion
1 tablespoon minced fresh parsley
1 teaspoon minced fresh dill or ½ teaspoon dry
6 chopped black olives
¼ teaspoon freshly ground black pepper
2 tablespoons lemon juice
¼ teaspoon dry mustard
Vegetable coating spray

Preheat oven to 400°. Spray a 4 × 8 loaf pan with vegetable coating spray. Mix all ingredients in a large bowl and then place in loaf pan. Bake for 30 minutes. Serve hot with dill sauce on pg. 78.

Servings: 4

Trisha Shirey

NUTRIENT VALUES					
PROTEIN 38%		CARBOHYDRATE 28%		FAT 34%	ALCOHOL 0%
CALORIES 175.0	PRO-GM 16.70		CARB-GM 12.20	FAT-GM 6.638	SOD-MG 478.0
FOOD EXCHANGES					
MILK 0.1	VEG. 0.3	FRUIT 0.0	BREAD 0.6	MEAT 1.9	FAT 0.5

CHEESY BAKED TUNA & ARTICHOKE HEARTS

1   4½-ounce can mushrooms, sliced and drained
1   green onion, chopped
1   6½-ounce can water packed tuna, drained
1   8½-ounce can artichoke hearts, diced
2   tablespoons reduced-calorie margarine
2   tablespoons unbleached white flour
1   cup skim milk
1   teaspoon low-sodium soy sauce
¼   teaspoon fresh ground white pepper
¼   cup plus 2 tablespoons freshly grated Parmesan cheese
Vegetable coating spray

Preheat oven to 375°. Spray an 8-inch square pan with vegetable coating spray. Combine mushrooms, onion, tuna and artichoke and place in pan. Melt margarine in a small saucepan until bubbling. Reduce heat and add flour, stirring constantly with a wire whisk. Cook flour one minute than add milk gradually, continually stirring until smooth, thick and bubbling. Remove from heat, add ¼ cup cheese, soy sauce and pepper and mix well. Pour over tuna mix and top with two tablespoons Parmesan. Bake uncovered 20 minutes until golden brown.

Servings: 6

Trisha Shirey

NUTRIENT VALUES					
PROTEIN	CARBOHYDRATE		FAT		ALCOHOL
43%	24%		34%		0%
CALORIES	PRO-GM	CARB-GM		FAT-GM	SOD-MG
126.0	13.80	7.618		4.801	251.0
FOOD EXCHANGES					
MILK	VEG.	FRUIT	BREAD	MEAT	FAT
0.2	0.6	0.0	0.3	1.3	0.5

LEMON-BROILED SCALLOPS

12 ounces scallops
1½ teaspoons reduced-
    calorie margarine,
    melted
2 tablespoons fresh lemon
    juice
¼ teaspoon dried savory or
    ½ teaspoon fresh
¼ teaspoon dried basil or
    ½ teaspoon fresh

Preheat broiler. Place scallops in a shallow baking dish. Combine remaining ingredients. Baste scallops with half of this mixture. Broil three inches from heat for five minutes. Turn scallops. Baste with remaining sauce and broil five minutes or until done.

Serve with fresh steamed vegetables.

Servings: 2

NUTRIENT VALUES			
PROTEIN	CARBOHYDRATE	FAT	ALCOHOL
75%	9%	16%	0%
CALORIES	PRO-GM	CARB-GM	FAT-GM	SOD-MG
208.0	39.60	4.606	3.827	483.0

FOOD EXCHANGES					
MILK	VEG.	FRUIT	BREAD	MEAT	FAT
0.0	0.0	0.0	0.0	4.5	0.3

CRAB CAKES/TUNA CAKES

6½–7 ounces crab meat or
    water-packed tuna,
    drained
6 whole grain crackers,
    finely crushed
¼ cup minced red bell
    pepper
2 tablespoons fresh,
    minced parsley
2 tablespoons minced
    onions
1 egg white
2 teaspoons reduced-
    calorie mayonnaise
1½ teaspoon lemon juice
1 teaspoon Worcestershire
⅛ teaspoon ground red
    pepper
1–2 teaspoons minced fresh
    basil
½ teaspoon marjoram
1 clove garlic, minced
Vegetable coating spray

Preheat oven to 375°. Spray nonstick baking sheet with vegetable coating spray. In large bowl, gently mix all ingredients, being careful not to break up lumps of crab meat. Using scant ¼ cup mixture for each, make 6 cakes. Shape mixture into circle, pressing flat. Place on prepared baking sheet. Bake 20–25 minutes or until golden brown.

Servings: 2 (3 cakes each)

NUTRIENT VALUES				
PROTEIN	CARBOHYDRATE		FAT	ALCOHOL
52%	23%		25%	0%
CALORIES	PRO-GM	CARB-GM	FAT-GM	SOD-MG
53.30	6.682	2.948	1.451	183.0

FOOD EXCHANGES					
MILK	VEG.	FRUIT	BREAD	MEAT	FAT
0.0	0.1	0.0	0.0	0.8	0.1

SHRIMP CREOLE

1   8-ounce can tomato sauce (low sodium)
4   ounces sliced, fresh mushrooms
½   cup dry white wine
½   chopped onion
2   cloves garlic, minced
½   cup chopped green pepper
½   cup chopped celery
2   bay leaves
¼   teaspoon Louisiana hot sauce
1   pound medium shrimp, peeled and deveined

In a large, heavy skillet, saute onion, garlic, mushrooms, celery, pepper in white wine for 3–4 minutes. Add tomato sauce, pepper sauce and bay leaves. Cover and bring to a boil, then simmer 10 minutes. Add shrimp and cook uncovered for 3–4 minutes until shrimp is done. Remove bay leaves and serve over rice.

Servings: 4 (1 cup serving)

Trisha Shirey

NUTRIENT VALUES						
PROTEIN 66%		CARBOHYDRATE 26%		FAT 8%		ALCOHOL 0%
CALORIES 179.0	PRO-GM 29.60		CARB-GM 11.70		FAT-GM 1.567	SOD-MG 30.30
FOOD EXCHANGES						
MILK 0.0	VEG. 1.6	FRUIT 0.0		BREAD 0.0	MEAT 3.0	FAT 0.0

SHRIMP AND SNOW PEAS

¾   pound shrimp, deveined, cut into thirds
1½ teaspoons vegetable oil
½   pound fresh snow peas
¼   cup green onions with tops, diced
2   tablespoons dry sherry
2   tablespoons soy sauce
1½ teaspoons brown sugar
½   teaspoon white pepper

Heat a nonstick skillet, add oil and shrimp. Cook over medium heat for five minutes. Add snow peas, onions, sherry, soy sauce, sugar and pepper. Cook, stirring constantly for 3–4 minutes.

Servings: 3

NUTRIENT VALUES						
PROTEIN 62%		CARBOHYDRATE 22%		FAT 17%		ALCOHOL 0%
CALORIES 204.0	PRO-GM 30.80		CARB-GM 10.80		FAT-GM 3.686	SOD-MG 690.0
FOOD EXCHANGES						
MILK 0.0	VEG. 1.2	FRUIT 0.0		BREAD 0.3	MEAT 3.0	FAT 0.5

SHRIMP VEGETABLE STIR FRY

1	pound shrimp, peeled and deveined
1	teaspoon baking soda
1	egg white
1½	teaspoons cornstarch
1	teaspoon grated ginger
2	green onions, trimmed and cut into 2-inch lengths
1	tablespoon peanut oil
1	tablespoon dry sherry or wine vinegar
8	ounces snow peas
8	ounces fresh mushrooms, sliced
1	red bell pepper, thinly sliced
2	cups broccoli florets

Rinse shrimp well after peeling and deveining. Add soda to shrimp and stir to mix. Let stand for 30 minutes. Rinse shrimp well in cold water to remove soda. Pat dry on paper towels or cloth. Mix egg white and cornstarch and beat. Add shrimp and gently coat. Refrigerate for 30 minutes. Combine ginger and onions and set aside. In a wok or cast iron skillet, heat the oil. When hot add the shrimp and cook for 2–3 minutes or until pink. Add green onions and ginger and cook for one additional minute. Remove shrimp and set aside. Add snow peas, mushrooms, bell pepper, and broccoli to wok. Cook 6–8 minutes, stirring constantly until tender crisp. Add shrimp back to wok with sherry and cook 1–2 minutes until heated through. Serve immediately over brown rice.

Servings: 4

NUTRIENT VALUES			
PROTEIN	CARBOHYDRATE	FAT	ALCOHOL
58%	22%	21%	0%
CALORIES	PRO-GM	CARB-GM	FAT-GM	SOD-MG
225.0	32.70	12.40	5.214	235.0
FOOD EXCHANGES					
MILK	VEG.	FRUIT	BREAD	MEAT	FAT
0.0	2.1	0.0	0.0	3.1	0.6

SHRIMP AND ASPARAGUS SALAD

1   **small red pepper**
2   **ounces watercress,**
    washed and dried
1   **teaspoon olive oil**
1   **teaspoon fresh minced**
    dill or ½ teaspoon dried
1   **teaspoon freshly ground**
    black pepper
16 **asparagus spears,**
    steamed
1   **tablespoon reduced-**
    calorie margarine
12 **medium raw shrimp,**
    (about 8 ounces), shelled,
    cut crosswise into thirds
½   **cup reserved asparagus**
    cooking liquid
2   **teaspoons fresh lemon**
    juice

Roast the red pepper by holding over gas flame on kitchen fork, turning to char the skin. Or roast pepper under broiler until charred. Put the charred pepper into a plastic food storage bag and put in the freezer until cool enough to handle, about 15 minutes. Peel off and discard the charred skin. Core and seed the pepper and cut into ½-inch pieces, set aside.

Toss the watercress with 1 teaspoon olive oil, dill and pepper and divide among three serving plates.

Cut the asparagus spears into ½-inch pieces, set aside.

Melt half the butter in a nonstick skillet over medium high heat. Add the shrimp and stir-fry until just cooked through, about one minute. Add the pepper and the asparagus and cook, stirring, until the vegetables are hot, about one minute more.

Divide the mixture over the watercress on the serving plates, set aside.

Add the asparagus cooking liquid to the skillet and reduce to half. Stir in the remaining butter. Remove from heat and stir in the lemon juice. Pour sauce over each salad and serve.

Servings: 3

NUTRIENT VALUES			
PROTEIN	CARBOHYDRATE	FAT	ALCOHOL
54%	21%	26%	0%
CALORIES	PRO-GM	CARB-GM	FAT-GM	SOD-MG
159.0	22.20	8.530	4.758	57.40
FOOD EXCHANGES					
MILK	VEG.	FRUIT	BREAD	MEAT	FAT
0.0	1.7	0.0	0.0	2.0	0.7

TUNA RICE SALAD

1 9¼-ounce can water packed tuna, drained
1 stalk celery, chopped
3 green onions, chopped
1 chili pepper, seeded and chopped
1 clove garlic, minced
1 tablespoon lemon juice
½ teaspoon celery seed
1 tablespoon low-sodium soy sauce
2 tablespoons apple juice concentrate, undiluted
1 teaspoon dried basil (or 2 teaspoons, if fresh)
1 cup frozen peas, thawed
1 8-ounce can water chestnuts, chopped
2 large carrots, grated
2 cups cooked brown rice, cold
¼ teaspoon finely grated peeled ginger
2 tablespoons minced fresh parsley

Mix all ingredients together in a large bowl and chill for several hours.

Servings: 7 (1 cup serving)

Variation: Omit pepper and ginger and add 2 tablespoons finely minced fresh mint leaves.

Trisha Shirey

NUTRIENT VALUES			
PROTEIN	CARBOHYDRATE	FAT	ALCOHOL
34%	61%	5%	0%
CALORIES	PRO-GM	CARB-GM	FAT-GM	SOD-MG
149.0	12.70	22.90	0.766	309.0
FOOD EXCHANGES					
MILK	VEG.	FRUIT	BREAD	MEAT	FAT
0.0	0.9	0.0	1.0	1.0	0.0

TUNA SALAD NICOISE

4 ripe black olives
3 cups green beans,
   steamed
4 tomatoes, cut into sixths
2 cups sliced cucumbers
2 cups sliced mushrooms,
   steamed
8 ounces new potatoes,
   steamed and sliced
2 6½-ounce cans solid,
   water-packed tuna
8 cups chopped lettuce

MARINADE
2 teaspoons safflower oil
2 tablespoons cider
   vinegar
1 tablespoon chopped
   fresh parsley
1 tablespoon chopped
   fresh chives
3 tablespoons lemon juice
¼ cup water
½ teaspoon chopped fresh
   oregano
½ cup lowfat buttermilk

Mix marinade in large bowl. Add green beans and mushrooms. Refrigerate for 2–4 hours. Drain and reserve marinade for dressing. Arrange vegetables and tuna on top of lettuce on serving plate. Divide remaining marinade and pour over beans, tomato, cucumber, mushrooms and potatoes.

Servings: 4

NUTRIENT VALUES					
PROTEIN	CARBOHYDRATE		FAT		ALCOHOL
40%	45%		15%		0%
CALORIES	PRO-GM	CARB-GM		FAT-GM	SOD-MG
291.0	31.40	35.00		5.219	398.0
FOOD EXCHANGES					
MILK	VEG.	FRUIT	BREAD	MEAT	FAT
0.1	3.5	0.1	0.9	2.5	0.6

CREOLE SEAFOOD GUMBO

½ teaspoon reduced-calorie margarine
½ cup chopped onion
1   clove garlic, minced
½ pound fresh shrimp, peeled and deveined
½ cup sliced celery
½ cup chopped green pepper
¼ cup uncooked brown rice
3½ cups water
10 ounces tomatoes, canned, undrained, chopped, no salt added
2   tablespoons wheat flour
⅛ teaspoon pepper
½ teaspoon Worcestershire sauce
½ pound white fish, cut in 1-inch chunks
5   ounces frozen, sliced okra
2   ounces pimiento, drained
½ teaspoon gumbo filé

Melt margarine over low heat, add onion and garlic; saute until tender. Add celery, green pepper, rice and water. Bring to a boil. Reduce heat; simmer uncovered for 30–35 minutes. Stir in tomatoes. Combine flour and pepper, add ½ cup liquid from gumbo and Worcestershire and mix well. Stir into gumbo. Cook over medium heat until mixture begins to thicken. Add fish, shrimp, okra and pimiento and add gumbo filé. Cook until fish is white and firm (about 10 minutes).

Servings: 7 (1 cup serving)

NUTRIENT VALUES				
PROTEIN 49%	CARBOHYDRATE 42%		FAT 9%	ALCOHOL 0%
CALORIES 116.0	PRO-GM 14.20	CARB-GM 12.30	FAT-GM 1.097	SOD-MG 114.0
FOOD EXCHANGES					
MILK 0.0	VEG. 0.8	FRUIT 0.0	BREAD 0.4	MEAT 1.4	FAT 0.1

FISH STEW

1 stalk celery, diced
1 carrot, diced
1 leek, white part only
2 green onions, chopped
1 tablespoon olive oil
2 cloves garlic, minced
½ teaspoon basil, dried
½ teaspoon oregano, dried
1 can tomato puree (20 ounces)
1 cup clam juice
½ cup dry white wine
2 bay leaves
½ teaspoon freshly ground black pepper
8 ounces bay scallops
12 ounces white fish fillets cut into 1-inch pieces
½ teaspoon grated zest of lemon peel
2 teaspoons minced parsley
8 ounces cooked crab meat torn into large pieces

In a large, heavy soup kettle, saute first four ingredients in oil, until onions are clear. Add garlic, basil, oregano, tomato puree, clam juice, wine and bay leaves. Bring to a boil and simmer 20 minutes. Add scallops, fish and lemon peel and simmer 10 minutes more. Fish should flake easily with a fork. Add crab and parsley and cook until heated through.

Servings: 4 (1½ cup serving)

Trisha Shirey

NUTRIENT VALUES					
PROTEIN	CARBOHYDRATE			FAT	ALCOHOL
49%	33%			18%	0%
CALORIES	PRO-GM	CARB-GM		FAT-GM	SOD-MG
291.0	36.50	24.90		5.827	436.0
FOOD EXCHANGES					
MILK	VEG.	FRUIT	BREAD	MEAT	FAT
0.0	3.5	0.0	0.0	3.5	0.6

TUNA CREOLE

½ cup chopped onion
½ cup chopped green
   pepper
½ cup vegetable stock
1 16-ounce can tomatoes,
   chopped
¼ teaspoon thyme or ½
   teaspoon minced lemon
   thyme
⅛ teaspoon cayenne pepper
¼ teaspoon gumbo filé
½ teaspoon black pepper
2 6½-ounce cans water-
   packed tuna, drained
5¼ cups hot cooked brown
   rice

Saute onions and green pepper in stock until tender, approximately 5 minutes. Stir in tomatoes, thyme, filé, cayenne, and black pepper. Simmer 5 minutes. Stir in tuna to break up, then cover and simmer 5 minutes. Serve over hot rice, using ¾ cup cooked brown rice per serving.

Servings: 7 (½ cup creole over ¾ cup rice)

NUTRIENT VALUES				
PROTEIN	CARBOHYDRATE		FAT	ALCOHOL
29%	66%		6%	0%
CALORIES	PRO-GM	CARB-GM	FAT-GM	SOD-MG
252.0	18.10	41.70	1.604	290.0
FOOD EXCHANGES					
MILK	VEG.	FRUIT	BREAD	MEAT	FAT
0.0	0.8	0.0	2.4	1.4	0.0

CRAB MANICOTTI

8 ounces manicotti shells
6 ounces crab meat, canned (undrained)
1½ cups part-skim ricotta cheese
½ cup nonfat yogurt
2 teaspoons cornstarch
2 tablespoons minced parsley
2 tablespoons grated onion
1 clove garlic, minced
1 teaspoon fresh minced oregano or ½ teaspoon dried
1½ cups sliced mushrooms
16 ounces tomato sauce
1 teaspoon sugar
1½ cups water
½ teaspoon dried basil or 1 teaspoon fresh minced
½ teaspoon dried oregano or 1 teaspoon fresh minced
1 clove garlic, minced
⅛ teaspoon dried thyme or ½ teaspoon fresh
Vegetable coating spray

Cook manicotti shells according to package directions. Drain. Combine crab, ricotta cheese, yogurt, cornstarch, parsley, onion, garlic, oregano, and mushrooms. Mix well. Fill manicotti with crab mixture and place in 13 × 9 baking dish that has been sprayed with vegetable coating spray. Combine remaining ingredients in a medium saucepan. Cook over medium heat for five minutes. Pour over filled shells and bake at 350° for 30 minutes or until heated.

Servings: 6 (2 shells per serving)

NUTRIENT VALUES					
PROTEIN	CARBOHYDRATE		FAT		ALCOHOL
24%	58%		18%		0%
CALORIES	PRO-GM	CARB-GM		FAT-GM	SOD-MG
330.0	20.20	47.80		6.587	249.0
FOOD EXCHANGES					
MILK	VEG.	FRUIT	BREAD	MEAT	FAT
0.1	1.7	0.0	2.2	1.8	0.5

LINGUINE WITH CLAM SAUCE

8 ounces dry linguine, cooked as directed on package
1 tablespoon olive oil
2 garlic cloves, minced
3 shallots, chopped
2 tablespoons cooking sherry
2 tablespoons Parmesan cheese
1 6½-ounce can minced clams, undrained
½ teaspoon dried oregano
¼ teaspoon white pepper
2 tablespoons fresh, chopped parsley

In a large skillet, heat oil over medium heat. Add garlic and shallots. Saute several minutes. Add clams, oregano and pepper. Mix well. Reduce heat. Simmer uncovered five minutes. Remove from heat. Add parsley, sherry and Parmesan and mix well. Place drained pasta in sauce. Toss well.

Servings: 4

NUTRIENT VALUES			
PROTEIN	CARBOHYDRATE	FAT	ALCOHOL
17%	64%	17%	2%
CALORIES	PRO-GM	CARB-GM	FAT-GM	SOD-MG
325.0	13.40	51.50	6.032	84.40
FOOD EXCHANGES					
MILK	VEG.	FRUIT	BREAD	MEAT	FAT
0.0	0.0	0.0	3.3	0.6	0.6

SALMON PASTA SALAD

1 **pound fresh salmon steaks or fillets**
½ **pound medium pasta shells (dry, eggless)**
2 **cups diced celery**
1 **14-ounce can hearts of palm, drained and sliced**
1 **14-ounce can artichoke hearts, drained and quartered**
⅓ **cup reduced-calorie mayonnaise**
¾ **cup nonfat yogurt**
2 **teaspoons dill weed**
½ **teaspoon white pepper**
Vegetable coating spray

Place salmon in a shallow nonstick baking dish that has been sprayed with vegetable coating spray. Bake at 325° for 15–20 minutes until the fish is thoroughly cooked and flakes easily. Set aside to cool. Boil pasta in water until tender. Drain, rinse in cool water and set aside. Mix mayonnaise and nonfat yogurt with dillweed and pepper. Add celery, hearts of palm, artichokes and drained pasta. Remove skin and bones from salmon, flake into chunks and mix with pasta. Chill until ready to serve.

Servings: 8 (1 cup serving)

NUTRIENT VALUES				
PROTEIN	CARBOHYDRATE		FAT	ALCOHOL
31%	45%		24%	0%
CALORIES	PRO-GM	CARB-GM	FAT-GM	SOD-MG
284.0	22.40	32.20	7.815	108.0
FOOD EXCHANGES					
MILK	VEG.	FRUIT	BREAD	MEAT	FAT
0.1	0.8	0.0	1.6	2.1	0.7

TUNA STUFFED POTATOES

4 large, hot baked potatoes
½ cup hot skim milk
2 green onions, minced
   (green tops included)
1 egg or egg substitute
1 egg white
1 tablespoon reduced-
   calorie margarine
½ teaspoon salt
1 teaspoon black pepper
1 cup diced tomato
1 7-ounce can water-
   packed tuna
2 tablespoons Parmesan
   cheese, grated

Cut a thin slice off the top of each baked potato, scoop out potato and combine with hot milk, green onions, beaten eggs and margarine. Whip well. Add salt, pepper and gently stir in tomato and tuna. Fill potato skins with this mixture—mounding it high. Sprinkle with Parmesan cheese. Place on baking sheet and cook at 400° for 10–15 minutes.

Servings: 4

Ellen McCullough

NUTRIENT VALUES					
PROTEIN 33%	CARBOHYDRATE 51%		FAT 16%		ALCOHOL 0%
CALORIES 255.0	PRO-GM 21.50	CARB-GM 33.00		FAT-GM 4.525	SOD-MG 557.0
FOOD EXCHANGES					
MILK 0.1	VEG. 0.3	FRUIT 0.0	BREAD 1.9	MEAT 1.9	FAT 0.4

OVEN FRIED FISH

20 ounces white fish fillets
    (4 5-ounce pieces)
½   cup lowfat buttermilk
½   cup melba toast crumbs
2   tablespoons minced
    fresh parsley
1   teaspoon paprika
Vegetable coating spray

Put buttermilk in a shallow bowl. Mix crumbs, parsley, and paprika and put in a shallow bowl. Dip fish fillets in buttermilk, then in crumb mixture. Place on a baking sheet that has been sprayed with vegetable coating spray. Bake at 450° for 12 minutes or until fish flakes easily.

Servings: 4

NUTRIENT VALUES					
PROTEIN 63%	CARBOHYDRATE 25%		FAT 12%		ALCOHOL 0%
CALORIES 149.0	PRO-GM 22.30	CARB-GM 8.806		FAT-GM 1.948	SOD-MG 180.0
FOOD EXCHANGES					
MILK 0.1	VEG. 0.0	FRUIT 0.0	BREAD 0.5	MEAT 2.1	FAT 0.1

SEAFOOD QUICHE

2 eggs or egg substitute
4 egg whites, beaten well
6 ounces shrimp, precooked
6 ounces crab meat
2 chopped green onions
10–12 medium mushrooms, sliced thinly (approximately 4 ounces)
1¼ cups evaporated skim milk
2 cups grated part-skim mozzarella or Swiss cheese
Vegetable coating spray

Mix all ingredients and pour into a 9-inch pan sprayed with vegetable coating spray. Bake at 350° 30–40 minutes until firm and lightly browned.

Servings: 8

Trisha Shirey

NUTRIENT VALUES					
PROTEIN 50%	CARBOHYDRATE 15%		FAT 35%	ALCOHOL 0%	
CALORIES 183.0	PRO-GM 22.20	CARB-GM 6.556	FAT-GM 6.819	SOD-MG 330.0	
FOOD EXCHANGES					
MILK 0.4	VEG. 0.1	FRUIT 0.0	BREAD 0.0	MEAT 2.4	FAT 0.6

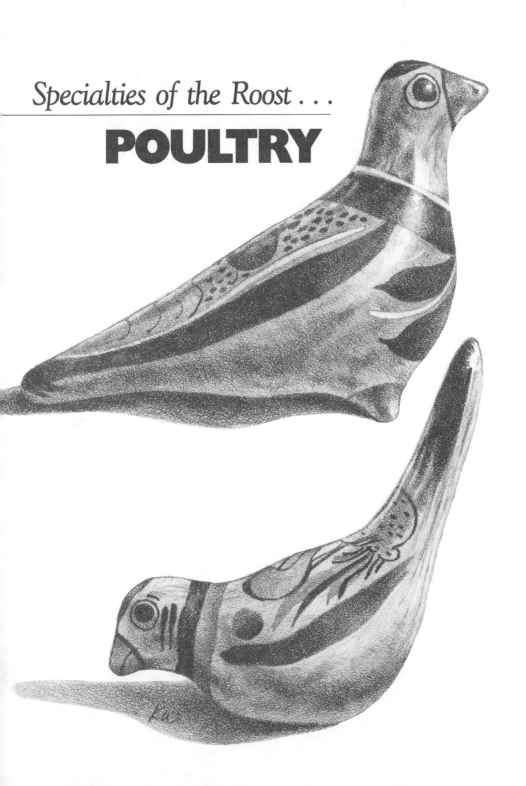

Specialties of the Roost . . .

POULTRY

CHICKEN PARMESAN

2½ slices whole wheat bread
    made into crumbs
2   tablespoons Parmesan
    cheese
2   tablespoons fresh
    chopped parsley
1   clove garlic, minced
2   tablespoons reduced-
    calorie margarine
3   chicken breast halves,
    skinned
Vegetable coating spray

Spray a 9 × 11 inch baking dish with vegetable coating spray. In a bowl, mix bread crumbs, cheese, parsley, and garlic. Melt margarine in a separate bowl.

Dip chicken breasts in margarine, then in bread crumb mixture. Place in baking dish sprayed with vegetable coating spray. Bake uncovered 45–55 minutes or until done.

Servings: 3

NUTRIENT VALUES					
PROTEIN	CARBOHYDRATE		FAT		ALCOHOL
45%	17%		38%		0%
CALORIES	PRO-GM	CARB-GM		FAT-GM	SOD-MG
261.0	29.60	11.30		11.20	298.0
FOOD EXCHANGES					
MILK	VEG.	FRUIT	BREAD	MEAT	FAT
0.0	0.0	0.0	0.7	2.3	3.2

HONEY CRUNCH CHICKEN

4   chicken breast halves,
    skinned
2   tablespoons reduced-
    calorie mayonnaise
2   tablespoons nonfat
    yogurt
1½ ounces Grape-Nuts
    cereal, crushed
1   tablespoon honey

Wash chicken and pat dry. Place in a shallow baking pan. Mix mayonnaise and yogurt together. Using a pastry brush, spread mayonnaise mixture over both sides of chicken. Process cereal in a blender or food processor. Sprinkle crushed cereal evenly over top side of chicken. Drizzle evenly with honey. Preheat oven to 350°, bake uncovered 40–45 minutes.

Servings: 4

NUTRIENT VALUES					
PROTEIN	CARBOHYDRATE		FAT		ALCOHOL
47%	26%		27%		0%
CALORIES	PRO-GM	CARB-GM		FAT-GM	SOD-MG
231.0	27.30	15.20		7.043	79.10
FOOD EXCHANGES					
MILK	VEG.	FRUIT	BREAD	MEAT	FAT
0.0	0.0	0.0	0.8	2.1	2.6

MEXICAN OVEN-FRIED CHICKEN

4   chicken breast halves, skinned
1   cup Snap-E-Tom or spiced tomato juice
½   cup crushed corn flakes cereal or wheat flakes
¼   cup wheat bran
½   teaspoon dried oregano
½   teaspoon ground cumin
½   teaspoon chili powder
½   teaspoon paprika
¼   teaspoon dried minced onion
¼   teaspoon garlic powder
Vegetable coating spray

Combine chicken and Snap-E-Tom mix in a large bowl; cover chicken and refrigerate six hours or overnight.

Combine next eight ingredients. Drain chicken, and dredge in cereal mixture. Place chicken breasts in a baking pan covered with coating spray. Bake at 350° for 50 to 60 minutes or until done.

Servings: 4

NUTRIENT VALUES				
PROTEIN	CARBOHYDRATE		FAT	ALCOHOL
52%	25%		23%	0%
CALORIES	PRO-GM	CARB-GM	FAT-GM	SOD-MG
206.0	28.10	13.40	5.556	398.0
FOOD EXCHANGES					
MILK	VEG.	FRUIT	BREAD	MEAT	FAT
0.0	0.4	0.0	0.6	2.1	2.3

OVEN FRIED CHICKEN

½ cup low-calorie Italian
    dressing (can use skim
    milk)
4   chicken breast halves,
    skinned
½ cup cornflakes, crushed
½ cup wheat bran
2   tablespoons Parmesan
    cheese

Clean and skin chicken breasts. Mix corn-flakes, bran and Parmesan together. Set aside. Dip chicken in low-calorie Italian dressing or skim milk. Then dip in cornflake mixture, turning to coat evenly. Place coated chicken onto nonstick baking pan. Bake at 350° for 35–45 minutes or until browned.

Servings: 4

If you prefer moister chicken, marinate chicken in lowfat buttermilk 2–3 hours before coating and baking.

NUTRIENT VALUES				
PROTEIN	CARBOHYDRATE		FAT	ALCOHOL
46%	22%		33%	0%
CALORIES	PRO-GM	CARB-GM	FAT-GM	SOD-MG
240.0	29.70	14.20	9.446	329.0
FOOD EXCHANGES					
MILK	VEG.	FRUIT	BREAD	MEAT	FAT
0.0	0.0	0.0	0.8	2.3	3.1

OVEN-FRIED SESAME CHICKEN

3   tablespoons sesame
    seeds
3   tablespoons whole wheat
    flour
¼ teaspoon pepper
4   chicken breast halves,
    skinned
2   tablespoons soy sauce
2   tablespoons reduced-
    calorie margarine,
    melted

Combine sesame seeds, flour, and pepper. Dip chicken pieces into soy sauce; dredge in sesame seed mixture, covering completely.

Arrange chicken in a large shallow baking dish; drizzle margarine over chicken. Bake uncovered at 350° for 40 to 45 minutes or until chicken is tender.

Servings: 4

NUTRIENT VALUES				
PROTEIN	CARBOHYDRATE		FAT	ALCOHOL
47%	11%		42%	0%
CALORIES	PRO-GM	CARB-GM	FAT-GM	SOD-MG
240.0	28.70	6.723	11.20	582.0
FOOD EXCHANGES					
MILK	VEG.	FRUIT	BREAD	MEAT	FAT
0.0	0.0	0.0	0.4	2.1	3.9

PARMESAN OVEN-FRIED CHICKEN

⅓ cup wheat bran
½ cup whole wheat breadcrumbs
⅓ cup grated Parmesan cheese
2 tablespoons chopped fresh parsley
¼ teaspoon garlic powder
¼ teaspoon black pepper
4 chicken breast halves, skinned
¼ cup low-calorie Italian dressing (see p. 166)
Vegetable coating spray

Combine first six ingredients; set aside.

Dip chicken in salad dressing; dredge in breadcrumb mixture. Place chicken in a 13 × 9 × 2 inch baking pan sprayed with coating spray. Bake uncovered at 350° for 45 minutes or until tender.

Servings: 4

NUTRIENT VALUES			
PROTEIN	CARBOHYDRATE	FAT	ALCOHOL
49%	17%	34%	0%
CALORIES	PRO-GM	CARB-GM	FAT-GM	SOD-MG
245.0	31.50	11.30	9.769	312.0
FOOD EXCHANGES					
MILK	VEG.	FRUIT	BREAD	MEAT	FAT
0.0	0.0	0.0	0.8	2.5	2.9

CHICKEN AND ARTICHOKES

3   chicken breasts, halved, skinned
1   8-ounce can artichoke hearts, drained, liquid reserved
1   tablespoon cornstarch
1   cup water
½   cup dry white wine
2   packets chicken bouillon, low-sodium
½   pound fresh mushrooms, sliced
2   tablespoons fresh chopped parsley

Drain artichoke hearts and cut in half. Set aside. In a nonstick skillet, add reserved liquid and chicken. Cook 10 minutes on medium heat, turning once. Remove chicken and set aside. Add cornstarch, water, wine, and bouillon. Mix well. Simmer until slightly thickened, stirring constantly. Add chicken, artichoke heart halves and sliced mushrooms. Cover and simmer 30 minutes or until done. Serve chicken with remaining sauce. Sprinkle with parsley.

Servings: 3

NUTRIENT VALUES				
PROTEIN	CARBOHYDRATE		FAT	ALCOHOL
55%	22%		23%	0%
CALORIES	PRO-GM	CARB-GM	FAT-GM	SOD-MG
214.0	30.10	12.30	5.665	5.080
FOOD EXCHANGES				
MILK	VEG.	FRUIT	BREAD	MEAT	FAT
0.0	1.7	0.0	0.2	3.3	0.0

CHICKEN DIJON

2 boneless chicken breast halves, skinned
¼ teaspoon pepper
4 teaspoons reduced-calorie margarine, melted
1 tablespoon Dijon mustard
1 teaspoon dried parsley flakes
¼ teaspoon dried rosemary, crumbled
¼ teaspoon paprika
¼ teaspoon dried thyme
Vegetable coating spray

Preheat oven to 350°. Place chicken in a shallow baking pan that has been sprayed with vegetable coating spray. Combine remaining ingredients in a small bowl. Mix well and spread over chicken. Cover and bake 30 minutes. Remove cover, baste chicken and bake 15 minutes more or until done.

Servings: 2

NUTRIENT VALUES					
PROTEIN 53%	CARBOHYDRATE 4%		FAT 43%	ALCOHOL 0%	
CALORIES 200.0	PRO-GM 25.80	CARB-GM 1.799	FAT-GM 9.242	SOD-MG 185.0	
FOOD EXCHANGES					
MILK 0.0	VEG. 0.0	FRUIT 0.0	BREAD 0.0	MEAT 2.3	FAT 3.0

CHICKEN IN ORANGE SAUCE

4 chicken breast halves, skinned
⅔ cup fresh orange juice
2 tablespoons dry sherry
1 tablespoon minced fresh parsley
1½ teaspoons cornstarch
¾ teaspoon grated orange rind
Paprika

Place chicken in a shallow baking dish. Combine next 5 ingredients in a small saucepan; bring to a boil, stirring constantly.

Pour sauce over chicken; cover and bake at 350° for 30 minutes. Uncover and bake an additional 25 to 30 minutes or until chicken is done. Sprinkle with paprika and serve.

Servings: 4

NUTRIENT VALUES					
PROTEIN 60%	CARBOHYDRATE 14%		FAT 26%	ALCOHOL 0%	
CALORIES 174.0	PRO-GM 26.00	CARB-GM 6.283	FAT-GM 5.064	SOD-MG 1.399	
FOOD EXCHANGES					
MILK 0.0	VEG. 0.0	FRUIT 0.3	BREAD 0.0	MEAT 2.1	FAT 2.1

CHICKEN PIQUANT

4   chicken breast halves,
     skinned
½   cup white wine
¼   cup low sodium soy
     sauce
1   tablespoon vegetable oil
2   tablespoons water
½   clove garlic, minced
¾   teaspoon ginger
½   teaspoon oregano
1½ teaspoons brown sugar
½   cup sliced fresh
     mushrooms

Arrange chicken breasts in baking dish. Combine all other ingredients except mushrooms and pour over chicken. Cover and bake for 1 hour. Add mushrooms, cover, and cook additional 15 minutes.

Servings: 4

NUTRIENT VALUES			
PROTEIN	CARBOHYDRATE	FAT	ALCOHOL
53%	10%	37%	0%
CALORIES	PRO-GM	CARB-GM	FAT-GM	SOD-MG
205.0	27.50	5.247	8.486	1030
FOOD EXCHANGES					
MILK	VEG.	FRUIT	BREAD	MEAT	FAT
0.0	0.1	0.0	0.3	2.1	2.8

MARSALA-BAKED CHICKEN

½ teaspoon dried oregano
  or 2 teaspoons minced
  fresh
1 teaspoon minced lemon
  basil
¼ cup whole wheat
  breadcrumbs
2 tablespoons grated
  Parmesan cheese
1 tablespoon minced fresh
  parsley
¼ teaspoon paprika
4 chicken breast halves,
  skinned
Vegetable coating spray
2 tablespoons reduced-
  calorie margarine
⅓ cup Marsala wine

Combine first six ingredients. Dredge chicken in breadcrumb mixture.

Arrange chicken in a shallow baking pan covered with coating spray. Dot with margarine; cover and bake at 350° for 20 minutes. Pour wine over chicken. Cover and bake 10 minutes; uncover and bake 10 additional minutes.

Servings: 4

NUTRIENT VALUES				
PROTEIN	CARBOHYDRATE		FAT	ALCOHOL
54%	6%		40%	0%
CALORIES	PRO-GM	CARB-GM	FAT-GM	SOD-MG
202.0	27.30	2.913	9.124	144.0
FOOD EXCHANGES					
MILK	VEG.	FRUIT	BREAD	MEAT	FAT
0.0	0.0	0.0	0.1	2.3	2.8

ROSEMARY-BAKED CHICKEN

2 teaspoons dried whole rosemary, crushed
¼ teaspoon pepper
4 chicken breast halves, skinned
½ cup unsweetened pineapple juice
¼ teaspoon ground ginger
4 tablespoons minced chives
Paprika

Rub rosemary and pepper into the chicken breasts. Place in a baking dish. Combine pineapple juice and ginger; pour over chicken. Sprinkle with chives and paprika. Place fresh rosemary sprigs in baking dish if available.

Cover and bake at 350° for 30 minutes; remove cover and bake 25 to 30 minutes or until done.

Servings: 4

NUTRIENT VALUES					
PROTEIN 59%	CARBOHYDRATE 14%		FAT 27%	ALCOHOL 0%	
CALORIES 174.0	PRO-GM 25.90	CARB-GM 6.159	FAT-GM 5.146	SOD-MG 0.875	
FOOD EXCHANGES					
MILK 0.0	VEG. 0.0	FRUIT 0.3	BREAD 0.0	MEAT 3.3	FAT 0.0

SESAME BAKED CHICKEN

4 chicken breast halves
1 medium garlic clove
¼ cup low sodium soy sauce
2 tablespoons chicken broth, defatted
2 teaspoons sesame oil
1 teaspoon sugar
1 teaspoon plum sauce
Vegetable coating spray

Clean and deskin chicken breasts and place in baking dish that has been sprayed with vegetable coating spray. Place all remaining ingredients in a blender or food processor and blend until smooth.

Drizzle sesame sauce evenly over chicken breasts. Bake uncovered at 350° for 45–50 minutes or until chicken is done.

Servings: 4

NUTRIENT VALUES					
PROTEIN 57%	CARBOHYDRATE 8%		FAT 35%	ALCOHOL 0%	
CALORIES 191.0	PRO-GM 27.40	CARB-GM 3.963	FAT-GM 7.461	SOD-MG 1029	
FOOD EXCHANGES					
MILK 0.0	VEG. 0.0	FRUIT 0.0	BREAD 0.1	MEAT 2.1	FAT 2.6

WINE-BAKED CHICKEN BREASTS

4   chicken breast halves, skinned
½   pound fresh mushrooms, halved
½   cup dry white wine
3   tablespoons chopped fresh parsley
½   teaspoon dried tarragon
¼   teaspoon freshly ground pepper

Arrange chicken breasts, bone side down, in baking dish. Arrange mushrooms around chicken. Pour wine over chicken; sprinkle with parsley, tarragon and pepper. Cover and bake at 350° for 40 to 50 minutes or until done.

Servings: 4

NUTRIENT VALUES					
PROTEIN 62%	CARBOHYDRATE 11%		FAT 27%		ALCOHOL 0%
CALORIES 172.0	PRO-GM 27.20	CARB-GM 4.742		FAT-GM 5.278	SOD-MG 4.678
FOOD EXCHANGES					
MILK 0.0	VEG. 0.6	FRUIT 0.0	BREAD 0.0	MEAT 2.1	FAT 2.1

CHICKEN FLORENTINE

3   chicken breast halves, skinned
4   cups water
1   cup chicken broth, defatted
2   garlic cloves, minced
½   pound fresh spinach, washed and drained
1   slice whole wheat bread made into crumbs
2   tablespoons Parmesan cheese, grated
Vegetable coating spray

Simmer chicken breast halves in water for 35–45 minutes or until done. Add additional water if necessary.

Saute garlic in chicken broth for 5 minutes. Add spinach, cover and simmer additional 5 minutes or until spinach is limp. Spray 8" baking dish with vegetable coating spray. Place spinach in baking dish. Place chicken on top of spinach.

Mix bread crumbs and cheese. Sprinkle over chicken. Bake at 350° for 20 minutes or until brown.

Servings: 3

NUTRIENT VALUES					
PROTEIN 55%	CARBOHYDRATE 15%		FAT 29%		ALCOHOL 0%
CALORIES 218.0	PRO-GM 31.10	CARB-GM 8.643		FAT-GM 7.242	SOD-MG 192.0
FOOD EXCHANGES					
MILK 0.0	VEG. 0.7	FRUIT 0.0	BREAD 0.3	MEAT 2.3	FAT 2.2

CORNBREAD

1 cup cornmeal (I prefer yellow)
2/3 cup flour   1 tsp. baking soda
2/3 tsp. salt   1 cup buttermilk
1 egg   1/4 cup Wesson oil plux
                                        1 tsp.

Preheat oven to 400.
Put 1 tsp. Wesson oil in 7" skillet (cast iron)
Mix all ingredients into a batter. Place skillet on
burner and heat. Pour batter into skillet. Place
on middle shelf in oven. Bake for 35 or 40 minutes
(or until done) Will serve 6.

                              Dot Owens

CHICKEN CACCIATORE

1   16-ounce can whole
    tomatoes, undrained and
    chopped
4   ounces tomato sauce
8   ounces fresh mushrooms,
    cleaned and sliced
¼   cup chopped onion
2   cloves garlic, minced
2   tablespoons chopped
    green pepper
¼   teaspoon celery seed
1   bay leaf
1   teaspoon sugar
1   teaspoon dried whole
    oregano
½   teaspoon pepper
4   boneless chicken breast
    halves, skinned
2   cups hot cooked whole
    wheat spaghetti (4
    ounces dry)

Combine all ingredients except chicken and vermicelli in a 2–3 quart saucepan and bring to a boil. Add chicken; cover, reduce heat and simmer 30 minutes. Uncover and simmer an additional 30 minutes. Discard bay leaves; serve chicken and sauce over spaghetti.

Servings: 4

NUTRIENT VALUES			
PROTEIN	CARBOHYDRATE	FAT	ALCOHOL
39%	44%	17%	0%
CALORIES	PRO-GM	CARB-GM	FAT-GM	SOD-MG
332.0	32.70	37.00	6.213	200.0
FOOD EXCHANGES			-		
MILK	VEG.	FRUIT	BREAD	MEAT	FAT
0.0	1.6	0.0	1.6	2.1	2.1

CHICKEN JAMBALAYA

4 chicken breast halves, skinned
1 cup chicken broth, defatted
½ cup dry white wine
1 16-ounce can tomatoes, chopped
½ cup chopped onion
¼ cup chopped green pepper
2 tablespoons chopped fresh parsley
½ teaspoon dried basil
¼ teaspoon thyme
1 bay leaf
½ teaspoon black pepper
¾ cup raw long-grain brown rice
Vegetable coating spray

Combine broth, wine, tomatoes, onion, green pepper, parsley, basil, thyme, bay leaf and pepper in a large saucepan. Bring to a boil. Reduce heat and cover, simmer for 5 minutes. Remove from heat. Remove bay leaves and add rice. Spray a 13 × 9 inch baking dish with vegetable coating spray. Pour rice mixture into dish. Place chicken on top of mixture. Cover and bake 55–65 minutes at 350° or until done. Add water if rice is dry.

Servings: 4

NUTRIENT VALUES			
PROTEIN	CARBOHYDRATE	FAT	ALCOHOL
49%	28%	23%	0%
CALORIES	PRO-GM	CARB-GM	FAT-GM	SOD-MG
229.0	28.40	16.60	5.918	185.0
FOOD EXCHANGES					
MILK	VEG.	FRUIT	BREAD	MEAT	FAT
0.0	1.1	0.0	0.5	2.1	2.3

CHICKEN WITH GRAINS

1 medium onion, chopped
1 clove garlic, minced
2 stalks celery, chopped
1 teaspoon minced rosemary or oregano
3 tablespoons minced parsley
½ cup water
½ cup barley
3 cups chicken stock, defatted
4 chicken breast halves, skinned
2 tablespoons reduced-calorie margarine
8 ounce can stewed tomatoes, undrained

In a large saucepan, saute onion, garlic, celery, rosemary and parsley in water until tender. Add barley and saute 2 minutes more, stirring constantly. Add stock and bring to boil. Stir, cover and simmer for 40 minutes.

Brown chicken in margarine. Place barley mix in a baking dish; place chicken on top. Cover with tomatoes. Bake uncovered for 40 minutes at 350°.

Servings: 4

NUTRIENT VALUES			
PROTEIN	CARBOHYDRATE	FAT	ALCOHOL
36%	38%	26%	0%
CALORIES	PRO-GM	CARB-GM	FAT-GM	SOD-MG
333.0	30.90	32.40	10.00	347.00
FOOD EXCHANGES					
MILK	VEG.	FRUIT	BREAD	MEAT	FAT
0.0	1.4	0.0	1.3	2.1	3.6

CHICKEN KIEV

6 chicken breast halves, skinned and boned
3 tablespoons reduced-calorie margarine
1½ tablespoons dry chives
2 tablespoons minced fresh parsley
3 egg whites
1 tablespoon water
2 cups whole wheat bread crumbs—4 slices
⅓ cup whole wheat flour

Mix margarine, chives and parsley together in small bowl. Place in freezer for 15 minutes. Pound chicken breast halves flat with meat mallet. Place 1 tablespoon of mixture in center of each chicken breast. Fold and secure with a toothpick. In a small bowl, beat together egg whites and water. Dredge each chicken breast in flour, dip in egg mixture, dredge in bread crumbs. Place on nonstick cookie sheet. Bake uncovered 55–60 minutes or until done.

Servings: 6

NUTRIENT VALUES			
PROTEIN	CARBOHYDRATE	FAT	ALCOHOL
47%	22%	31%	0%
CALORIES	PRO-GM	CARB-GM	FAT-GM	SOD-MG
251.0	29.70	13.90	8.641	197.0

FOOD EXCHANGES					
MILK	VEG.	FRUIT	BREAD	MEAT	FAT
0.0	0.0	0.0	0.8	2.3	2.9

PESTO-STUFFED CHICKEN BREASTS

4 boneless chicken breast halves
Freshly ground pepper
1 clove garlic, minced
3 tablespoons basil pesto (see p. 66)
4 teaspoons Parmesan cheese, freshly grated
4 large sprigs fresh basil
Vegetable coating spray

Remove skin from chicken. Slightly flatten each chicken breast. Sprinkle with pepper and garlic. Then spread each breast with 2 teaspoons pesto and sprinkle with 1 teaspoon grated Parmesan.

Place the basil sprigs in the middle of each breast and roll up, starting with the wider end. Place them seam-side down in a baking dish, covered with vegetable coating spray. Top with the remaining pesto and bake for 30 minutes at 350°.

Servings: 4

NUTRIENT VALUES			
PROTEIN	CARBOHYDRATE	FAT	ALCOHOL
60%	5%	35%	0%
CALORIES	PRO-GM	CARB-GM	FAT-GM	SOD-MG
185.0	27.70	2.313	7.235	72.40

FOOD EXCHANGES					
MILK	VEG.	FRUIT	BREAD	MEAT	FAT
0.0	0.0	0.0	0.0	2.3	2.1

CHICKEN CROQUETTES

2 cups cooked chicken, chopped or shredded fine
1 cup chicken stock, defatted
½ cup chopped onion
½ teaspoon thyme
½ teaspoon marjoram
3 tablespoons flour
3 tablespoons fresh parsley, chopped
3 tablespoons skim milk
1 tablespoon Dijon mustard
¼ teaspoon black pepper
2 egg whites
¼ cup Parmesan cheese
3 tablespoons reduced-calorie margarine

Saute onion in chicken stock until tender, approximately 10 minutes. Add next 7 ingredients, stirring constantly until smooth. Remove from heat and add chicken, egg whites and Parmesan. Mix well. Place in freezer 20 minutes or until stiff. Shape into 12 patties. Brown patties in margarine in a nonstick skillet for 10–12 minutes or until browned.

Servings: 12

NUTRIENT VALUES			
PROTEIN	CARBOHYDRATE	FAT	ALCOHOL
49%	9%	42%	0%
CALORIES	PRO-GM	CARB-GM	FAT-GM	SOD-MG
113.0	13.30	2.531	5.080	125.0
FOOD EXCHANGES					
MILK	VEG.	FRUIT	BREAD	MEAT	FAT
0.0	0.1	0.0	0.1	1.6	0.3

CHICKEN AND DUMPLINGS

1   **chicken breast (whole, skinned)**
2   **quarts water**
½   **cup sliced carrots**
½   **cup sliced celery**
1   **cup chopped onion**
½   **teaspoon black pepper**
5   **whole wheat flour tortillas, quartered**
3   **tablespoons minced fresh parsley**

Place chicken, water, carrots, celery, and onions in a large saucepan. Bring to a boil, then reduce heat. Cover and simmer for one hour. Remove chicken and set aside to cool. When cool, remove chicken from bone and chop. Remove vegetables from broth and set aside. Chill broth and defat. Heat defatted broth, add chicken and vegetables. Bring to a boil, add pepper and parsley. Drop tortilla quarters into broth one at a time. Cover and cook 15 minutes.

Servings: 4 (1½ cup serving)

NUTRIENT VALUES			
PROTEIN 31%	CARBOHYDRATE 46%	FAT 23%	ALCOHOL 0%
CALORIES 208.0	PRO-GM 16.50	CARB-GM 24.10	FAT-GM 5.297	SOD-MG 223.0
FOOD EXCHANGES					
MILK 0.0	VEG. 0.8	FRUIT 0.0	BREAD 1.3	MEAT 1.2	FAT 1.9

TURKEY RICE CASSEROLE

1 tablespoon vegetable oil
1 medium onion, finely chopped
1 clove garlic, finely chopped
1 pound ground raw turkey
1 teaspoon dried oregano or 1 tablespoon chopped fresh
1 teaspoon dried basil or 1 tablespoon chopped fresh
½ teaspoon crushed red pepper flakes
1 celery stalk, finely chopped
1 16-ounce can tomatoes
1 8-ounce can tomato sauce
½ cup water
3 cups long grain brown rice, cold
1 cup lowfat cottage cheese
2 egg whites
6 ounces part-skim mozzarella cheese, grated
¼ cup freshly grated Parmesan

Heat the oil in a heavy or non-stick pan and saute the onion and garlic until tender but not browned. Add the turkey and cook, stirring, until all pink has disappeared.

Add oregano, basil, pepper flakes, celery, tomatoes, tomato sauce and water. Bring to a boil and simmer for 25 minutes.

Combine cottage cheese, egg whites and mozzarella. Set aside.

Mix turkey and tomato mixture. Layer in a 13 × 9 inch baking dish: turkey and tomato mixture, rice, cheese. Repeat for 2nd layer. Sprinkle with Parmesan and bake for 35 minutes at 350°. Freezes well.

Servings: 10

Double this recipe and freeze one casserole for an easy company dinner.

NUTRIENT VALUES					
PROTEIN	CARBOHYDRATE		FAT		ALCOHOL
26%	43%		30%		0%
CALORIES	PRO-GM	CARB-GM		FAT-GM	SOD-MG
165.0	10.90	17.80		5.551	313.0
FOOD EXCHANGES					
MILK	VEG.	FRUIT	BREAD	MEAT	FAT
0.0	0.6	0.0	0.9	1.2	0.6

STIR-FRIED CHICKEN WITH BROCCOLI

1 tablespoon low-sodium soy sauce
1 tablespoon cornstarch
3 tablespoons cold water
1 teaspoon sesame oil
¼ teaspoon sugar
1 whole boneless, chicken breast, skinned
3 cups broccoli florets, broken into bite-sized pieces
2 teaspoons fresh minced ginger
1 medium garlic clove, peeled and minced
¼ cup water

To make marinade, combine the soy sauce, cornstarch, cold water, sesame oil, and sugar. Set aside.

Cut the chicken breast in half lengthwise, then cut into thin strips. Put in a large bowl and pour in the marinade. Stir to coat the chicken and marinate, uncovered, at room temperature for 30 minutes.

Heat a wok or a large skillet over medium high heat. Add the chicken and marinade and stir-fry until the chicken turns white, about 2 minutes. Remove chicken and set aside. Add broccoli, ginger, and garlic and stir until tender crisp, about 2 minutes. Stir in chicken and water, cook 1 additional minute. Serve hot over brown rice.

Servings: 3 (1 cup stir-fry per serving)

NUTRIENT VALUES					
PROTEIN 50%		CARBOHYDRATE 22%		FAT 28%	ALCOHOL 0%
CALORIES 156.0	PRO-GM 20.40		CARB-GM 9.118	FAT-GM 5.161	SOD-MG 368.0
FOOD EXCHANGES					
MILK 0.0	VEG. 1.0	FRUIT 0.0	BREAD 0.2	MEAT 1.5	FAT 1.8

STIR-FRIED GINGER CHICKEN

2 skinless chicken breast halves, boned
1 tablespoon safflower oil
4 cups broccoli, separated into florets and sliced stems
8 ounces snow peas
1 cup chicken stock, defatted
1 tablespoon fresh grated ginger
2 cloves garlic, chopped
1 tablespoon cornstarch
3 tablespoons cold water
2 tablespoons soy sauce
1 tablespoon dry sherry
1 teaspoon sesame oil

Cut the chicken into 1-inch strips and stir-fry it in the oil in a wok or nonstick skillet for about 2 minutes over high heat. Remove chicken and set aside. Stir-fry the broccoli florets and snow peas until tender crisp. Remove and set aside. Add the chicken stock, ginger, and garlic to wok and bring to a boil. Cook for approximately 5 minutes. Combine the cornstarch with the cold water. Stir it into the chicken stock and boil the mixture until it has thickened. Add the soy sauce, sherry, sesame oil, chicken and vegetables to the sauce and heat through.

Serve with brown rice.

Servings: 4 (1 cup stir-fry per serving)

NUTRIENT VALUES					
PROTEIN	CARBOHYDRATE		FAT		ALCOHOL
36%	26%		34%		4%
CALORIES	PRO-GM	CARB-GM		FAT-GM	SOD-MG
193.0	18.40	13.40		7.549	542.0
FOOD EXCHANGES					
MILK	VEG.	FRUIT	BREAD	MEAT	FAT
0.0	2.0	0.0	0.3	1.1	2.0

CHICKEN PAILLARD

4   4-ounce boneless chicken
    breast halves, skinned
2   tablespoons rum or 2
    teaspoons rum extract
2   tablespoons reduced-
    sodium soy sauce
3   tablespoons lime juice
1   tablespoon plus 1½
    teaspoons brown sugar
1   tablespoon
    Worcestershire sauce
1   tablespoon vegetable oil
⅛   teaspoon pepper
Vegetable coating spray
1   tablespoon minced fresh
    parsley
1   lime, cut into 4 wedges

Place the chicken between 2 sheets of waxed paper, flatten to ¼″ thickness, using a meat mallet or rolling pin; set aside. Combine next 7 ingredients in a shallow dish; mixing well. Add chicken to marinade, turning to coat well; cover and marinate in refrigerator 30 minutes. Coat a nonstick skillet or ridged grill pan with cooking spray, and place over medium heat until hot. Remove chicken from marinade, and place in skillet; cook 4 minutes on each side or until tender. Transfer chicken to a platter, and garnish with parsley. Squeeze lime over chicken before serving.

Servings: 4

NUTRIENT VALUES					
PROTEIN	CARBOHYDRATE		FAT		ALCOHOL
44%	17%		32%		7%
CALORIES	PRO-GM	CARB-GM		FAT-GM	SOD-MG
235.0	26.70	10.20		8.468	555.0
FOOD EXCHANGES					
MILK	VEG.	FRUIT	BREAD	MEAT	FAT
0.0	0.0	0.1	0.4	3.3	0.6

MARINATED GRILLED CHICKEN I

4   chicken breast halves,
    skinned
6   lemons (1 cup juice)
¼   cup Dijon mustard
4–5 cloves garlic
1   tablespoon olive oil
2   tablespoons black pepper

Place chicken in a large bowl. Squeeze juice from lemons. Mix with remaining ingredients. Marinate chicken 4–6 hours before grilling. Use marinade to baste chicken as it cooks.

Servings: 4

NUTRIENT VALUES					
PROTEIN	CARBOHYDRATE		FAT		ALCOHOL
48%	18%		35%		0%
CALORIES	PRO-GM	CARB-GM		FAT-GM	SOD-MG
225.3	26.51	9.753		8.505	198.3
FOOD EXCHANGES					
MILK	VEG.	FRUIT	BREAD	MEAT	FAT
0.0	0.0	0.4	0.3	2.1	2.8

MARINATED GRILLED CHICKEN II

4 chicken breast halves, skinned

6 teaspoons rum or 1 teaspoon rum extract

2 tablespoons low-sodium soy sauce

3 tablespoons fresh lime juice

5 teaspoons brown sugar

1 tablespoon Worcestershire sauce

1 tablespoon olive oil

¼ teaspoon white pepper

Mix all ingredients except chicken. Marinate chicken 4–6 hours, turning every 2 hours.

Grill until done. Use marinade to baste chicken while grilling.

Servings: 4

NUTRIENT VALUES					
PROTEIN 53%	CARBOHYDRATE 12%		FAT 31%		ALCOHOL 4%
CALORIES 196.0	PRO-GM 26.20	CARB-GM 5.920		FAT-GM 6.695	SOD-MG 313.0
FOOD EXCHANGES					
MILK 0.0	VEG. 0.9	FRUIT 0.1	BREAD 0.4	MEAT 5.3	FAT 5.8

OVEN-BARBECUED CHICKEN

6 chicken breast halves, skinned

½ cup water

½ cup light ketchup

⅓ cup cider vinegar or herbal vinegar

1 tablespoon Worcestershire sauce

2 teaspoons minced onion

½ teaspoon pepper

¼ teaspoon garlic powder

¼ teaspoon dry mustard

Place chicken in a shallow baking dish and set aside.

Combine remaining ingredients in a small saucepan; bring to a boil. Pour barbecue sauce over chicken; cover and refrigerate. Allow to marinate at least 2 hours.

Bake at 350° for 45 minutes or until chicken is done. Turn chicken occasionally as it cooks.

Servings: 6

NUTRIENT VALUES					
PROTEIN 61%	CARBOHYDRATE 12%		FAT 26%		ALCOHOL 0%
CALORIES 168.0	PRO-GM 26.10	CARB-GM 5.210		FAT-GM 5.007	SOD-MG 171.0
FOOD EXCHANGES					
MILK 0.0	VEG. 0.0	FRUIT 0.0	BREAD 0.2	MEAT 2.2	FAT 2.2

ARROZ CON POLLO (RICE WITH CHICKEN)

5   chicken breast halves, skinned
½   teaspoon olive oil
½   clove garlic
½   onion, quartered
1   tomato, fresh or canned
1½ cups chicken stock, defatted
½   cup raw brown rice
½   teaspoon oregano
½   teaspoon black pepper
¼   cup fresh parsley, minced
1½ teaspoons pimentos, including juice
¼   cup frozen peas
¼   cup sliced carrots
White wine (optional)

Brown chicken in nonstick skillet with oil. Remove and set aside. Mince garlic and onions, and set aside. If using fresh tomato, peel and deseed. Place the tomato pulp and broth in skillet. Cook over medium heat for about 1 minutes. Add rice, oregano and pepper (and wine if desired). Bring to a boil and add chicken pieces. Cover and simmer over low heat for 20–30 minutes or until liquid is absorbed (adding additional stock as needed to prevent sticking). Don't stir rice. Add parsley, pimento, peas and carrots. Cover, simmer 4–5 minutes.

Servings: 5

NUTRIENT VALUES			
PROTEIN	CARBOHYDRATE	FAT	ALCOHOL
54%	20%	26%	0%
CALORIES	PRO-GM	CARB-GM	FAT-GM	SOD-MG
204.0	27.70	10.40	5.881	12.00
FOOD EXCHANGES					
MILK	VEG.	FRUIT	BREAD	MEAT	FAT
0.0.	0.4	0.0	0.4	2.1	2.3

CHICKEN ENCHILADAS VERDES

2 cups cooked chicken, chopped (remove all skin and visible fat)
2 green onions, chopped
⅛ teaspoon garlic powder
10 corn tortillas
1 cup chicken broth, defatted
½ cup nonfat yogurt
2 teaspoons skim milk
Thinly sliced onion
Salsa verde (recipe page 66)

Make salsa verde.

Combine chicken, green onions, garlic powder, and 3 tablespoons salsa verde. Mix well.

Heat ¼ cup chicken broth in small skillet, until hot. Slip 1 tortilla into skillet, cook until softened. (Or soften tortillas in microwave.)

Drain on paper towel. Repeat with remaining tortillas, adding additional chicken broth every 3–4 tortillas or as needed.

Fill each tortilla with 3 tablespoons of chicken mixture; roll up. Fill all tortillas and arrange seam-side down, in a single layer in shallow baking dish. Pour salsa verde over tortillas. Bake until sauce is bubbly, about 20 minutes in 350° oven.

Mix yogurt and skim milk and spoon over enchiladas. Top with onion slices.

Servings: 5 (2 enchiladas per serving)

NUTRIENT VALUES					
PROTEIN	CARBOHYDRATE		FAT		ALCOHOL
26%	58%		16%		0%
CALORIES	PRO-GM	CARB-GM		FAT-GM	SOD-MG
250.0	16.60	37.20		4.437	175.0
FOOD EXCHANGES					
MILK	VEG.	FRUIT	BREAD	MEAT	FAT
0.1	0.1	0.0	1.7	0.9	1.3

CHICKEN FAJITAS

3 chicken breast halves,
    skinned
½ cup fresh lime juice
3 cloves garlic, mashed
3 tablespoons minced
    fresh cilantro
2 teaspoons cumin powder

Combine all ingredients and marinate for 4 hours minimum. Grill chicken breasts over hot coals until done. Use leftover marinade to baste chicken as it grills.

Servings: 4

Allow chicken to cool and slice julienne. Serve in a whole wheat flour tortilla (80 calories) with mock sour cream, guacamole surprise, lettuce, and fresh pico de gallo.

NUTRIENT VALUES					
PROTEIN 59%	CARBOHYDRATE 13%		FAT 28%		ALCOHOL 0%
CALORIES 129.0	PRO-GM 19.70	CARB-GM 4.377		FAT-GM 4.080	SOD-MG 8.825
FOOD EXCHANGES					
MILK 0.0	VEG. 0.0	FRUIT 0.1	BREAD 0.0	MEAT 2.4	FAT 0.0

EL RANCHO GRANDE

1 pound ground turkey
¼ cup chopped celery
¼ cup chopped green
    pepper
¼ cup chopped onion
6 ounces eggless noodles
½ cup grated part-skim
    mozzarella
1 16-ounce can tomatoes,
    chopped and undrained
2 cups water

Brown turkey and onions over low heat in a nonstick skillet. Add tomatoes, celery, and green pepper. Cook until vegetables are tender, approximately 10 minutes. Add noodles and water and cook 20 more minutes. Sprinkle cheese evenly over servings.

Servings: 6 (1¼ cup servings)

NUTRIENT VALUES					
PROTEIN 18%	CARBOHYDRATE 69%		FAT 13%		ALCOHOL 0%
CALORIES 162.0	PRO-GM 7.137	CARB-GM 27.60		FAT-GM 2.312	SOD-MG 177.0
FOOD EXCHANGES					
MILK 0.0	VEG. 0.7	FRUIT 0.0	BREAD 1.6	MEAT 0.3	FAT 0.2

FETTUCCINI CON POLLO

2 chicken breasts (whole, skinned)
1 medium onion, julienned
½ pound mushrooms, sliced
1 large clove garlic, minced
2 tablespoons reduced-calorie margarine
12 ounces spinach fettuccini
2 cups skim evaporated milk
½ teaspoon pepper to taste
¼ teaspoon nutmeg
3 tablespoons tomato paste

Poach and cool the chicken breasts. Remove bone and slice into bite-sized pieces. Saute the onion, mushrooms and garlic in margarine until soft. Cook the pasta al dente according to the directions on the package and drain. Combine the evaporated milk, pasta, and seasonings. Add the tomato puree, vegetables, and chicken. Mixture will appear watery but will thicken into a creamy sauce when baked. Place the mixture in a 13 × 9 baking dish that has been sprayed with vegetable coating spray. Bake at 350° for 30 minutes.

Servings: 8 (1 cup serving)

NUTRIENT VALUES			
PROTEIN	CARBOHYDRATE	FAT	ALCOHOL
30%	57%	14%	0%
CALORIES	PRO-GM	CARB-GM	FAT-GM	SOD-MG
338.0	24.40	46.60	5.024	121.0

FOOD EXCHANGES					
MILK	VEG.	FRUIT	BREAD	MEAT	FAT
0.6	0.7	0.0	2.3	1.1	1.4

POLLA EN MOLA

4   chicken breast halves, skinned
1   small onion, sliced
2   tablespoons flour
2   teaspoons chili powder
1   clove garlic, minced
1   cup chicken broth, defatted
2   tablespoons peanut butter
¼   teaspoon salt
⅛   teaspoon ground cloves
1   teaspoon dried oregano or 2 teaspoons minced fresh
½   teaspoon cumin

Boil chicken and onion in water to cover for 20 minutes. Remove from heat. Allow 1½ cups broth to chill in freezer to congeal fat. Heat skillet over low heat, add flour and brown. Add chili powder, garlic and reserved, defatted broth and stir until mixture is smooth. Add peanut butter, salt, ground cloves, oregano, cumin, and chicken. Cook for 20 minutes over medium heat.

Servings: 4

NUTRIENT VALUES			
PROTEIN	CARBOHYDRATE	FAT	ALCOHOL
52%	16%	31%	0%
CALORIES	PRO-GM	CARB-GM	FAT-GM	SOD-MG
213.0	28.40	8.904	7.496	155.0

FOOD EXCHANGES					
MILK	VEG.	FRUIT	BREAD	MEAT	FAT
0.0	0.5	0.0	0.3	2.3	2.5

SOFT TURKEY/CHICKEN TACOS

5   whole wheat tortillas
5   ounces cooked turkey
    breast or chicken
1½ cups taco sauce (recipe
    follows)
¾   cups fresh diced
    tomatoes
5   tablespoons chopped
    onion
1¼ cups chopped lettuce
10 teaspoons grated
    Cheddar cheese or part-
    skim mozzarella

Combine all ingredients for taco sauce in a large saucepan. Bring to a boil, reduce heat and simmer 30 minutes. (Yields 1½ cups.) To assemble taco place 1 ounce warm turkey/chicken in warm flour tortilla. Add 4–5 tablespoons taco sauce, 2 tablespoons chopped tomato, 1 tablespoon chopped onion, ¼ cup chopped lettuce, and 2 teaspoons grated cheese. Fold tortilla in half and serve.

Servings: 5

TACO SAUCE:
1   16-ounce can tomatoes,
    chopped (undrained)
1½ teaspoons chili powder
1   teaspoon cumin
¼   teaspoon cayenne pepper
1   clove garlic, minced
1   cup water
1   teaspoon dried oregano
    or 2 teaspoons fresh
    minced

NUTRIENT VALUES			
PROTEIN	CARBOHYDRATE	FAT	ALCOHOL
30%	46%	25%	0%
CALORIES	PRO-GM	CARB-GM	FAT-GM	SOD-MG
187.0	14.20	21.90	5.268	378.0

FOOD EXCHANGES					
MILK	VEG.	FRUIT	BREAD	MEAT	FAT
0.0	1.2	0.0	0.9	1.2	0.7

TURKEY LOAF

1 cup onion (1 large) diced
½ cup diced green pepper
2 cloves garlic, minced
½ teaspoon freshly ground black pepper
1 piece whole wheat bread, cubed
1 egg white
1 teaspoon Worcestershire sauce
¼ teaspoon Tabasco
1 teaspoon oregano
1 tablespoon chopped fresh parsley
12 ounces tomato sauce
1 pound raw ground turkey
Vegetable coating spray

Preheat oven to 425°. Mix all ingredients reserving ½ cup tomato sauce. Spray a 4 × 8 loaf pan with vegetable coating spray and place mixture in pan. Pat down until firm and top with remaining sauce. Bake at 425° for 1 hour until lightly browned around edges.

Servings: 8

Makes good sandwiches, too.

Trisha Shirey

NUTRIENT VALUES			
PROTEIN	CARBOHYDRATE	FAT	ALCOHOL
61%	23%	16%	0%
CALORIES	PRO-GM	CARB-GM	FAT-GM	SOD-MG
127.0	18.80	7.250	2.157	82.50
FOOD EXCHANGES					
MILK	VEG.	FRUIT	BREAD	MEAT	FAT
0.0	0.3	0.0	0.4	0.1	0.0

TURKEY SAUSAGE

¼ **cup chicken or turkey stock, defatted**
½ **cup green pepper, finely minced**
½ **cup onions, finely minced**
1 **pound ground turkey, uncooked**
1½ **cups grated zucchini**
¼ **teaspoon ground sage**
¼ **teaspoon dried thyme**
¼ **teaspoon dried marjoram**
½ **teaspoon pepper**
¼ **teaspoon salt**
1 **clove garlic, minced**

In a medium nonstick skillet, cook peppers and onions in stock until tender, about 10 minutes.

In a large bowl, combine turkey with peppers and onions. Add remaining ingredients and mix well.

Form mixture into 6 thin patties. Cook on a nonstick skillet over medium heat, until lightly browned on both sides. Can also be baked at 425° for 30–40 minutes or until browned.

Servings: 6

Good served in whole wheat pita with fresh vegetables or for breakfast.

NUTRIENT VALUES					
PROTEIN	CARBOHYDRATE			FAT	ALCOHOL
73%	9%			18%	0%
CALORIES	PRO-GM		CARB-GM	FAT-GM	SOD-MG
133.0	23.50		2.990	2.590	132.0
FOOD EXCHANGES					
MILK	VEG.	FRUIT	BREAD	MEAT	FAT
0.0	0.5	0.0	0.0	0.0	0.0

TURKEY AND ARTICHOKE QUICHE

2 teaspoons minced fresh
  dill
2 tablespoons minced
  fresh parsley
2 eggs
4 egg whites, beaten
  slightly
1 cup diced turkey breast
1 14-ounce can artichoke
  hearts, quartered
2 cups grated part-skim
  mozzarella
1 cup evaporated skim
  milk
Vegetable coating spray

Spray a 9" round or square baking dish with
vegetable coating spray. Place turkey and artichokes in baking dish. Top with cheese.
Mix milk, herbs, and eggs together. Pour
milk mixture over eggs. Bake at 350°, 30–40
minutes or until firm in the center and lightly
browned.

Servings: 8

Trisha Shirey

NUTRIENT VALUES				
PROTEIN	CARBOHYDRATE		FAT	ALCOHOL
45%	18%		37%	0%
CALORIES	PRO-GM	CARB-GM	FAT-GM	SOD-MG
156.0	17.40	6.707	6.281	221.0
FOOD EXCHANGES					
MILK	VEG.	FRUIT	BREAD	MEAT	FAT
0.3	0.4	0.0	0.0	1.9	0.6

CHICKEN SALAD

2   chicken breasts, skinned and washed
4   cups water
2   small celery stalks with leaves
2   tablespoons reduced-calorie mayonnaise
1   cup celery, diced fine
⅓   cup sweet pickle, diced fine
2   tablespoons fresh chopped parsley
3   tablespoons nonfat yogurt
½   teaspoon black pepper

In a 2-quart saucepan, add chicken breasts, water and celery stalks. Bring to a boil then reduce heat. Simmer 45 minutes. Remove chicken and cool broth. When cool, remove chicken from bone. Chop chicken fine. In a medium mixing bowl, add chicken, mayonnaise, celery, pickle, parsley, yogurt and pepper. Mix well. cover and chill. Serve as a spread on crackers or as a sandwich filling.

Servings: 6 (¼ cup serving)

NUTRIENT VALUES			
PROTEIN	CARBOHYDRATE	FAT	ALCOHOL
50%	20%	30%	0%
CALORIES	PRO-GM	CARB-GM	FAT-GM	SOD-MG
141.0	17.70	7.085	4.705	135.0

FOOD EXCHANGES					
MILK	VEG.	FRUIT	BREAD	MEAT	FAT
0.1	0.0	0.0	0.3	1.4	1.8

CHICKEN SALAD WITH BASIL PESTO

3　cups diced cooked
　　chicken breast
1½ cups diced celery
¼　cup minced onion
3　tablespoons fresh lemon
　　juice
¼　teaspoon coriander
½　teaspoon black pepper
1　cup green grapes
Lettuce leaves
¼　cup basil pesto, see page
　　69

Combine all ingredients except lettuce and pesto. Toss well. Serve on lettuce leaves. Garnish with lemon wedges. Top with 1 tablespoon pesto. Pesto can be mixed with salad ingredients also.

Servings: 4 (generous 1 cup serving)

NUTRIENT VALUES					
PROTEIN 49%	CARBOHYDRATE 21%		FAT 30%	ALCOHOL 0%	
CALORIES 169.0	PRO-GM 21.30	CARB-GM 9.318	FAT-GM 5.812	SOD-MG 85.10	
FOOD EXCHANGES					
MILK 0.0	VEG. 0.1	FRUIT 0.4	BREAD 0.1	MEAT 1.6	FAT 1.6

CHICKEN RICE SALAD

1½ cups chicken, cooked
　　and coarsely diced
½　cup diced celery
2　green onions, chopped
1½ cups cooked brown rice,
　　cold
1　tablespoon reduced-
　　calorie mayonnaise
¼　cup nonfat yogurt
1½ teaspoons lemon juice
½　teaspoon honey
2　tablespoons raw,
　　unsalted cashew nuts
Lettuce leaves

Combine chicken, celery, onion, and rice in a large bowl. In a small bowl, mix mayonnaise, yogurt, lemon juice and honey. Pour dressing over chicken and mix. Add cashews just before serving. Serve on lettuce leaves.

Servings: 3 (1⅓ cups each)

NUTRIENT VALUES					
PROTEIN 32%	CARBOHYDRATE 37%		FAT 31%	ALCOHOL 0%	
CALORIES 262.0	PRO-GM 20.70	CARB-GM 24.10	FAT-GM 8.883	SOD-MG 72.00	
FOOD EXCHANGES					
MILK 0.2	VEG. 0.0	FRUIT 0.0	BREAD 1.2	MEAT 2.5	FAT 0.8

DILLED CHICKEN AND PASTA SALAD

6 **ounce package shell or elbow pasta, cooked**
2 **cups diced cooked chicken**
2 **cups chopped tomato**
½ **cup diced celery**
1 **cup grated carrots**
¼ **cup diced red onion**
¼ **cup chopped fresh parsley**
½ **cup chopped red peppers**

DRESSING
2 **cloves garlic, minced**
2 **tablespoons herbal vinegar (dill vinegar)**
1 **tablespoon safflower oil**
1½ **teaspoons dried whole dillweed (or 1 tablespoon fresh)**
2 **teaspoons Parmesan cheese**
½ **teaspoon pepper**

Combine first eight ingredients. Make dressing. Pour over salad. Mix well.

Chill at least 2 hours to blend flavors. Serve on leaf lettuce. Garnish with tomato wedges, lemon twists and melba toast.

Servings: 6 (1 heaping cup per serving)

NUTRIENT VALUES			
PROTEIN	CARBOHYDRATE	FAT	ALCOHOL
26%	54%	20%	0%
CALORIES	PRO-GM	CARB-GM	FAT-GM	SOD-MG
213.0	14.30	29.50	4.922	33.00

FOOD EXCHANGES					
MILK	VEG.	FRUIT	BREAD	MEAT	FAT
0.0	0.8	0.0	1.6	0.8	1.2

PASTA AND CHICKEN SALAD

4 ounces whole wheat or
   eggless elbow macaroni
¼ pound snow peas,
   trimmed
1 cup julienned zucchini
1 tablespoon vegetable oil
¼ cup cider vinegar or
   herbal vinegar
¼ cup chopped onion
¼ teaspoon black pepper
1½ cups cooked chicken or
   turkey, cubed
1 sweet red pepper,
   julienned
1 bell pepper, julienned
2 tablespoons reduced-
   calorie mayonnaise
¼ cup nonfat yogurt

Cook the pasta following label directions. Steam the snow peas and zucchini until tender crisp. Mix the cooked pasta and steamed vegetables in a large bowl. Add the oil, vinegar, onion, and pepper, tossing until well blended. Add green peppers, yogurt, chicken and mayonnaise. Mix well.

Serve on a bed of lettuce.

Servings: 5 (1½ cup serving)

NUTRIENT VALUES			
PROTEIN	CARBOHYDRATE	FAT	ALCOHOL
35%	34%	31%	0%
CALORIES	PRO-GM	CARB-GM	FAT-GM	SOD-MG
296.0	25.80	25.00	10.30	58.80

FOOD EXCHANGES					
MILK	VEG.	FRUIT	BREAD	MEAT	FAT
0.1	0.9	0.0	1.3	2.6	0.9

ROQUEFORT CHICKEN SALAD

3   chicken breast halves,
    skinned
1   pound zucchini, cut into
    julienne strips
¼   pound mushrooms,
    thinly sliced
3   celery stalks, cut into
    julienne strips
1   pound spinach, cleaned

DRESSING
½   teaspoon curry powder
2   tablespoons grated onion
2   ounces blue cheese or
    Roquefort
¼   cup reduced-calorie
    mayonnaise
¼   cup nonfat yogurt
2   tablespoons lemon juice

Boil chicken breasts until done. Cool, debone and shred. In a mixing bowl, combine the zucchini, mushrooms, celery and chicken.

In a separate bowl, mix the curry powder, onion, blue cheese, mayonnaise, yogurt and lemon juice. Pour over chicken mixture and toss to coat evenly.

Mound the chicken mixture in the center of spinach leaves.

Servings: 6

NUTRIENT VALUES			
PROTEIN	CARBOHYDRATE	FAT	ALCOHOL
40%	20%	40%	0%
CALORIES	PRO-GM	CARB-GM	FAT-GM	SOD-MG
180.0	19.00	9.447	8.401	219.0
FOOD EXCHANGES					
MILK	VEG.	FRUIT	BREAD	MEAT	FAT
0.2	1.4	0.0	0.2	1.3	2.0

SMOKED TURKEY SALAD

¾ **pound jicama, julienned**
¾ **pound carrots, julienned**
¾ **pound smoked turkey,**
    julienned
½ **cup fresh orange juice**
¼ **cup white wine vinegar**
2   **tablespoons soy sauce**
2   **tablespoons honey**
¼ **teaspoon white pepper**

Steam the julienned jicama and carrots for 2–3 minutes. Remove from heat and place vegetables in a large bowl. Add julienned turkey. Set aside. Combine remaining ingredients and pour over turkey salad.

Servings: 6 (1 cup serving)

NUTRIENT VALUES					
PROTEIN	CARBOHYDRATE		FAT		ALCOHOL
45%	51%		3%		0%
CALORIES	PRO-GM	CARB-GM		FAT-GM	SOD-MG
162.0	18.30	20.90		0.622	393.0
FOOD EXCHANGES					
MILK	VEG.	FRUIT	BREAD	MEAT	FAT
0.0	0.9	0.2	0.8	1.8	0.0

TURKEY SALAD DIJONAISE

DRESSING

1½ teaspoons Dijon mustard
2 tablespoons red wine
   vinegar or herbal
   vinegar
1 tablespoon olive oil
1 teaspoon sweet basil

12 ounces skinned, boned
   and cubed turkey breast
   (or chicken)
4 ounces part skim Swiss
   cheese, diced
1 cup cooked brown rice,
   chilled
¼ cup diced red bell
   pepper
¼ cup diced green bell
   pepper
3 tablespoons diced sour
   gherkin pickles

Mix dressing ingredients together and set aside.

Mix all salad ingredients together in a large bowl. Add dressing to turkey mixture and toss gently.

Servings: 4 (1 cup serving)

A quick meal when using leftover rice.

Ellen McCullough

NUTRIENT VALUES					
PROTEIN 36%	CARBOHYDRATE 26%		FAT 37%		ALCOHOL 0%
CALORIES 299.0	PRO-GM 27.40	CARB-GM 19.60		FAT-GM 12.50	SOD-MG 257.0
FOOD EXCHANGES					
MILK 0.8	VEG. 0.1	FRUIT 0.0	BREAD 0.6	MEAT 1.6	FAT 3.3

GRILLED TURKEY CHEESE SANDWICHES

4 slices whole wheat bread
2 ounces cooked turkey, sliced
1 ounce part-skim Swiss cheese, sliced
4 thin tomato slices
2 egg whites
¼ cup skim milk
Pinch of cayenne pepper

Arrange 1 slice of turkey (1 ounce), ½ slice cheese and 2 tomato slices on bread. Sprinkle with pepper. Top with the remaining 2 slices of bread.

Beat the egg whites with the milk and cayenne in a shallow dish. Dip the sandwiches in the egg mixture to coat both sides. Brown the sandwiches on a nonstick pan, turning to brown both sides and melt the cheese.

Servings: 2

NUTRIENT VALUES					
PROTEIN 34%	CARBOHYDRATE 48%		FAT 18%		ALCOHOL 0%
CALORIES 249.0	PRO-GM 21.70	CARB-GM 30.50		FAT-GM 5.091	SOD-MG 403.0
FOOD EXCHANGES					
MILK 0.8	VEG. 0.3	FRUIT 0.0	BREAD 1.5	MEAT 1.3	FAT 1.0

OPEN FACE TURKEY SANDWICHES

1 slice dark rye or whole wheat bread
2 ounces cooked sliced turkey breast

GARNISHES
Lettuce leaf
Purple onion ring
Tomato slice
2 tablespoons Curry Mayonnaise (see p. 72)

Place lettuce leaf on bread. Place turkey, onion ring and tomato slice on top of bread. Serve sandwich with 2 tablespoons Curry Mayonnaise.

Servings: 1

NUTRIENT VALUES					
PROTEIN 43%	CARBOHYDRATE 33%		FAT 24%		ALCOHOL 0%
CALORIES 189.0	PRO-GM 20.40	CARB-GM 15.50		FAT-GM 4.945	SOD-MG 233.0
FOOD EXCHANGES					
MILK 0.0	VEG. 0.5	FRUIT 0.0	BREAD 1.5	MEAT 1.5	FAT 0.0

Special Endings . . .

DESSERTS

CARROT CAKE

3 cups whole wheat flour
1½ teaspoons baking powder
1 teaspoon baking soda
1 tablespoon cinnamon
½ teaspoon ground cloves
½ teaspoon ground ginger
4 egg whites
2 tablespoons safflower oil
6 tablespoons water
½ cup lowfat buttermilk
¼ cup honey
2 teaspoons vanilla
2 cups grated carrots
8 ounces unsweetened crushed pineapple, drained (water packed)
½ cup raisins
Vegetable coating spray

Sift together dry ingredients into a large bowl and set aside. In a separate bowl, slightly beat egg whites. Add oil, water, buttermilk, honey, and vanilla. Mix well. Add carrots, pineapple, and raisins. Add liquid mixture to dry mixture, mixing well.

Spray a 9 × 13 inch baking pan with vegetable coating spray. Pour batter into baking pan. Bake at 350° for 40 minutes or until done. Allow cake to cool, then ice.

ICING (OPTIONAL)
1½ cups nonfat yogurt cheese
¼ cup apple juice concentrate

Mix together and spread over cake.

Servings: 16

NUTRIENT VALUES				
PROTEIN	CARBOHYDRATE		FAT	ALCOHOL
13%	76%		11%	0%
CALORIES	PRO-GM	CARB-GM	FAT-GM	SOD-MG
172.0	5.804	32.80	2.087	142.0
FOOD EXCHANGES					
MILK	VEG.	FRUIT	BREAD	MEAT	FAT
0.3	0.2	0.5	1.3	0.1	0.3

FRUIT CAKE

1 cup graham cracker crumbs
3 tablespoons sugar
¼ teaspoon ground cinnamon
⅛ teaspoon cloves
⅛ teaspoon allspice
⅛ teaspoon nutmeg
¾ teaspoon baking powder
1 egg beater (equivalent to 1 egg)
1 teaspoon rum extract
6 tablespoons pineapple juice (diluted)
½ cup chopped pineapple
½ cup chopped apples
½ cup sliced bananas
3 tablespoons raisins
1 egg white
Vegetable coating spray

In a medium bowl, combine graham cracker crumbs, sugar, spices, and baking powder. Stir in egg beater, rum extract and pineapple juice. Add fruit and raisins. Mix well.

In a separate bowl, beat egg white on high speed of an electric mixer until stiff. Fold into fruit mixture gently.

Spoon batter into a 4 × 8 inch loaf pan that has been sprayed with a vegetable coating spray.

Bake at 350° for 40 minutes. Cool in pan before removing.

Servings: 12

NUTRIENT VALUES				
PROTEIN	CARBOHYDRATE		FAT	ALCOHOL
14%	76%		10%	0%
CALORIES	PRO-GM	CARB-GM	FAT-GM	SOD-MG
71.10	2.700	14.40	0.827	92.70
FOOD EXCHANGES					
MILK	VEG.	FRUIT	BREAD	MEAT	FAT
0.0	0.0	0.4	0.5	0.2	0.1

CAROB COOKIES

½   cup whole wheat flour
½   cup all-purpose flour
½   cup carob powder
1   teaspoon baking powder
1   teaspoon cinnamon
¼   teaspoon cloves
¼   teaspoon salt
½   cup margarine, soft-tub
⅔   cup packed brown sugar
4   egg whites
¾   cup skim milk
3   cups quick cooking rolled oats
Vegetable coating spray

Preheat oven to 350°. Stir together flours, carob powder, baking powder, cinnamon, cloves, and salt. With a mixer, beat butter 30 seconds, add brown sugar and beat until fluffy. Add egg whites, beat well. Add the dry ingredients and milk alternately, beating after each addition. Stir in oats. Drop by rounded teaspoons 2 inches apart onto cookie sheet sprayed with vegetable coating spray. Bake at 350° for about 12 minutes. Cookies will appear moist when removed from oven, but will harden as they cool.

Yields: 4 dozen (1 cookie per serving)

NUTRIENT VALUES					
PROTEIN 8%		CARBOHYDRATE 54%		FAT 38%	ALCOHOL 0%
CALORIES 45.50	PRO-GM 0.816	CARB-GM 5.215		FAT-GM 1.625	SOD-MG 43.70
FOOD EXCHANGES					
MILK 0.0	VEG. 0.0	FRUIT 0.0	BREAD 0.0	MEAT 0.0	FAT 0.5

CARROT COOKIES

1¾ cups rolled oats
½ cup all-purpose flour
½ cup whole wheat flour
¼ cup nonfat dry milk powder
1 teaspoon baking powder
¼ teaspoon baking soda
½ teaspoon salt
¼ teaspoon ground nutmeg
¼ teaspoon ground cinnamon
2 tablespoons safflower oil
2 tablespoons brown sugar
½ cup molasses, light
2 egg whites
1 cup grated carrots
1 teaspoon vanilla

Combine the oats, flours, dry milk, baking powder, baking soda, salt, nutmeg and cinnamon. Combine oil, sugar, and molasses; add the egg whites, carrots, and vanilla. Add dry ingredients. Stir just until moistened. Drop cookie dough by tablespoons onto non-stick cookie sheet. Bake at 350° for 8–10 minutes. Allow to cool.

Makes: 4 dozen (1 cookie per serving)

NUTRIENT VALUES					
PROTEIN	CARBOHYDRATE		FAT		ALCOHOL
10%	72%		19%		0%
CALORIES	PRO-GM	CARB-GM		FAT-GM	SOD-MG
39.10	0.965	7.087		0.815	37.10
FOOD EXCHANGES					
MILK	VEG.	FRUIT	BREAD	MEAT	FAT
0.0	0.0	0.0	0.4	0.1	0.1

GINGER COOKIES

1 cup whole wheat pastry flour
1 cup all-purpose flour
¼ cup brown sugar, not packed
1 teaspoon baking soda
1 teaspoon ground cinnamon
1 teaspoon ground ginger
½ teaspoon salt
½ teaspoon ground cloves
½ cup reduced-calorie margarine
¼ cup lowfat buttermilk
¼ cup light molasses
2 egg whites, slightly beaten

Combine first eight ingredients, mixing well. Add margarine and stir until mixture is in coarse crumbs. Stir in buttermilk, molasses, and egg whites.

Shape dough into 1-inch balls. Place on ungreased baking sheets and bake at 325° for 8–10 minutes. Remove from baking sheets immediately. Cookies will firm as they cool.

Yields: 2½ dozen (1 cookie per serving)

NUTRIENT VALUES					
PROTEIN	CARBOHYDRATE		FAT		ALCOHOL
7%	67%		26%		0%
CALORIES	PRO-GM	CARB-GM		FAT-GM	SOD-MG
56.20	0.976	9.461		1.616	102.0
FOOD EXCHANGES					
MILK	VEG.	FRUIT	BREAD	MEAT	FAT
0.0	0.0	0.0	0.5	0.1	0.3

ORANGE MERINGUE COOKIES

3   egg whites, room
    temperature
¼   teaspoon cream of tartar
4   tablespoon sugar
¼   cup sliced almonds
1   tablespoon grated orange
    rind
Vegetable coating spray

Preheat oven to 250°. Spray two nonstick cookie sheets with vegetable coating spray. Beat egg whites until foamy with electric mixer. Add cream of tartar, and beat on high speed to soft peaks. Beat in 1 tablespoon of sugar at a time, beating to stiff peaks. Add almonds and orange rind and gently fold in. Drop meringue by heaping tablespoons onto cookie sheets. Bake 1 hour. Turn off oven and don't open door. Let cool 1 hour, then transfer to wire racks to cool completely. Store in tightly covered container.

Servings: 24 (1 cookie per serving)

NUTRIENT VALUES			
PROTEIN	CARBOHYDRATE	FAT	ALCOHOL
15%	50%	35%	0%
CALORIES	PRO-GM	CARB-GM	FAT-GM	SOD-MG
17.70	0.692	2.367	0.738	6.419

FOOD EXCHANGES					
MILK	VEG.	FRUIT	BREAD	MEAT	FAT
0.0	0.0	0.0	0.1	0.1	0.1

RAISIN-CARROT COOKIES

½ cup water
1 tablespoon safflower oil
¼ cup honey
2 tablespoons apple juice
   concentrate
4 egg whites
1 teaspoon vanilla
1¼ cups whole wheat flour
½ cup wheat germ
1 teaspoon soda
2 teaspoons cinnamon
1 teaspoon nutmeg
½ cup raisins
2 cups rolled oats
4 cups grated raw carrots
Vegetable coating spray

In a large mixing bowl blend water, oil, honey, and juice concentrate. Beat in egg whites and vanilla. Mix well. Stir in remaining ingredients, except coating spray. Make large drop cookies well apart on cookie sheet, which has been sprayed with vegetable coating spray. Use ¼ cup batter for each. Bake at 350° for 12–15 minutes.

Yields: 26 cookies

NUTRIENT VALUES					
PROTEIN	CARBOHYDRATE		FAT		ALCOHOL
12%	74%		14%		0%
CALORIES	PRO-GM	CARB-GM		FAT-GM	SOD-MG
88.60	2.820	16.80		1.364	46.40
FOOD EXCHANGES					
MILK	VEG.	FRUIT	BREAD	MEAT	FAT
0.0	0.3	0.2	0.8	0.1	0.2

BANANA BREAD

1 cup all-purpose flour
½ cup whole wheat pastry flour
¼ cup sugar
2 teaspoons baking powder
1 teaspoon baking soda
½ teaspoon salt
½ cup wheat bran
3 ripe bananas, mashed
¾ cup lowfat buttermilk or nonfat yogurt
2 tablespoons vegetable oil
4 egg whites
½ teaspoon cinnamon
½ teaspoon allspice
1 teaspoon vanilla
Vegetable coating spray

Sift together the flour, sugar, baking powder, baking soda and salt. Mix in wheat bran.

Add all remaining ingredients and beat until well blended. Place in loaf pan sprayed with vegetable coating spray. Bake at 350° for about 1 hour or until done.

One loaf makes 20 slices. Slice loaf into 20 thin slices or 10 slices, then cut slices in half.

Servings: 20

NUTRIENT VALUES			
PROTEIN	CARBOHYDRATE	FAT	ALCOHOL
11%	71%	17%	0%
CALORIES	PRO-GM	CARB-GM	FAT-GM	SOD-MG
83.00	2.522	15.80	1.704	144.0
FOOD EXCHANGES					
MILK	VEG.	FRUIT	BREAD	MEAT	FAT
0.1	0.0	0.3	0.7	0.1	0.3

BANANA BRAN BARS

½ cup whole wheat flour
½ cup wheat bran
1 teaspoon baking powder
¼ teaspoon ground allspice
2 egg whites
2 tablespoons brown sugar
1 tablespoon vegetable oil
¼ cup skim milk
½ teaspoon vanilla
1 banana, mashed
1 ounce Neufchatel cheese, softened (or 2 tablespoons light sour cream)
2 tablespoons powdered sugar
¼ teaspoon vanilla
1 to 2 tablespoon skim milk
2 tablespoons pecans, finely chopped
Vegetable coating spray

Spray an 8 × 8 inch nonstick pan with vegetable coating spray. Stir together flour, bran, baking powder and allspice. Set aside. Stir together the egg whites, brown sugar, oil, milk, banana and vanilla. Beat until well combined. Stir dry ingredients into banana mixture. Spread batter evenly in prepared baking pan. Bake in a 350° oven for 20 to 25 minutes or until done. Cool.

For frosting, stir together the Neufchatel cheese, powdered sugar and the vanilla. Add milk to thin. Spread over bars. Sprinkle pecans on top.

Servings: 12

NUTRIENT VALUES					
PROTEIN	CARBOHYDRATE		FAT		ALCOHOL
12%	60%		28%		0%
CALORIES	PRO-GM	CARB-GM		FAT-GM	SOD-MG
80.10	2.637	13.30		2.736	29.70
FOOD EXCHANGES					
MILK	VEG.	FRUIT	BREAD	MEAT	FAT
0.0	0.0	0.2	0.6	0.1	0.5

PEACH CRUMB BAKE

2 cups fresh peaches, sliced
3 tablespoons graham cracker crumbs
¼ teaspoon ground cinnamon
Dash of ground nutmeg
1 teaspoon reduced-calorie margarine, melted

Layer peaches in bottom of an 8-inch square baking dish. Mix remaining ingredients and sprinkle over peach slices. Bake for 15 minutes at 350°. Serve warm or chilled.

Servings: 3

NUTRIENT VALUES					
PROTEIN	CARBOHYDRATE		FAT		ALCOHOL
6%	80%		14%		0%
CALORIES	PRO-GM	CARB-GM		FAT-GM	SOD-MG
75.10	1.226	16.60		1.246	50.80
FOOD EXCHANGES					
MILK	VEG.	FRUIT	BREAD	MEAT	FAT
0.0	0.0	0.8	0.2	0.0	0.3

PEAR COBBLER

⅓ loaf cinnamon bread (5–6 slices)
3 pears, cored and cubed
7 tablespoons skim milk
1½ teaspoons honey
1½ teaspoons cinnamon
1½ teaspoons nutmeg
1½ teaspoons vanilla
¾ teaspoon almond extract
Vegetable coating spray

Crumble cinnamon bread to make bread crumbs. Mix crumbs, milk, honey, spices and extracts. Add pears. Add more milk or water if it seems too dry. Spoon into an 8 × 8 inch baking pan that has been sprayed with vegetable coating spray. Cover and bake at 350° for 30 minutes.

Servings: 9

NUTRIENT VALUES					
PROTEIN	CARBOHYDRATE		FAT		ALCOHOL
9%	81%		11%		0%
CALORIES	PRO-GM	CARB-GM		FAT-GM	SOD-MG
90.70	2.045	19.20		1.135	69.60
FOOD EXCHANGES					
MILK	VEG.	FRUIT	BREAD	MEAT	FAT
0.1	0.0	0.6	0.6	0.0	0.1

COFFEE YOGURT

1 cup nonfat yogurt
1 teaspoon instant decaffeinated coffee (or to taste)
1½ teaspoons sugar (or to taste)

Mix all ingredients together and chill.

Servings: 1 (1 cup)

Trisha Shirey

NUTRIENT VALUES					
PROTEIN	CARBOHYDRATE		FAT		ALCOHOL
33%	67%		0%		0%
CALORIES	PRO-GM	CARB-GM		FAT-GM	SOD-MG
133.0	11.00	22.00		0.000	160.0
FOOD EXCHANGES					
MILK	VEG.	FRUIT	BREAD	MEAT	FAT
1.5	0.0	0.0	0.5	0.0	0.0

LEMON YOGURT

1 cup nonfat yogurt
2 teaspoons maple syrup
¼ teaspoon lemon extract
2 tablespoons fresh lemon juice

Combine the yogurt, maple syrup and lemon extract and juice in a small bowl until well mixed. Serve chilled.

Servings: 1

NUTRIENT VALUES					
PROTEIN	CARBOHYDRATE		FAT		ALCOHOL
29%	71%		0%		0%
CALORIES	PRO-GM	CARB-GM		FAT-GM	SOD-MG
151.0	11.10	27.30		0.000	162.0
FOOD EXCHANGES					
MILK	VEG.	FRUIT	BREAD	MEAT	FAT
1.5	0.0	0.0	0.5	0.5	0.0

STRAWBERRY YOGURT

½ **cup frozen whole strawberries**
½ **cup nonfat yogurt**
1 **teaspoon maple syrup**
⅛ **teaspoons vanilla extract**

Allow the strawberries to thaw. Place the yogurt in a small bowl then stir the strawberries, maple syrup and vanilla into the yogurt. Continue stirring until the strawberries are mashed and the yogurt is pink.

Servings: 1

NUTRIENT VALUES					
PROTEIN	CARBOHYDRATE		FAT		ALCOHOL
23%	76%		1%		0%
CALORIES	PRO-GM	CARB-GM	FAT-GM		SOD-MG
97.70	5.815	19.10	0.080		82.50
FOOD EXCHANGES					
MILK	VEG.	FRUIT	BREAD	MEAT	FAT
0.5	0.0	0.5	0.0	0.0	0.0

VANILLA YOGURT

1½ **cups nonfat yogurt**
1½ **teaspoons vanilla extract**
1½ **tablespoons maple syrup**

Combine all ingredients and chill.

Yields: 3 (½ cup serving)

NUTRIENT VALUES					
PROTEIN	CARBOHYDRATE		FAT		ALCOHOL
28%	73%		0%		0%
CALORIES	PRO-GM	CARB-GM	FAT-GM		SOD-MG
80.00	5.500	14.50	0.000		81.50
FOOD EXCHANGES					
MILK	VEG.	FRUIT	BREAD	MEAT	FAT
0.7	0.0	0.0	0.3	0.2	0.0

CHOCOLATE PUDDING

¾ cup water
1 envelope unflavored gelatin
⅔ cup nonfat dry milk powder
2 tablespoons sugar
4 teaspoons cocoa, unsweetened
1 teaspoon vanilla
¼ teaspoon almond extract
7 ice cubes

Place water in a small saucepan. Sprinkle gelatin over water and let soften one minute. Place over low heat and continue stirring until gelatin is dissolved. Remove from heat.

In a blender, combine dry milk, sugar, cocoa, and extracts. Add gelatin mixture.

Add ice cubes, one at a time, while blending. Blend until ice is gone. Pour into serving dishes. Refrigerate for 15–20 minutes before serving.

Servings: 4 (⅔ cup serving)

NUTRIENT VALUES			
PROTEIN	CARBOHYDRATE	FAT	ALCOHOL
30%	63%	7%	0%
CALORIES	PRO-GM	CARB-GM	FAT-GM	SOD-MG
89.00	6.768	14.10	0.690	65.30
FOOD EXCHANGES					
MILK	VEG.	FRUIT	BREAD	MEAT	FAT
0.5	0.0	0.0	0.4	0.0	0.0

VANILLA PUDDING

2 cups skim milk
2 tablespoons cornstarch
3 tablespoons brown sugar
1 teaspoon vanilla extract

Gently heat 1½ cups of the milk in a double boiler. Combine cornstarch with remainder of milk. In top of double boiler add cornstarch mixture to warm milk. Stir in remaining ingredients and cook over very low heat until thick. Reduce heat further and cook gently about 10 more minutes.

Serve warm or pour into bowls and chill. Serve with fresh fruit.

Servings: 4 (½ cup serving)

NUTRIENT VALUES			
PROTEIN	CARBOHYDRATE	FAT	ALCOHOL
18%	79%	3%	0%
CALORIES	PRO-GM	CARB-GM	FAT-GM	SOD-MG
97.90	4.388	19.60	0.305	68.10
FOOD EXCHANGES					
MILK	VEG.	FRUIT	BREAD	MEAT	FAT
0.5	0.0	0.0	0.8	0.0	0.0

RICE PORRIDGE

1 **cup cooked brown rice,
cold**
½ **cup apple juice**
½ **cup water**
2 **tablespoons raisins or
other dried fruit**

Place all ingredients in a saucepan. Bring to a boil, then reduce heat and simmer, covered, 15 minutes, stirring frequently. Most of the liquid should be absorbed. Serve warm. If creamier porridge is desired, puree half.

Servings: 2 (½ cup each)

NUTRIENT VALUES			
PROTEIN	CARBOHYDRATE	FAT	ALCOHOL
6%	91%	3%	0%
CALORIES	PRO-GM	CARB-GM	FAT-GM	SOD-MG
143.0	2.129	32.90	0.562	2.813
FOOD EXCHANGES					
MILK	VEG.	FRUIT	BREAD	MEAT	FAT
0.0	0.0	1.0	1.3	0.0	0.0

AMBROSIA PIE

2 **envelopes gelatin**
1 **cup boiling water**
1 **tablespoon finely grated
zest of orange**
¼ **cup fresh squeezed
orange juice and pulp**
6 **tablespoons orange juice
concentrate**
¼ **cup sugar**
2 **cups yogurt cheese**
1 **8-ounce can unsweetened
pineapple tidbits,
crushed & juice**

Dissolve gelatin in boiling water and stir until gelatin is well dissolved (about 2 minutes). Mix in all remaining ingredients and stir well with a wire whisk or mixer on low speed.

Pour into a 9-inch glass pie pan and chill until firm (about 2 hours).

Servings: 8

Trisha Shirey

NUTRIENT VALUES			
PROTEIN	CARBOHYDRATE	FAT	ALCOHOL
26%	74%	0%	0%
CALORIES	PRO-GM	CARB-GM	FAT-GM	SOD-MG
114.0	7.444	21.50	0.064	83.00
FOOD EXCHANGES					
MILK	VEG.	FRUIT	BREAD	MEAT	FAT
0.7	0.0	0.6	0.3	0.0	0.0

FRUIT PIE

2 **cups cherries, halved and pitted (fresh or frozen)**
1 **cup blueberries**
3 **tablespoons orange juice**
1 **tablespoon lemon juice**
½ **teaspoon cinnamon**
2 **teaspoons cornstarch**
1 **tablespoon water**

TOPPING:
¼ **cup graham cracker crumbs**
2 **tablespoons wheat bran**
¼ **teaspoon cinnamon**
2 **teaspoons reduced-calorie margarine, melted**

To make filling: In a medium-sized saucepan, combine cherries, blueberries, orange juice, lemon juice, and cinnamon. Simmer 10 minutes or until fruit is tender.

Blend together cornstarch and water in a small cup, quickly stir into fruit. Bring to boiling point, stirring constantly, until mixture thickens. Divide mixture among six 8-ounce dessert dishes.

For topping: Combine graham cracker crumbs, wheat bran, cinnamon and margarine in a small bowl. Sprinkle mixture evenly over fruit dishes.

Servings: 6

May use raspberries or strawberries in place of cherries.

NUTRIENT VALUES			
PROTEIN	CARBOHYDRATE	FAT	ALCOHOL
7%	77%	16%	0%
CALORIES	PRO-GM	CARB-GM	FAT-GM	SOD-MG
69.60	1.404	15.20	1.388	40.40
FOOD EXCHANGES					
MILK	VEG.	FRUIT	BREAD	MEAT	FAT
0.0	0.0	0.8	0.3	0.0	0.3

GRAPEFRUIT PIE

2 envelopes unflavored
   gelatin
1 cup boiling water
½ cup sugar
1 tablespoon grated
   grapefruit peel
1½ cups grapefruit juice,
   fresh squeezed with
   pulp (2–3 large
   grapefruit)
3 cups nonfat yogurt
   cheese
2 drops red food coloring
   (optional)

Add gelatin to water and stir until dissolved, about 1 minute. Add sugar, juice and grapefruit peel and mix well. Mix in yogurt cheese one cup at a time with a wire whisk or mixer on low speed. Blend until smooth. Add food coloring if desired. Pour into a 9-inch glass pie pan and chill until firm (2 hours). Garnish with mint or lemon balm.

Servings: 10

Trisha Shirey

NUTRIENT VALUES					
PROTEIN	CARBOHYDRATE		FAT		ALCOHOL
26%	74%		0%		0%
CALORIES	PRO-GM	CARB-GM	FAT-GM		SOD-MG
121.0	7.995	22.70	0.040		98.00
FOOD EXCHANGES					
MILK	VEG.	FRUIT	BREAD	MEAT	FAT
0.8	0.0	0.3	0.6	0.0	0.0

KEY LIME PIE

2 envelopes unflavored
   gelatin
1 cup boiling water
½ cup sugar
⅔ cup fresh lime juice
2 tablespoons finely grated
   zest of lime
3 cups nonfat yogurt
   cheese

Mix sugar and gelatin in a large bowl. Pour in boiling water, stir one minute until gelatin is dissolved. Stir in lime juice and peel; mix well. Add yogurt cheese one cup at a time and mix until well blended and smooth.

Pour into a 9-inch glass pie pan and chill until firm (2–3 hours). Garnish with fresh mint sprigs and lime slices if desired.

Servings: 10

Trisha Shirey

NUTRIENT VALUES					
PROTEIN	CARBOHYDRATE		FAT		ALCOHOL
27%	72%		0%		0%
CALORIES	PRO-GM	CARB-GM	FAT-GM		SOD-MG
111.0	7.890	20.90	0.021		97.80
FOOD EXCHANGES					
MILK	VEG.	FRUIT	BREAD	MEAT	FAT
0.8	0.0	0.1	0.6	0.0	0.0

CINNAMON YOGURT CHEESECAKE

2 envelopes unflavored
  gelatin
½ cup sugar
1 cup boiling water
4 cups yogurt cheese
2 teaspoons vanilla
1 teaspoon cinnamon
Vegetable coating spray

In a large bowl, mix gelatin with sugar. Add boiling water and stir until dissolved. With electric mixer, beat in yogurt cheese and vanilla until smooth. Pour into an 8–9 inch springform pan that has been sprayed with vegetable coating spray. Sprinkle cinnamon over top of cheesecake. With a knife, swirl cinnamon through cheesecake. Chill until firm.

Servings: 12

NUTRIENT VALUES					
PROTEIN	CARBOHYDRATE		FAT		ALCOHOL
31%	69%		1%		0%
CALORIES	PRO-GM	CARB-GM	FAT-GM		SOD-MG
109.0	8.341	18.80	0.066		108.0
FOOD EXCHANGES					
MILK	VEG.	FRUIT	BREAD	MEAT	FAT
0.9	0.0	0.0	0.5	0.0	0.0

REFRIGERATOR YOGURT CHEESECAKE

2 envelopes unflavored
  gelatin
½ cup sugar
1 cup boiling water
4 cups nonfat yogurt
  cheese
2 tablespoons vanilla
Vegetable coating spray

In a large bowl, mix gelatin with sugar. Add boiling water and stir until dissolved. With electric mixer, beat in yogurt cheese and vanilla until smooth. Pour into an 8–9 inch springform pan that has been sprayed with vegetable coating spray. Chill until firm. Top with fresh fruit or canned fruit in its own juice thickened with cornstarch.

Servings: 12

NUTRIENT VALUES					
PROTEIN	CARBOHYDRATE		FAT		ALCOHOL
31%	69%		0%		0%
CALORIES	PRO-GM	CARB-GM	FAT-GM		SOD-MG
108.0	8.333	18.70	0.060		108.0
FOOD EXCHANGES					
MILK	VEG.	FRUIT	BREAD	MEAT	FAT
0.9	0.0	0.0	0.5	0.0	0.0

STRAWBERRY CHEESECAKE

2 cups yogurt cheese
2 tablespoons cornstarch
½ cup sugar
1 tablespoon lemon juice
½ teaspoon vanilla
½ teaspoon strawberry extract
2 egg whites
3 tablespoons Smucker's low-sugar strawberry spread
Vegetable Coating Spray

Combine yogurt cheese, cornstarch, sugar, lemon juice, vanilla, strawberry extract, and strawberry spread in a medium mixing bowl. Mix on medium speed with an electric mixer. Set aside. Beat egg whites until stiff in a separate bowl. Fold egg whites into yogurt cheese mixture. Spray a 9-inch springform pan with vegetable coating spray. Pour batter into prepared pan. Bake at 300° for 35–45 minutes. Cool before removing from pan.

Servings: 10

NUTRIENT VALUES			
PROTEIN	CARBOHYDRATE	FAT	ALCOHOL
21%	79%	1%	0%
CALORIES	PRO-GM	CARB-GM	FAT-GM	SOD-MG
97.20	5.081	19.40	0.072	79.20
FOOD EXCHANGES					
MILK	VEG.	FRUIT	BREAD	MEAT	FAT
0.6	0.0	0.0	0.8	0.1	0.0

APRICOT COFFEE CAKE

2   egg whites, lightly
    beaten
1   cup nonfat yogurt
1   6-ounce can frozen
    pineapple juice
    concentrate (reserve 1
    tablespoon)
¼   cup water
2½ cups whole wheat flour
½   cup wheat bran
2   teaspoons baking
    powder
1   teaspoon baking soda
½   teaspoon salt
½   cup dried apricots,
    chopped
Vegetable coating spray

TOPPING:
3   tablespoons water
1   teaspoon nonfat dry
    milk powder
1   teaspoon cinnamon
1   tablespoon pineapple
    juice concentrate
    (reserved from above)

In a small bowl combine egg whites, yogurt, juice concentrate, and water. In a separate bowl, combine dry ingredients and apricots. Add liquids and mix just until moistened.

Spray a 9-inch square baking dish with vegetable coating spray. Pour in batter. Bake at 350° for 45 minutes.

Combine the reserved 1 tablespoon juice concentrate with water, nonfat dry milk and cinnamon. Drizzle mixture over the warm coffee cake.

Servings: 12

NUTRIENT VALUES					
PROTEIN	CARBOHYDRATE		FAT	ALCOHOL	
13%	85%		3%	0%	
CALORIES	PRO-GM	CARB-GM	FAT-GM	SOD-MG	
153.0	4.992	33.30	0.459	233.0	
FOOD EXCHANGES					
MILK	VEG.	FRUIT	BREAD	MEAT	FAT
0.1	0.0	0.7	1.4	0.1	0.0

STRAWBERRY GELATIN

1 **envelope unflavored gelatin**
1 **cup pineapple juice**
⅓ **cup skim milk**
1 **cup fresh or frozen strawberries**

Soften gelatin in ¼ cup pineapple juice. Heat remaining juice to boiling. Remove from heat. Stir into softened gelatin until dissolved. Add milk, beating until blended. Chill mixture until partially set. Blend fruit and jelled mixture in blender until smooth. Chill until firm.

Servings: 5 (½ cup serving)

NUTRIENT VALUES			
PROTEIN 17%	CARBOHYDRATE 79%	FAT 3%	ALCOHOL 0%
CALORIES 47.70	PRO-GM 2.120	CARB-GM 9.792	FAT-GM 0.190	SOD-MG 11.00
FOOD EXCHANGES					
MILK 0.1	VEG. 0.0	FRUIT 0.7	BREAD 0.0	MEAT 0.0	FAT 0.0

CHOCOLATE MOUSSE

2 **egg whites**
1 **envelope unflavored gelatin**
1 **cup boiling water**
½ **cup part-skim ricotta cheese**
½ **cup skim milk**
2 **tablespoons unsweetened cocoa powder**
¼ **cup sugar**

In a blender or food processor, combine the egg whites, gelatin and 1 tablespoon of cold water. Blend until combined. Let stand until the gelatin softens, about 1 minute. Add the boiling water and blend until the gelatin is dissolved, about 20 seconds.

Add the ricotta cheese, skim milk, cocoa, and sugar. Blend until smooth, about 1 minute.

Pour the mousse into seven dessert dishes and chill until set.

Servings: 7 (½ cup serving)

NUTRIENT VALUES			
PROTEIN 27%	CARBOHYDRATE 53%	FAT 20%	ALCOHOL 0%
CALORIES 64.60	PRO-GM 4.439	CARB-GM 8.753	FAT-GM 1.436	SOD-MG 81.60
FOOD EXCHANGES					
MILK 0.0	VEG. 0.0	FRUIT 0.0	BREAD 0.5	MEAT 0.5	FAT 0.0

PUMPKIN MOUSSE

1 **envelope unflavored gelatin**
½ **cup water**
⅔ **cup instant nonfat dry milk powder**
½ **cup mashed canned pumpkin**
2 **tablespoons orange juice concentrate, undiluted**
½ **teaspoon vanilla extract**
½ **teaspoon cinnamon**
⅛ **teaspoon cloves**
⅛ **teaspoon nutmeg**
8–10 **ice cubes**

Combine gelatin and 2 tablespoons water in blender. Process for 10 seconds, let stand 1 minute. Add 6 tablespoons boiling water. Process until gelatin is dissolved. Add remaining ingredients except ice cubes to blender and process until smooth. Add ice cubes to container and process until smooth.

Servings: 4 (½ cup serving)

NUTRIENT VALUES				
PROTEIN	CARBOHYDRATE		FAT	ALCOHOL
34%	64%		3%	0%
CALORIES	PRO-GM	CARB-GM	FAT-GM	SOD-MG
69.90	6.006	11.40	0.229	66.10
FOOD EXCHANGES					
MILK	VEG.	FRUIT	BREAD	MEAT	FAT
0.5	0.0	0.3	0.1	0.0	0.0

BANANA SOUFFLE

3 firm bananas
2 tablespoons lemon juice
2 tablespoons honey
2 tablespoons water
1 tablespoon cornstarch
¾ cup skim milk
2 egg beaters (egg substitute)
2 egg whites
1 teaspoon vanilla

Peel and slice bananas and sprinkle with lemon juice. In a saucepan mix the honey, water and cornstarch. Add milk and mix well. Stir and cook over medium heat until thickened. Add a little of the hot mixture to the egg beaters, then mix with remaining hot mixture. Stir in sliced bananas. Beat egg whites until they stand in stiff peaks. Fold into custard mixture along with vanilla. Turn into a 1½-quart souffle dish. Place in a pan of hot water. Bake at 350° for 1 hour or until firm.

Servings: 6

NUTRIENT VALUES			
PROTEIN	CARBOHYDRATE	FAT	ALCOHOL
16%	81%	3%	0%
CALORIES	PRO-GM	CARB-GM	FAT-GM	SOD-MG
107.0	4.515	23.30	0.362	53.90
FOOD EXCHANGES					
MILK	VEG.	FRUIT	BREAD	MEAT	FAT
0.2	0.0	1.0	0.4	0.3	0.0

RUM SOUFFLE

1½ teaspoons cornstarch
1   tablespoon cold water
½   cup evaporated skim
    milk
2   egg beaters (egg
    substitute or 2 whole
    eggs)
¼   cup sugar
1½ teaspoons unflavored
    gelatin
2   tablespoons cold water
¼   teaspoon vanilla
1   tablespoon rum extract
2   egg whites

Mix cornstarch and 1 tablespoon cold water until smooth. Stir in evaporated milk and cook over low heat until thickened. Remove from heat.

Beat egg beaters and sugar together. Add to the milk mixture.

Dissolve gelatin in 2 tablespoons cold water. Add to the milk mixture and cook over low heat for about 5 minutes. Stir in vanilla and rum extract. Remove from heat.

Whip egg whites until soft peaks form. Gently fold into the milk mixture. Spoon into four serving dishes and refrigerate 2–3 hours. Garnish with fresh mint and fresh fruit.

Servings: 4 (¾ cup serving)

NUTRIENT VALUES			
PROTEIN	CARBOHYDRATE	FAT	ALCOHOL
35%	65%	0%	0%
CALORIES	PRO-GM	CARB-GM	FAT-GM	SOD-MG
109.0	9.428	17.80	0.000	123.0

FOOD EXCHANGES					
MILK	VEG.	FRUIT	BREAD	MEAT	FAT
0.3	0.0	0.0	0.8	0.8	0.0

BAKED APPLES

3 red apples, cored
2 tablespoons lemon juice
1 tablespoon honey
⅛ teaspoon cinnamon
⅛ teaspoon cardamon
⅛ teaspoon allspice
⅛ teaspoon ginger
1 tablespoon amaretto
2 tablespoons raisins

Cut apples in half. Place apples in baking pan. Blend other ingredients and partially fill each apple cavity; sprinkle with cinnamon. Add ¼ inch water to pan and cover with foil; bake 10–15 minutes. Remove foil and baste with juices in pan. Cook another 10 minutes or until tender.

Servings: 6

NUTRIENT VALUES				
PROTEIN	CARBOHYDRATE		FAT	ALCOHOL
1%	96%		3%	0%
CALORIES	PRO-GM	CARB-GM	FAT-GM	SOD-MG
57.10	0.211	15.20	0.214	0.563
FOOD EXCHANGES					
MILK	VEG.	FRUIT	BREAD	MEAT	FAT
0.0	0.0	0.8	0.2	0.0	0.0

APPLE CRISP

4 apples
2 teaspoons lemon juice
½ teaspoon cinnamon
1 tablespoon whole wheat flour
¼ cup raisins
¾ cup water
Vegetable coating spray

TOPPING
½ cup rolled oats
½ cup wheat bran
¼ cup whole wheat flour
1 teaspoon cinnamon
1 tablespoon brown sugar
1½ teaspoons vegetable oil

Preheat oven to 375°. Spray 8 × 8 baking dish with vegetable coating spray. Slice apples and mix in a bowl with lemon juice, cinnamon, flour and raisins and place them in the baking dish. Cover with ¾ cup water. Mix topping in a bowl and sprinkle evenly over top of apples. Cover dish and bake 15 minutes. Remove cover, stir ingredients together and bake 15–20 additional minutes or until apples are done.

Servings: 6 (⅔ cup serving)

NUTRIENT VALUES				
PROTEIN	CARBOHYDRATE		FAT	ALCOHOL
8%	80%		12%	0%
CALORIES	PRO-GM	CARB-GM	FAT-GM	SOD-MG
156.0	3.592	35.40	2.445	1.931
FOOD EXCHANGES					
MILK	VEG.	FRUIT	BREAD	MEAT	FAT
0.0	0.0	1.2	1.2	0.0	0.4

JAMAICAN BAKED BANANAS

2 **bananas, peeled and halved, lengthwise**
1½ **teaspoons brown sugar**
1½ **teaspoons dark rum or ¾ teaspoon rum extract**
⅛ **teaspoon ground cinnamon**
3 **tablespoons lemon or orange juice**
¼ **orange, peeled and sliced**
Pinch of allspice
Vegetable coating spray

Arrange bananas in pan sprayed with vegetable coating spray. Sprinkle brown sugar and spices on bananas. Mix together rum, lemon or orange juice. Place orange slices over bananas and pour rum mixture over and bake at 350° for 25 minutes.

Servings: 4 (½ banana per serving)

NUTRIENT VALUES					
PROTEIN	CARBOHYDRATE		FAT		ALCOHOL
4%	90%		6%		0%
CALORIES	PRO-GM	CARB-GM		FAT-GM	SOD-MG
71.30	0.763	17.80		0.495	1.423
FOOD EXCHANGES					
MILK	VEG.	FRUIT	BREAD	MEAT	FAT
0.0	0.0	1.3	0.1	0.0	0.0

BLUEBERRIES AND PINEAPPLE

1 **cup blueberries, fresh or frozen**
1 **cup pineapple, diced, fresh or juice packed**
½ **cup nonfat yogurt**

Mix all ingredients well. Dish up in small bowls and top with mint leaf. Serve immediately or pineapple will discolor.

Servings: 4

NUTRIENT VALUES					
PROTEIN	CARBOHYDRATE		FAT		ALCOHOL
12%	83%		5%		0%
CALORIES	PRO-GM	CARB-GM		FAT-GM	SOD-MG
53.50	1.768	11.90		0.303	22.50
FOOD EXCHANGES					
MILK	VEG.	FRUIT	BREAD	MEAT	FAT
0.1	0.0	0.8	0.0	0.0	0.0

BLUEBERRIES IN YOGURT

½ cup frozen or fresh
blueberries
½ cup nonfat yogurt

Mix blueberries and yogurt and chill.

Servings: 2 (½ cup serving)

NUTRIENT VALUES					
PROTEIN	CARBOHYDRATE		FAT		ALCOHOL
24%	73%		2%		0%
CALORIES	PRO-GM	CARB-GM	FAT-GM		SOD-MG
48.00	2.993	9.125	0.138		42.30
FOOD EXCHANGES					
MILK	VEG.	FRUIT	BREAD	MEAT	FAT
0.3	0.0	0.3	0.0	0.0	0.0

FRUIT FANTASIA

2 cups nonfat yogurt
8 whole strawberries,
sliced
2 teaspoons fresh lemon
juice
2 teaspoons honey
1 cup cantalope, cut in ¼-
inch chunks
Nutmeg
Fresh mint sprigs

Mix first five ingredients together in a large
bowl. Place into serving dishes and garnish
with sprinkle of nutmeg and sprig of mint.

Servings: 4 (⅔ cup serving)

NUTRIENT VALUES					
PROTEIN	CARBOHYDRATE		FAT		ALCOHOL
27%	71%		2%		0%
CALORIES	PRO-GM	CARB-GM	FAT-GM		SOD-MG
86.30	5.973	15.70	0.179		83.90
FOOD EXCHANGES					
MILK	VEG.	FRUIT	BREAD	MEAT	FAT
0.6	0.0	0.4	0.1	0.0	0.0

FRUIT KABOB

¼ cup pineapple chunks, (fresh or canned)
4 strawberries, halved
¼ banana, sliced
¼ apple, sliced
½ kiwi, sliced thick
Lime

Alternate fruit on wooden skewers. Squeeze lime over fruit. Serve chilled.

Servings: 1

NUTRIENT VALUES				
PROTEIN	CARBOHYDRATE		FAT	ALCOHOL
4%	90%		6%	0%
CALORIES	PRO-GM	CARB-GM	FAT-GM	SOD-MG
98.80	1.108	24.80	0.715	3.048
FOOD EXCHANGES					
MILK	VEG.	FRUIT	BREAD	MEAT	FAT
0.0	0.0	2.0	0.0	0.0	0.0

ORANGES POACHED IN RED WINE

2 cups red wine
2 tablespoons honey
1 star anise pod
½ cinnamon stick
Juice from 3 oranges (¾ cup)
1 tablespoon grated orange rind
1½ teaspoons orange liqueur
2 oranges, sliced, pith removed, seeded

Combine wine, honey, spices, and juice; simmer 10 minutes. Remove from heat. Add orange liqueur and orange rind and cool. Add the orange slices and marinate for 1 hour.

Serve 2–3 slices on lettuce bed.

Servings: 4

NUTRIENT VALUES				
PROTEIN	CARBOHYDRATE		FAT	ALCOHOL
4%	91%		1%	4%
CALORIES	PRO-GM	CARB-GM	FAT-GM	SOD-MG
88.70	0.911	21.60	0.153	1.625
FOOD EXCHANGES					
MILK	VEG.	FRUIT	BREAD	MEAT	FAT
0.0	0.0	0.9	0.5	0.0	0.0

PEACHES WITH AMARETTO

3 large ripe peaches
2 tablespoons amaretto
2 tablespoons almonds, chopped
6 fresh strawberries, sliced

Drop peaches into boiling water, cover 1 minute, drain and run under cold water. Peel off skins. Cut peaches in half, remove stones, spoon liquid into cavities of peaches, sprinkle in chopped almonds, garnish with strawberries and chill.

Servings: 6

NUTRIENT VALUES					
PROTEIN 4%	CARBOHYDRATE 70%		FAT 2%		ALCOHOL 24%
CALORIES 38.10	PRO-GM 0.441	CARB-GM 7.258		FAT-GM 0.094	SOD-MG 0.833
FOOD EXCHANGES					
MILK 0.0	VEG. 0.0	FRUIT 0.4	BREAD 0.1	MEAT 0.0	FAT 0.0

BAKED PEARS

2 large ripe firm pears
2 tablespoons apple juice concentrate
¼ cup frozen blueberries
2 tablespoons water

Wash pears, halve and scoop out core. Place cut side down in glass baking dish. Mix blueberries, water and apple juice concentrate. Scatter blueberries over pears. Bake at 400° for 15–20 minutes until easily pierced with fork and sauce is bubbling. Serve pear with blueberries and sauce spooned over top.

Servings: 4

Trisha Shirey

NUTRIENT VALUES					
PROTEIN 2%	CARBOHYDRATE 93%		FAT 5%		ALCOHOL 0%
CALORIES 68.90	PRO-GM 0.366	CARB-GM 17.40		FAT-GM 0.392	SOD-MG 3.063
FOOD EXCHANGES					
MILK 0.0	VEG. 0.0	FRUIT 1.3	BREAD 0.0	MEAT 0.0	FAT 0.0

GINGERSNAP-BAKED PEARS

2 **pears, halved and cored**
4 **gingersnaps, finely crushed**
1 **teaspoon brown sugar**
1 **teaspoon reduced-calorie margarine**

Put gingersnaps in running blender to make crumbs. Place crumbs in small bowl and add brown sugar and margarine. Mix until combined. Divide into fourths and place in middle of pear. Bake at 300° for 20 minutes.

Servings: 4

NUTRIENT VALUES					
PROTEIN 3%	CARBOHYDRATE 75%		FAT 22%		ALCOHOL 0%
CALORIES 91.80	PRO-GM 0.651	CARB-GM 18.40		FAT-GM 2.425	SOD-MG 31.40
FOOD EXCHANGES					
MILK 0.0	VEG. 0.0	FRUIT 0.9	BREAD 0.3	MEAT 0.0	FAT 0.4

PEARS WITH BLUE CHEESE

2 **large pears**
1 **ounce blue cheese**
4 **teaspoons chopped walnuts**
¼ **cup nonfat yogurt**

Wash pears, halve and core. Crumble blue cheese and mix with walnuts and yogurt. Divide mixture and place in center of pear. Serve chillled.

Servings: 4

NUTRIENT VALUES					
PROTEIN 12%	CARBOHYDRATE 54%		FAT 33%		ALCOHOL 0%
CALORIES 96.70	PRO-GM 3.163	CARB-GM 14.00		FAT-GM 3.840	SOD-MG 110.0
FOOD EXCHANGES					
MILK 0.1	VEG. 0.0	FRUIT 0.9	BREAD 0.0	MEAT 0.3	FAT 0.5

MAPLE-BAKED PEARS

2 pears
1 tablespoon maple syrup
¼ teaspoon vanilla extract
2 teaspoons wheat germ
2 teaspoons reduced-
    calorie margarine
Vegetable coating spray

Preheat oven to 350°. Spray a nonstick baking dish with vegetable coating spray. Cut pears in half and core. Place in baking dish. Mix syrup, almond extract and vanilla. Drizzle over pears. Sprinkle with wheat germ. Divide butter among pears. Bake 10 minutes or until tender.

Servings: 4 servings

NUTRIENT VALUES					
PROTEIN 3%	CARBOHYDRATE 79%		FAT 17%		ALCOHOL 0%
CALORIES 75.70	PRO-GM 0.638	CARB-GM 16.30		FAT-GM 1.585	SOD-MG 23.00
FOOD EXCHANGES					
MILK 0.0	VEG. 0.0	FRUIT 0.9	BREAD 0.1	MEAT 0.1	FAT 0.3

PEAR WITH PUREED STRAWBERRIES

2 pears, peeled
¼ cup pineapple or lemon
    juice
1 cup strawberries
Mint for garnish

Slice, seed and peel two pears lengthwise. Dip in pineapple juice (or lemon) to prevent browning. Chill.

Clean and cut tops off the strawberries. Put in blender and puree. Chill. Spoon pureed strawberries into pear halves. Garnish with sprig of mint.

Servings: 4

NUTRIENT VALUES					
PROTEIN 3%	CARBOHYDRATE 91%		FAT 6%		ALCOHOL 0%
CALORIES 68.90	PRO-GM 0.603	CARB-GM 17.30		FAT-GM 0.480	SOD-MG 1.125
FOOD EXCHANGES					
MILK 0.0	VEG. 0.0	FRUIT 1.0	BREAD 0.0	MEAT 0.0	FAT 0.0

FRUIT CUP

1 **banana, sliced**
1 **cup strawberries, sliced**
1 **cup blueberries, sliced**

OR:
1 **cup diced cantalope**
1 **kiwi, sliced**
1 **cup watermelon, diced**
1 **banana**

This consists of several fresh fruits (in season) of your choice, peeled and cubed. Mix together in bowl with dash of vanilla and cinnamon. Place in cups or bowl. Garnish with mint sprigs.

Servings: 5 (½ cup serving)

NUTRIENT VALUES					
PROTEIN	CARBOHYDRATE		FAT		ALCOHOL
5%	90%		5%		0%
CALORIES	PRO-GM	CARB-GM		FAT-GM	SOD-MG
47.20	0.622	11.80		0.334	2.438
FOOD EXCHANGES					
MILK	VEG.	FRUIT	BREAD	MEAT	FAT
0.0	0.0	1.0	0.0	0.0	0.0

GINGERED FRUIT

2 **apples, cored and sliced**
2 **oranges, peeled and sectioned**
1 **banana, sliced**
⅓ **cup orange juice**
1 **tablespoon grated fresh ginger**

Combine all ingredients. Cover and chill for two hours.

Servings: 6 (½ cup serving)

NUTRIENT VALUES					
PROTEIN	CARBOHYDRATE		FAT		ALCOHOL
4%	92%		4%		0%
CALORIES	PRO-GM	CARB-GM		FAT-GM	SOD-MG
69.30	0.776	17.60		0.309	0.653
FOOD EXCHANGES					
MILK	VEG.	FRUIT	BREAD	MEAT	FAT
0.0	0.0	1.2	0.0	0.0	0.0

YOGURT AMBROSIA

½ cup cubed oranges
½ cup bananas
½ cup seedless grapes
1 cup nonfat yogurt
5 teaspoons shredded
    coconut

Mix fruit with yogurt. Top each serving with 1 teaspoon shredded coconut.

Servings: 5 (½ cup serving)

NUTRIENT VALUES					
PROTEIN	CARBOHYDRATE		FAT		ALCOHOL
19%	71%		11%		0%
CALORIES	PRO-GM	CARB-GM		FAT-GM	SOD-MG
53.10	2.605	9.944		0.669	32.70
FOOD EXCHANGES					
MILK	VEG.	FRUIT	BREAD	MEAT	FAT
0.3	0.0	0.5	0.0	0.0	0.1

BANANA AND PINEAPPLE SORBET

3 cups ripe pineapple, cut
    into 1-inch chunks
2 ripe bananas, cut into 1-
    inch chunks
2 tablespoons frozen apple
    juice concentrate
1 cup lowfat evaporated
    milk, chilled in freezer
1 teaspoon vanilla extract

Freeze fruit until ready to use. Place ½ of each ingredient in blender container. Process until smooth. Empty blender. Process remaining half of ingredients. Spoon into serving dishes. Freeze for one hour before serving.

Servings: 6 (⅔ cup serving)

Replace pineapple with 4 cups whole strawberries for banana/strawberry sorbet.

NUTRIENT VALUES					
PROTEIN	CARBOHYDRATE		FAT		ALCOHOL
12%	84%		4%		0%
CALORIES	PRO-GM	CARB-GM		FAT-GM	SOD-MG
118.0	3.710	26.00		0.520	52.60
FOOD EXCHANGES					
MILK	VEG.	FRUIT	BREAD	MEAT	FAT
0.4	0.0	1.5	0.0	0.0	0.0

BLUEBERRY SORBET

2 **cups blueberries**
2 **ripe bananas**
2 **tablespoons apple juice concentrate**
1 **cup skim evaporated milk**
1 **teaspoon vanilla**

Blend all ingredients in food processor until smooth. Pour into serving dishes and freeze. Freeze at least two hours.

Servings: 6 (⅔ cup serving)

NUTRIENT VALUES					
PROTEIN	CARBOHYDRATE			FAT	ALCOHOL
13%	84%			3%	0%
CALORIES	PRO-GM	CARB-GM		FAT-GM	SOD-MG
107.0	3.733	23.20		0.374	55.10
FOOD EXCHANGES					
MILK	VEG.	FRUIT	BREAD	MEAT	FAT
0.4	0.0	1.3	0.0	0.0	0.0

BANANA YOGURT FREEZE

4 **medium ripe bananas**
1 **cup nonfat yogurt**
2 **teaspoons vanilla**
Freshly grated nutmeg

Cut bananas into chunks and freeze in plastic bag for 24 hours.

Place yogurt and vanilla in a food processor or blender to mix. Gradually add the banana chunks and process until smooth. Pour into serving dishes, garnish with nutmeg. Serve immediately. Can hold in freezer up to two hours before serving.

Servings: 6 (½ cup serving)

NUTRIENT VALUES					
PROTEIN	CARBOHYDRATE			FAT	ALCOHOL
11%	86%			3%	0%
CALORIES	PRO-GM	CARB-GM		FAT-GM	SOD-MG
91.00	2.653	21.30		0.381	27.50
FOOD EXCHANGES					
MILK	VEG.	FRUIT	BREAD	MEAT	FAT
0.3	0.0	1.3	0.0	0.0	0.0

ORANGE SHERBET

12 ounces frozen orange
   juice concentrate,
   undiluted
1½ cups nonfat dry milk
   powder
4 cups skim milk
1 teaspoon vanilla

Combine all ingredients in a blender or food processor and blend until well mixed. Process in two batches if necessary. Pour into an ice cream freezer and process until frozen or pour into a plastic bowl, cover and freeze. Once mixture freezes solid you may need to let it sit at room temperature 10–15 minutes to soften before serving.

Servings: 24 (½ cup serving)

NUTRIENT VALUES					
PROTEIN	CARBOHYDRATE		FAT		ALCOHOL
25%	73%		3%		0%
CALORIES	PRO-GM	CARB-GM		FAT-GM	SOD-MG
52.80	3.291	9.679		0.162	45.40
FOOD EXCHANGES					
MILK	VEG.	FRUIT	BREAD	MEAT	FAT
0.4	0.0	0.4	0.0	0.0	0.0

PEACH SHERBET

12 ounces frozen pineapple
   juice concentrate
1½ cups nonfat dry milk
   powder
4 cups skim milk
1 teaspoon vanilla
4 cups fresh or frozen
   peaches (pureed in
   blender)

Combine all ingredients in a blender or food processor and blend until well mixed. Process in two batches if necessary. Pour into an ice cream freezer and process until frozen or pour into a plastic bowl, cover and freeze. Once mixture freezes solid you may need to let it sit at room temperature 10–15 minutes to soften before serving.

Servings: 24 (½ cup serving) (yields 3 quarts)

NUTRIENT VALUES					
PROTEIN	CARBOHYDRATE		FAT		ALCOHOL
22%	75%		3%		0%
CALORIES	PRO-GM	CARB-GM		FAT-GM	SOD-MG
55.20	3.150	10.50		0.159	47.30
FOOD EXCHANGES					
MILK	VEG.	FRUIT	BREAD	MEAT	FAT
0.4	0.0	0.4	0.0	0.0	0.0

PINEAPPLE SHERBET

12 ounces frozen pineapple juice concentrate, undiluted
1½ cups nonfat dry milk powder
4 cups skim milk
1 teaspoon vanilla
2 cups unsweetened crushed pineapple, drained

Combine all ingredients in a blender or food processor and blend until well mixed. Process in two batches if necessary. Pour into an ice cream freezer or pour into a plastic bowl, cover and freeze. Once mixture freezes solid you may need to let it sit at room temperature 10–15 minutes to soften before serving.

Servings: 24 (½ cup serving)

NUTRIENT VALUES			
PROTEIN	CARBOHYDRATE	FAT	ALCOHOL
19%	79%	2%	0%
CALORIES	PRO-GM	CARB-GM	FAT-GM	SOD-MG
66.80	3.040	13.00	0.151	46.70
FOOD EXCHANGES					
MILK	VEG.	FRUIT	BREAD	MEAT	FAT
0.4	0.0	0.1	0.4	0.0	0.0

STRAWBERRY SHERBET

12 ounces frozen pineapple juice concentrate
1½ cups nonfat dry milk
4 cups skim milk
1 teaspoon vanilla
4 cups sliced strawberries

Combine all ingredients in a blender or food processor and blend until well mixed. Process in two batches if necessary. Pour into an ice cream freezer and process until frozen or pour into a plastic bowl, cover and freeze. Once mixture freezes solid you may need to let it sit at room temperature 10–15 minutes to soften before serving.

Servings: 24 (½ cup serving) (yields 3 quarts)

NUTRIENT VALUES			
PROTEIN	CARBOHYDRATE	FAT	ALCOHOL
24%	72%	4%	0%
CALORIES	PRO-GM	CARB-GM	FAT-GM	SOD-MG
50.50	3.104	9.126	0.224	47.40
FOOD EXCHANGES					
MILK	VEG.	FRUIT	BREAD	MEAT	FAT
0.4	0.0	0.3	0.0	0.0	0.0

ORANGE SNOW

1   **large orange**
½   **envelope unflavored**
     gelatin
¾   **cup orange juice**
1   **teaspoon sugar**
1   **egg white**

Peel orange, divide into segments, set aside.

Sprinkle gelatin over ¼ cup orange juice in a small saucepan. Let stand to soften. Place saucepan over low heat, stir constantly until gelatin dissolves. Remove from heat.

Meanwhile, in a medium saucepan, heat remaining ½ cup orange juice and sugar. Stir in melted gelatin. Pour into large bowl, chill until mixture is semi-set.

In a medium-sized bowl, beat egg white with a mixer set at high speed, until very stiff. Beat semi-set gelatin until foamy. Fold egg white into gelatin mixture. Drain reserved orange pieces. Fold into mixture.

Spoon into 4 serving dishes. Chill.

Servings: 4 (½ cup serving)

NUTRIENT VALUES			
PROTEIN	CARBOHYDRATE	FAT	ALCOHOL
18%	80%	2%	0%
CALORIES	PRO-GM	CARB-GM	FAT-GM	SOD-MG
45.90	2.169	9.546	0.108	14.60
FOOD EXCHANGES					
MILK	VEG.	FRUIT	BREAD	MEAT	FAT
0.0	0.0	0.6	0.0	0.1	0.0

PEACH PINEAPPLE CREAM

¼ cup nonfat yogurt
⅓ cup skim evaporated milk
½ cup fresh or canned pineapple
1½ cups fresh or frozen, thawed peaches (cut into small pieces)
¼ cup pineapple juice
1 tablespoon lemon juice
½ teaspoon cinnamon
½ teaspoon vanilla

Mix all ingredients together in large bowl. Pour into individual serving bowls. Place in freezer for 1–2 hours. Allow to sit at room temperature for 15 minutes before serving.

Servings: 4 (½ cup serving)

NUTRIENT VALUES			
PROTEIN	CARBOHYDRATE	FAT	ALCOHOL
15%	84%	1%	0%
CALORIES	PRO-GM	CARB-GM	FAT-GM	SOD-MG
71.20	2.840	15.70	0.110	36.00

FOOD EXCHANGES					
MILK	VEG.	FRUIT	BREAD	MEAT	FAT
0.4	0.0	0.8	0.0	0.0	0.0

FROZEN PEACH YOGURT

1½ pounds fresh peaches, peeled, halved and pitted, or frozen (unsweetened) peaches thawed
⅓ cup sugar
2 cups nonfat yogurt
2 teaspoons vanilla
⅛ teaspoon cinnamon
1 cup evaporated skim milk, chilled until almost frozen

Slice peaches and process in a blender or processor until pureed. You should have 3 cups peach puree.

In a large bowl mix peach puree, sugar, yogurt, vanilla and cinnamon. Set aside. Whip evaporated skim milk until whipped and thick. Add whipped milk to yogurt mixture.

Place in ice cream maker and churn according to manufacturer's directions. Eat immediately or freeze. If mixture freezes solid, let it stand at room temperature 15–20 minutes to soften.

Servings: 16 (½ cup serving)

NUTRIENT VALUES			
PROTEIN	CARBOHYDRATE	FAT	ALCOHOL
18%	81%	1%	0%
CALORIES	PRO-GM	CARB-GM	FAT-GM	SOD-MG
59.50	2.798	12.50	0.040	39.00
FOOD EXCHANGES					
MILK	VEG.	FRUIT	BREAD	MEAT	FAT
0.3	0.0	0.3	0.2	0.0	0.0

Recipe for _____

_____

_____

_____

_____

_____

_____

_____

_____

_____

_____

_____

_____

_____

_____

_____

_____

_____

_____

NUTRIENT VALUES			
PROTEIN	CARBOHYDRATE	FAT	ALCOHOL
CALORIES	PRO-GM	CARB-GM	FAT-GM	SOD-MG
FOOD EXCHANGES					
MILK	VEG.	FRUIT	BREAD	MEAT	FAT

Recipe for _____

_____

_____

_____

_____

_____

_____

_____

_____

_____

_____

_____

_____

_____

_____

_____

_____

NUTRIENT VALUES				
PROTEIN	CARBOHYDRATE		FAT	ALCOHOL
CALORIES	PRO-GM	CARB-GM	FAT-GM	SOD-MG
FOOD EXCHANGES				
MILK	VEG.	FRUIT	BREAD	MEAT	FAT

Recipe for _____

_____

_____

_____

_____

_____

_____

_____

_____

_____

_____

_____

_____

_____

_____

_____

_____

NUTRIENT VALUES			
PROTEIN	CARBOHYDRATE	FAT	ALCOHOL
CALORIES	PRO-GM	CARB-GM	FAT-GM	SOD-MG

FOOD EXCHANGES					
MILK	VEG.	FRUIT	BREAD	MEAT	FAT

Recipe for _____

_____

_____

_____

_____

_____

_____

_____

_____

_____

_____

_____

_____

_____

_____

_____

_____

_____

_____

NUTRIENT VALUES			
PROTEIN	CARBOHYDRATE	FAT	ALCOHOL
CALORIES	PRO-GM CARB-GM	FAT-GM	SOD-MG
FOOD EXCHANGES			
MILK VEG.	FRUIT BREAD	MEAT	FAT

392

Recipe for _____

_____

_____

_____

_____

_____

_____

_____

_____

_____

_____

_____

_____

_____

_____

_____

_____

NUTRIENT VALUES				
PROTEIN	CARBOHYDRATE		FAT	ALCOHOL
CALORIES	PRO-GM	CARB-GM	FAT-GM	SOD-MG
FOOD EXCHANGES				
MILK	VEG.	FRUIT	BREAD	MEAT	FAT

Recipe for _____

_____

_____

_____

_____

_____

_____

_____

_____

_____

_____

_____

_____

_____

_____

_____

_____

_____

NUTRIENT VALUES			
PROTEIN	CARBOHYDRATE	FAT	ALCOHOL
CALORIES	PRO-GM	CARB-GM	FAT-GM	SOD-MG
FOOD EXCHANGES					
MILK	VEG.	FRUIT	BREAD	MEAT	FAT

Recipe for _____

_____

_____

_____

_____

_____

_____

_____

_____

_____

_____

_____

_____

_____

_____

_____

NUTRIENT VALUES				
PROTEIN	CARBOHYDRATE		FAT	ALCOHOL
CALORIES	PRO-GM	CARB-GM	FAT-GM	SOD-MG
FOOD EXCHANGES					
MILK	VEG.	FRUIT	BREAD	MEAT	FAT

Recipe for _____

_____

_____

_____

_____

_____

_____

_____

_____

_____

_____

_____

_____

_____

_____

_____

_____

_____

_____

_____

NUTRIENT VALUES				
PROTEIN	CARBOHYDRATE		FAT	ALCOHOL
CALORIES	PRO-GM	CARB-GM	FAT-GM	SOD-MG
FOOD EXCHANGES					
MILK	VEG.	FRUIT	BREAD	MEAT	FAT

Recipe for _____

_____

_____

_____

_____

_____

_____

_____

_____

_____

_____

_____

_____

_____

_____

_____

_____

_____

_____

NUTRIENT VALUES			
PROTEIN	CARBOHYDRATE	FAT	ALCOHOL
CALORIES	PRO-GM	CARB-GM	FAT-GM	SOD-MG

FOOD EXCHANGES					
MILK	VEG.	FRUIT	BREAD	MEAT	FAT

Recipe for _____

_____

_____

_____

_____

_____

_____

_____

_____

_____

_____

_____

_____

_____

_____

_____

_____

NUTRIENT VALUES				
PROTEIN	CARBOHYDRATE		FAT	ALCOHOL
CALORIES	PRO-GM	CARB-GM	FAT-GM	SOD-MG
FOOD EXCHANGES				
MILK	VEG.	FRUIT	BREAD	MEAT	FAT

Recipe for _____

_____

_____

_____

_____

_____

_____

_____

_____

_____

_____

_____

_____

_____

_____

_____

_____

_____

NUTRIENT VALUES				
PROTEIN	CARBOHYDRATE		FAT	ALCOHOL
CALORIES	PRO-GM	CARB-GM	FAT-GM	SOD-MG
FOOD EXCHANGES				
MILK	VEG.	FRUIT	BREAD	MEAT	FAT

Recipe for _____

_____

_____

_____

_____

_____

_____

_____

_____

_____

_____

_____

_____

_____

_____

_____

_____

_____

_____

_____

NUTRIENT VALUES				
PROTEIN	CARBOHYDRATE		FAT	ALCOHOL
CALORIES	PRO-GM	CARB-GM	FAT-GM	SOD-MG
FOOD EXCHANGES					
MILK	VEG.	FRUIT	BREAD	MEAT	FAT

Recipe for _____

_____

_____

_____

_____

_____

_____

_____

_____

_____

_____

_____

_____

_____

_____

_____

_____

_____

NUTRIENT VALUES				
PROTEIN	CARBOHYDRATE		FAT	ALCOHOL
CALORIES	PRO-GM	CARB-GM	FAT-GM	SOD-MG
FOOD EXCHANGES					
MILK	VEG.	FRUIT	BREAD	MEAT	FAT

Recipe for _____

_____

_____

_____

_____

_____

_____

_____

_____

_____

_____

_____

_____

_____

_____

_____

_____

_____

NUTRIENT VALUES				
PROTEIN	CARBOHYDRATE		FAT	ALCOHOL
CALORIES	PRO-GM	CARB-GM	FAT-GM	SOD-MG
FOOD EXCHANGES					
MILK	VEG.	FRUIT	BREAD	MEAT	FAT

402

Recipe for _____

_____

_____

_____

_____

_____

_____

_____

_____

_____

_____

_____

_____

_____

_____

_____

_____

_____

NUTRIENT VALUES			
PROTEIN	CARBOHYDRATE	FAT	ALCOHOL
CALORIES	PRO-GM	CARB-GM	FAT-GM	SOD-MG

FOOD EXCHANGES					
MILK	VEG.	FRUIT	BREAD	MEAT	FAT

HOW TO USE OUR INDEX

We endeavored to make *Spa Specialties* an easy-to-use cookbook packed with information to use in meal planning, weight loss and for basic nutritional information.

When planning the index, we tried to think of every way you might look for information or recipes and arranged it so you could look things up quickly.

Here's how to look up recipes:

By Name—All recipes are listed alphabetically by name. So you will find blueberry muffins under Blueberries in the B's.

By Ingredient—If you are looking for a way to serve chicken, look for heading *Chicken* for a listing of all recipes that include chicken. When your garden is inundating you with squash, look for *Squash* recipes in the index. You can use what is in season or what you have on hand in your pantry to create meals by utilizing the index in this way.

For Menu Planning—See our **Suggested Menu** section for well-balanced meals for breakfast, lunch and dinner. Menu planning will help make your shopping trips easier by enabling you to get all the needed ingredients for several days in one shopping trip.

If You are Out of an Ingredient or Want to Reduce Calories in "old favorite" recipes, see our **Substitutions** list or **Low Fat/Low Calorie Hints** list for 34 hints on reducing calories. Also reference our **Equivalents** list.

For a Fast Meal—On those extra busy days, see our **Quick and Easy** category for fast main dishes. These are ready to eat in 20-30 minutes.

For Foreign Flavors—The next time you're feeling festive and want to cook up a Mexican meal, look under the **Southwestern Cuisine** heading. Also listed are **Italian Cuisine** and **Oriental Cuisine.** These listings can help you plan a party menu from appetizer to dessert with an exotic cuisine.

For Ease in Shopping—Use **Stocking Your Pantry** as a shopping checklist for ensuring that you always have healthy foods on hand.

Index

SPA SPECIALTIES ORDER FORM

Please send me _____ copies of *SPA SPECIALTIES* at $17.95 each plus $2.00 postage and handling per copy.

Total enclosed $ _____. ☐ Check   ☐ MasterCard   ☐ VISA
☐ American Express

Account Number   Expiration Date

Signature

Name

Address

City _____ State _____ Zip

Lake Austin Resort   1705 Quinlan Park Rd.,   Austin, TX 78732
In the U.S call **1-800-847-5637** or Canada **1-800-338-6651**

Yes, I am interested in receiving additional information about Lake Austin Resort and the programs. Please send a free brochure to:

Name

Address

City

State   Zip Code

Lake Austin Resort   1705 Quinlan Park Rd.,   Austin, TX 78732
In the U.S call **1-800-847-5637** or Canada **1-800-338-6651**

Yes, I am interested in having my name added to the Lake Austin Resort mailing list for *SPA SPECIALTIES* updates and/or the Lake Austin Resort Cooking Newsletter. (Please circle information requested).

Name

Address

City

State   Zip Code

Lake Austin Resort   1705 Quinlan Park Rd.,   Austin, TX 78732
In the U.S call **1-800-847-5637** or Canada **1-800-338-6651**

Let us hear from you! Do you have a question or comment about a recipe in *SPA SPECIALTIES* or do you have a low fat, low calorie idea you would like to share?

Name

Address

City   State Zip

Comments:

Lake Austin Resort   1705 Quinlan Park Rd.,   Austin, TX 78732

Really Creamy™
YOGURT CHEESE FUNNEL

Turns yogurt into yogurt cheese!